£26.50

PLAYING WITH SIGNS

PLAYING WITH SIGNS

A SEMIOTIC INTERPRETATION OF CLASSIC MUSIC

V. Kofi Agawu

PRINCETON UNIVERSITY PRESS, 1991

PRINCETON, NEW JERSEY

LIBRARY OF CONGRESS CATALOGING-IN-PUBLICATION DATA

AGAWU, V. KOFI (VICTOR KOFI)
PLAYING WITH SIGNS:
A SEMIOTIC INTERPRETATION OF CLASSIC MUSIC
INCLUDES BIBLIOGRAPHICAL REFERENCES (P.145) AND INDEX.
ISBN 0-691-09138-2 (ALK. PAPER)
1. MUSIC—SEMIOTICS. 2. MUSICAL ANALYSIS. 3. CLASSICISM IN MUSIC. I. TITLE
ML3838.A317 1991 781.6'8111—dc20 90-8569

THIS BOOK HAS BEEN COMPOSED IN ADOBE SABON

PRINTED IN THE UNITED STATES OF AMERICA BY
PRINCETON UNIVERSITY PRESS, PRINCETON, NEW JERSEY

1 3 5 7 9 10 8 6 4 2

To the memory of my father
Rev. R. F. Agawu-Kakraba

CONTENTS

PREFACE

THE AIM of this book is to point out certain features of a small group of compositions by Haydn, Mozart, and Beethoven that might enhance understanding and appreciation of the Classic repertoire. My title includes the article "a" not to deflect attention from the book's shortcomings by acknowledging the possibility of multiple interpretations of the same piece of music, but rather to recognize—indeed, to celebrate—the activity of music analysis as a never-ending process. I know of no analysis that is finished or complete; the best analyses, in my view, are those that spur the musician on to further analysis. It is my hope that some readers will find it difficult to resist arguing with the book's premises and method. Reading another musician's analyses of well-known works can never be a passive process.

To the extent that there exists an underlying strategy or plot for this book, it resides in a number of conflicts and loose ends that are maintained throughout. First, I have chosen analysis rather than theory, because analyzing comes to me more easily than theorizing. While it is true that no analysis can take place in a theoretical vacuum, it is also true that there is a world of difference between an analysis that takes its theoretical premises for granted and one that is self-conscious about theory. The state of blindness adopted in the first approach may prove to be a liberating force, enabling the writer simply to get on with the job of exploration. In the latter approach, a measure of intellectual responsibility may be brought to bear on the theoretical enterprise, so that, even if no new insights into specific works emerge, the process by which we arrive at those insights may be clarified. My own approach sits precariously and ambivalently on the divide between the two approaches, as even a cursory comparison of the interpretative Chapter 4 to the theoretical Chapter 7 will reveal.

A second conflict grows out of an uncertainty about the exact nature of the relationship between historical theory and contemporary analysis. No one writing about the music of the late eighteenth century can afford to ignore what its theorists have written about that repertoire. But insofar as today's writer necessarily proceeds from an aesthetic response to the musical object, he or she cannot take the eighteenth-century writing as law. These earlier writings must be incorporated into the horizon of the contemporary writer's own musical experience. The practical consequence of this conflict for me is that, while I acknowledge the contributions of Mattheson, Koch, Quantz, and others, I do not downplay my greater reliance on modern writers such as Schenker, Rosen, and Ratner.

A third conflict exists between what the musician conceives and what he or she perceives. There is no shortage of conceptual constructs in the theoretical literature, but we all know that the dictates of these constructs do not necessarily find corroboration in aural perception. Yet we need both frameworks, if for no other reason than that perception is not static, and therefore whatever temporal gap exists between what we conceive and what we perceive now is subject to closure at a future date. On a number of occasions throughout this book, I have succumbed to the lure of musical detail without seeking a governing conceptual construct for those details; on other occasions I have abandoned the musical surface in search of abstract constructs that have little to do with what I perceive.

A fourth and final conflict stems from the two modes of discourse employed in this book— verbal (words) and graphic (music). Both are necessarily mediated by some sort of conceptual apparatus, but, being two distinct systems, they are clearly nonequivalent. We use words to convey information about a piece of music, and I have done so throughout this book. But there are occasions when the limitations of words become especially severe, as, for example, when I have to make a summary statement about the significance or meaning of a particular piece or passage. The necessarily simple statements that represent endlessly complex musical phenomena must be seen as necessary evils. By contrast, the use of music notation to represent analytic decisions, while no less concept-dependent, has the advantage of narrowing the gap between music as object-language and music as metalanguage. To understand a voice-leading graph, one must hear it as well. There is then a graphic self-sufficiency that makes extensive verbal gloss redundant.

At each stage in the preparation of this book, I have been aware of the provisional nature of its results. Doubtless it would have been a better book had I waited another decade to write it. But the illusion of a definitive analysis, which must remain one of those fictive categories that we simultaneously attack (in practice) and uphold (in theory), may well be the only authority to which I can appeal in imposing arbitrary closure on the present discourse.

Ithaca, New York
December 1989

ACKNOWLEDGMENTS

ALTHOUGH I cannot mention everyone who has contributed either directly or indirectly to the writing of this book, a few specific acknowledgments must be made. Leonard Ratner introduced a deeply skeptical graduate student to the notion of expression in Classic music. I am grateful for his patience and counsel as teacher and advisor. It was in the company of my friends Valentin Mudimbe, Elizabeth Mudimbe-Boyi, and Arnd Bohm that I first heard the word "semiotics." I am not certain whether they will approve of the uses to which the word has been put here, but I am grateful to them for introducing me to a new and rich world of ideas. Arnd Bohm read several chapters in draft and offered many valuable comments. I am grateful to Laurence Dreyfus for reading and commenting on the second and third chapters, and particularly for making me realize the scope of the theoretical issues involved in this kind of investigation. Jonathan Berger and I first toyed with the idea of a project like this while attending Ratner's courses. I am grateful to him for allowing me to appropriate the results of those preliminary discussions. Arnold Whittall has been a constant source of encouragement and inspiration to me ever since I took the M. Mus. in Analysis at King's College London in 1978. While this book may not show what I have learned from him in the way of intellectual rigor, it could not have assumed even the present form without extensive conversations with him. I would also like to thank my friends and former colleagues Curtis Price, Mark Everist, Nicholas Marston, Nicola Lefanu, and David Lumsdaine, as well as the students in the Department of Music at King's College, who provided a stimulating and challenging environment in which to work. Finally, I owe a debt of gratitude to Christie, without whose love and encouragement this book might have taken considerably longer to write.

PLAYING WITH SIGNS

ONE

INTRODUCTION

I

HOW do composers reach their audiences? If we accept as valuable the traditional distinction among composers, performers, and listeners—roles that are not mutually exclusive of one another—then we might say that the search for an answer to this question forms an essential component of the activities of various musicians, irrespective of their individual callings as historians, theorists, analysts, and critics. The subject is just as relevant today as it was in 1781 when Wolfgang Amadeus Mozart, writing to his father from Vienna, described in fascinating detail the composition of portions of his opera *Die Entführung aus dem Serail*.[1] I will begin the present study by drawing attention to certain passages from this well-known letter, because the "communication problem" is succinctly captured here by one who not only understood it very well but developed successful, if individual, solutions to it. An analysis of Mozart's words can therefore provide a framework for studying some of the ways in which composers reach their audiences.

The specific subject of Mozart's letter is operatic composition. There is, first of all, the usual concern with singers and their particular voices. The composer is to take advantage of Herr Fischer's "excellent voice" for the part of Osmin. Similarly, Constanze's aria has been "sacrificed" a bit to accommodate the "flexible throat" of Mlle. Cavalieri. Mozart then anticipates the likely impact of certain passages of music. He plans to use "Turkish music" to inject a note of comedy into the scene in which Osmin expresses his rage. There is no question that the composer bears his audience very much in mind, for he is certain that this strategy will "have a good effect." In other words, Mozart expected his audience to be able to identify Turkish music and its traditional associations, and to react accordingly. And such a response was, in turn, possible because among the communicative codes he shared with his audience was one constituted by elements of an eighteenth-century affinity with the exotic, of which "Turkish music" formed a category. In addition to this kind of "extramusical" competence, Mozart exploits an assumed level of intramusical competence in the matter of the perception of closure: he seeks to surprise his listeners with a change of key and meter at the end of this aria. The crucial phrase, "when the aria seems to be at an end," presumes that the audience would recognize certain generic signals of closure, and would therefore be "fooled" into thinking that the piece was about to end. Other aspects of compositional manipulation are also alluded to by Mozart. Harmonic distance is one such issue; Mozart decides in favor of a modulation from F major to "the more remote A minor," rather than to "the nearest D minor." He also includes an element of the learned code, "a fairly respectable piece of real three-part writing" in the Trio at the end of Act 1 "because the words lend themselves to it." Elsewhere, he considers broader aspects of the thorny problem of music and words.

Mozart was, of course, writing to his mentor, so it may be argued that these comments are of no more than biographical interest—"shop talk" in today's parlance. Yet the numerous references to the audience found throughout his letters are, at the very least, an indication that strategies for effective communication were of more than average interest to him. This was a preoccupation

---

[1] This letter, dated 26 September 1781, appears as L(426) in Emily Anderson, ed., *The Letters of Mozart and His Family*, 768–70.

that he shared with several of his contemporaries, including Franz Joseph Haydn and, to a lesser extent, Ludwig van Beethoven. These composers, perhaps more explicitly than any others in the history of Western music, wrote decidely listener-oriented music. It is this public music of the later eighteenth century, commonly referred to as the Classic era (roughly 1770–1830), that forms the subject of this book.[2]

My point of departure is an implication drawn from Mozart's letter: if a central task of the composer is to reach his audience, then a central problem for the analyst is to uncover the various dimensions of this communicative process. Framed this way, the task is potentially forbidding. On one hand, it calls for a historical account of the psychology of audience response, and on the other, it requires the formulation of a critical apparatus that is both internally coherent and properly authorized by this historical interpretation. But even if the attainment of such an ideal seems difficult, it must not prevent us from taking a few steps in that direction. My broad aim, then, is to examine in detail a handful of works from this repertoire, paying particular attention to their meaning and significance as communicated through two channels, describable as "structural" and "expressive" attributes. I hope not only that the individual analyses will enhance an appreciation (or at least clarify the nature of our understanding) of these particular pieces, but also that the approach developed will contribute to the development of a theory of meaning for Classic music.

The analytical approach adopted in this book, broadly described as "semiotic," is defended more fully below, but it is worth noting the sense in which this semiotic interpretation draws on traditional categories of theory, analysis, and criticism. To analyze is to take apart and to show how constituent elements interact with one another to create a larger, not necessarily unified, whole. To criticize is to spice this analytical activity with evaluative comment, to return the clinical dissection to a humane environment. Both these activities, however, retain a dialectical relationship with theory. To analyze or criticize is necessarily to invoke certain theoretical postulates, whether or not these are made explicit. There is no such thing as a "neutral" analysis, an analysis free of theoretical prejudice. When people sometimes complain in the face of analytical orthodoxies that they are interested only in illuminating "the music," they all too often forget that their discourse cannot possibly be neutral even if they wished it to be. A semiotic interpretation uses the descriptive mechanism of semiotics to forge a *reading* of a particular work. Since this reading falls within the purview of both analysis and criticism, it is clear that a semiotic interpretation necessarily retains bonds with traditional analysis.

It is this play of critical modes that has dictated the shape of the book's argument. Chapter 1 outlines the broad parameters of the study. In Chapters 2 and 3, I defend theoretically the two central tools of my subsequent analyses. Chapter 2 deals with the referential or expressive aspects of Classic music as embodied in the notion of "topic," and Chapter 3 takes up notions of syntax and formal structure, proposing a simplified but, I believe, effective model for the analysis of harmonic rhetoric. The interpretive exercise in Chapters 4, 5, and 6 is conceived as an *explication*

---

[2] There is, of course, nothing sacred about the dates 1770–1830, except that they encompass the period in which all the music analyzed in this book was composed. (Only in the closing chapter on Romanticism do we overstep these boundaries.) Although considering the various phases of classicism is tangential to my concerns, the results of my analyses may well stimulate such discussion. A concise summary of the issues involved in periodization may be found in Reinhard G. Pauly, *Music in the Classic Period*, 1–10. See also Ludwig Finscher, *Studien zur Geschichte des Streichquartetts*—which, although it is restricted by both genre and composer, nevertheless includes a valuable diachronic history of the classical style. A more theoretical approach to the issues of periodization may be found in Carl Dahlhaus, *Foundations of Music History*, 15–18. For a recent survey of the meanings associated with the terms "Classic" and "classical" as they apply to this and other periods of music history, see Daniel Heartz, "Classical," in *The New Grove Dictionary of Music and Musicians*. In this book, I shall use "Classic" throughout.

de texte, but, to mitigate the potential boundlessness of such an exercise, I have slanted my readings in particular ways to reflect what I perceive to be essential in each work analyzed. Chapter 7 sets out in abstract and summary form the theory underlying the analyses, and an Epilogue speculates on some possible applications of the method pursued here to Romantic music.

The recurring question for me throughout these pages concerns *meaning* in Classic music—not "what does this piece mean?" but, rather, "*how* does this piece mean?" In other words, it seems more useful, in the face of the multiplicity of potential meanings of any single work, to frame the analytical question in terms of the dimensions that make meaning possible; only then can we hope to reduce away the fanciful meanings that are likely to crop up in an unbridled discussion of the phenomenon, and to approach the preferred meanings dictated by both historical and theoretical limitations. This is one reason why I have borrowed certain concepts from semiotics, for semiotics provides a useful searchlight for understanding the nature and sources of meaning, even if it ultimately evades—or declares irrelevant—the "what" question.

While acknowledging the usefulness of semiotics, I should also point out that this book is addressed first and foremost to the musical community. Linguists and literary critics will not find any advances in theory or methodology here; nor will they find rank definitions of basic musical terms for amateurs. It will be apparent that I operate within a familiar tradition of music analysis, and this discovery may even lead my critics to argue that the appeal to semiotics is a private one, one that need not be brought out into the open. To this charge I plead guilty, but offer the defense that because the present attempt to engage literary-critical discourse forms part of the contemporary history of music theory (whose antecedents, in any case, include borrowings of concepts as well as terminology from grammar, rhetoric, logic, and other areas), any attempt to suppress this affinity is likely to have been motivated by a resistance to theory—which should be construed as patently ahistorical. But this is where and why we need to be specific about the usefulness of semiotics. The best way for me to discuss this issue—indeed to demystify the supposed novelty of semiotics—is to re-create the context of previous studies of Classic music (which means essentially summarizing the approaches of Charles Rosen and Leonard Ratner), and to extract from the nature of these discourses an explicit concern with language. We will then be in a position to show the extent to which a semiotic awareness is already implicit in these and other efforts.[3]

II

According to Rosen, the classical style is to be seen and heard in the works of its three major exponents, Haydn, Mozart, and Beethoven. Theirs is a profoundly dramatic musical style based on the strategic exploitation of certain potent tonal relationships. These relationships were established in the works of earlier eighteenth-century composers such as Bach and Handel, but exploited for their own sake in the works of later eighteenth-century composers. The explicit

---

[3] See Charles Rosen, *The Classical Style* and Leonard G. Ratner, *Classic Music: Expression, Form, and Style*. Because a great deal has been written about the music of the Classic era, the choice of two representative studies becomes a difficult and ultimately personal decision. In isolating these two studies, I have not overlooked style-critical attempts, such as Guido Adler's *Der Stil in der Musik*, Jan La Rue's *Guidelines for Style Analysis*, or Eugene Wolf's *The Symphonies of Johann Stamitz*, all of whose emphases are on taxonomic frameworks. Nor have I overlooked the style-historical synthesis of Finscher (cited in Note 2). Of more immediate relevance to my concerns are discussions of style in Giorgio Pestelli, *The Age of Mozart and Beethoven*, Friedrich Blume, *Classic and Romantic Music*, and Joseph Kerman, *The Beethoven Quartets*. Other studies will be referred to in conjunction with specific works.

concern with the dramatic element in a work's beginning, middle, or end was, Rosen implies, quite without precedent and has since been without rival in the history of Western music. The most fundamental source of dramatic tension in this style is the tonic-dominant polarity, which serves to sustain the power of musical discourse in genres as diverse as opera, concerto, string quartet, and symphony. Rosen's way of justifying his hypothesis is to cite numerous passages, some typical, but most atypical, to support his single recurring point that the music of the late eighteenth century is overtly dramatic in intent, and that the apprehension of this drama constitutes the most valuable challenge for the listener. His method may be described as critical insofar as his observations are always spiced with evaluative comment. The net effect of such an approach, however, is that the classical style, ostensibly the subject of the book, is left undefined. Its normative features are taken as axiomatic, rather than stated in the form of abstractions. Rosen invites us to see the style in action, not to seek a comprehensive definition of it.

Although there are points of contact between their respective books, the approaches of Rosen and Ratner differ significantly in their ultimate emphases. Ratner's aim is "to describe the stylistic premises of Classic music" from its simplest to its most elaborate manifestations. The normative thus assumes an important role in his study, and there is a constant invocation of various formulas culled from the prescriptions of numerous eighteenth-century theorists. More important, the analytical principles extracted from these theoretical works are applied to various pieces. Thus, "expression," without which "no [Classic] piece was fit to be heard," is described in terms of conventional topics or "subjects of musical discourse," and illustrated by excerpts from a wide range of works by the three major composers of the period, as well as by several minor ones. Similarly, "musical rhetoric" is defined with respect to the norms of periodic organization, which include harmony, rhythm, texture, melody, and performance. The same approach is extended to "form" in its myriad manifestations as sonata form, couplet forms, forms of the learned style, aria, concerto, and fantasia. Normative national styles are also isolated, as are high and low styles reflecting the stratification of eighteenth-century society. Ratner's book closes with a description of three major compositions—Mozart's *Don Giovanni*, Haydn's Piano Sonata in E♭ Major, Hob. XVI: 52, and Beethoven's String Quartet Op. 59, No.1—chosen not because they typify the classical style, but because they utilize, challenge, and thereby affirm its premises.

If we can assume that the studies by Rosen and Ratner are representative of the range of methodologies followed by students of Classic music, we can go on to observe that the specific concern with normative procedures—whether these are treated axiomatically as with Rosen, or spelled out in the form of formulaic recipes as with Ratner—grows out of the feeling that the classical style approximates a *language* "spoken" by Haydn, Mozart, Beethoven, and their contemporaries. Most scholars acknowledge the exemplary and polished nature of this music, hence the terms "Classic," "classical," and "classic," even where attempts are made to dispense with the label altogether.[4] The uniformity of intent necessary for this style to attain the status of a language can therefore be inferred from this characterization. But inference is weaker than explicit demonstration—hence my reference to a "feeling," by which I mean a persistent current that informs these writings in the form of a subtext; it guides the formulation of the authors' concepts but it is never made explicit. What is the precise nature and the extent of the linguistic analogy in writings about Classic music? To answer this question, we need to examine a few characteristic descriptions of the music.

---

[4] Misconceptions generated by the use of the word "classical" lead Kerman, for example, to "take the plunge and eliminate it entirely" from his book *Listen*, 245.

Descriptions of music in terms of language or language-based disciplines are commonplace in the musicological literature. In the seventeenth and eighteenth centuries, rhetoric provided a useful model for such discourse, and theorists freely borrowed the language and terminology of rhetoricians.[5] Thus Joachim Burmeister, in his *Musica Poetica* of 1601, drew on literary concepts to characterize compositional strategy as a threefold process—*exordium, confirmatio*, and *conclusio*. Johann Mattheson also relied a great deal on rhetorical terms in characterizing the process of a piece of music. In his *Vollkommene Capellmeister* of 1739, Mattheson extended Burmeister's three-stage model to a six-stage one as follows: *exordium* (introduction), *narratio* (report), *propositio* (proposal), *confirmatio* (corroboration), *confutatio* (refutation), and *peroratio* (conclusion). Later in the century, Heinrich Koch continued, on the one hand, to borrow from rhetoric while, on the other hand, showing a decisive shift from rhetoric to (or, more accurately, *back* to) linguistics, from rhetorical terms to grammatical ones. These trends have continued to the present day, both informally in music criticism, and more formally in the recent theories of Allan Keiler, Mario Baroni, David Lidov, and Lerdahl and Jackendoff, among others.[6]

What distinguishes writing about Classic music from that about other music is not merely a general awareness of the affinities between music and language, but a persistent concern with a shadowy linguistic analogy at all levels. Is it perhaps the case that Mozart and Haydn "spoke one language" whereas Brahms and Wagner, Schumann and Chopin, or Bach and Rameau spoke different languages? Certainly a hasty response to this question might cite the fact that it is, at least superficially, easier to mistake, for example, Haydn for Mozart (and vice versa) than it is to mistake Brahms for Wagner or Rameau for Bach. One might then go on to cite sociological factors—such as the presence of a certain societal uniformity in the late eighteenth century, which was then overthrown in the nineteenth, leading to a profound individualization in artistic expression—to support such a viewpoint.[7] Yet our hasty response will still have left many questions unanswered.

I have assembled a number of passages from the writings of Rosen, Ratner, and Friedrich Blume to buttress my claim for a "persistent concern with a shadowy linguistic analogy," by which I mean that extensive use continues to be made of an analogy whose meaning and significance are anything but clear. The ensuing exercise is, however, strictly a look at the nature of the authors' discourse, not an evaluation of their specific viewpoints.

The first sentence of *The Classical Style* already contains the word "language," and one need not look beyond the table of contents to see the importance attached to it: two chapters called "The Musical Language of the Late Eighteenth Century" and "The Coherence of the Musical Language" are announced. But there does not seem to be a specific sense in which Rosen uses the word "language." We are first told that the classical style is an "art," but that as a style it "creates

---

[5] Sources of the most frequently used rhetorical terms as applied to music may be found in George Buelow, "Rhetoric and Music," *The New Grove Dictionary of Music and Musicians*. See also Hans Heinrich Unger, *Die Beziehungen zwischen Musik und Rhetorik*, and the digest in Ian Bent, *Analysis*, 6–11. Also of interest is Bent's "The 'Compositional Process' in Music Theory, 1713–1850," which includes a concise summary of the terms used by theorists such as Mattheson, Koch, Lobe, Sulzer, and Czerny to describe aspects of musical form.

[6] See Allan Keiler, "Bernstein's 'The Unanswered Question' and the Problem of Musical Competence," idem, "Two Views of Musical Semiotics," Mario Baroni, "The Concept of Musical Grammar," David Lidov, "Nattiez's Semiotics of Music," idem, "Musical and Verbal Semantics," idem, "The Allegretto of Beethoven's Seventh," and Fred Lerdahl and Ray Jackendoff, *A Generative Theory of Tonal Music*. For a comprehensive survey of the language-music analogy, including references to non-Western music, see Harold Powers, "Language Models and Music Analysis."

[7] Rose Rosengard Subotnik discusses this historical shift in "The Cultural Message of Musical Semiology."

a mode of understanding." Style becomes an "isolatable" and "definable [system] of expression." Style is then described "figuratively" as "a way of focusing a language, which then becomes a dialect or language in its own right." Rosen acknowledges that "analogies with language break down because a style is finally itself treated as a work of art." This, however, does not prevent him from continuing to invoke linguistic analogies. He writes: "the relation of the classical style to the 'anonymous' style of musical vernacular of the late eighteenth century is that it represents not only a synthesis of the artistic possibilities of the age, but also a purification of the irrelevant residue of past traditions." A "musical vernacular" has now entered into the picture, although its relationship to the "musical language" remains obscure. Then we are told plainly that "the musical language which made the classical style possible is that of tonality, which was not a massive immobile system but a living, gradually changing language from its beginning." Presumably, then, the classical style is not the language but, rather, tonality? Or is tonality the language and the classical style a sort of metalanguage? Here, it must be said that the issues are especially imprecise.

Other linguistic terms continue to be used freely throughout the book. For example, "if we do not feel the 'second' theme of the Appassionata Sonata as a variant of the opening, we have missed an important part of the discourse." There are references to "the discursive logic of [Classic music]," to a "syntactic and often dramatic movement," and to "the blending of genres." Taking a larger historical context, Rosen sees the classical style as "a step in the progressive realization of the musical language as it had existed and developed since the fifteenth century." The four-measure phrase is described as "paradigm" as distinct from the "model." And so on.

In these randomly chosen passages, we have encountered a variety of terms whose origin in linguistic and language-based disciplines is self-evident: "language," "dialect," "vernacular," "style," "logic," "discourse," "model," "paradigm," and "syntax." It is, of course, true that writers on music have always borrowed terminology from other disciplines, but this concentration on terms associated with language transcends what one normally finds. There is clearly a need for a systematic analysis of the nature of discourse on Classic music. Attractive though such a project might be, however, it is tangential to my concerns here. So long as the basic point—that writing about Classic music seems to require reference to a language model—is acceptable, we can proceed with the terms in which this can be carried out. But before doing that, let us consider other manifestations of this same general tendency.

In the preface to *Classic Music*, Ratner acknowledges the linguistic analogy as a point of departure for "a full-scale explication of the stylistic premises of classic music." He refers to "universally accepted formulas" that were used by composers. The following passage captures the extent of his dependence on the linguistic analogy:

> This consistency [in composers' handling of material] bespeaks a *language* understood throughout Europe and parts of the New World. Moreover, to speak of 18th-century music as a language is not simply to use a figure of speech. Structural parallels between music and oratory follow a clear path through music theory of the 17th and 18th centuries. Just as there were rules for organizing an oratorical discourse, so were there explicit prescriptions for building a musical progression. Both language and music had their vocabulary, syntax, and arrangement of formal structures, subsumed under the title *Rhetoric*.[8]

Here we have, in capsule form, the entire semiotic enterprise spelled out by one who does not claim a semiotic orientation: a syntax, a syntagmatic chain ("arrangement of formal

[8] Ratner, *Classic Music*, xiv.

structures"), and rules of transformation ("explicit prescriptions for building a musical progression"). However, Ratner, like Rosen, treats the language analogy as a figure of speech—this in spite of his words to the contrary. How appropriate is the use of the term "speak" for the transmission of a piece of music? If music, like language, has a vocabulary, what are its words, and what do they mean? Do we all possess musical competence just as we do linguistic competence? Ratner is less interested in confronting these basic questions than he is in retaining the analogical use of the terms.[9]

And finally, Friedrich Blume: the fourth chapter of his *Classic and Romantic Music* is entitled "The Nations, 'Mixed Taste,' and the 'Universal Language'." Like Ratner, he advocates the idea of universals in musical expression. The following passage identifies two phases in the evolution of the Classical style, and it is in this description that the language analogy is again strongly invoked:

> The genetic history of [the classical] style may be divided into two phases, an early Classic, which extends from the beginnings (1740) into the 1770s and includes the so-called style galant and style of "sensibility"(*Empfindsamkeit*) and a High Classic, in which forms and stylistic means remained basically constant (grammar and syntax of the universal language had been developed, so to speak) and composers were in a position to shape ideas that sprang from their free imagination in a fully evolved language, according to their personal capacity. The elementary forms of the style were all fashioned in the early Classic phase; seen from the point of view of literary style history, the High Classic phase brought their further development only in the distinctive modes of speech of the individual masters.[10]

Here, too, Blume's expression speaks for itself: "style," "grammar," "syntax," "universal language," "fully evolved language," and "distinctive modes of speech" all underline his fundamental reliance on the linguistic analogy and metaphor.

For language to provide a useful model for musical analysis, it must do at least three things: first, it must explain the laws that govern the moment-by-moment succession of events in a piece, that is, the syntax of music. Second and consequently, it must explain the constraints affecting organization at higher levels—the levels of sentence, paragraph, chapter, and beyond. It must, in other words, provide a framework for understanding the *discourse* of music.[11] Third, it must demonstrate, rather than merely assume, that music represents a *bona fide* system of communication, and must then go on to show what is being communicated and how. The predominant concern of music theory so far has been with the development of a syntax for music—thus, Schenker's theory of tonal music, various eighteenth-century theorists' prescriptions for composition, and Fred Lerdahl and Ray Jackendoff's recent theory of tonal music: all these are attempts to formulate a syntax for tonal music.[12] Although accounts of syntax can themselves be hierarchic and hence, as in Schenker, vitally involved with higher levels of "meaning," one often has to infer these levels of meaning by reading between the lines rather than reading the lines themselves. And the communication issue, because it is so closely bound up with the status of

---

[9] For further discussion, see Keiler, "Bernstein's 'The Unanswered Question'" and Lerdahl and Jackendoff, *A Generative Theory of Tonal Music*, 314–330

[10] Blume, *Classic and Romantic Music*, 30.

[11] Antony Easthope, *Poetry as Discourse*, 8.

[12] Schenker's theory of tonal music, developed over a period of thirty years, reaches its most refined form in *Der freie Satz (Free Composition)*. The prescriptions of eighteenth-century theorists are quoted extensively throughout Ratner, *Classic Music*. Lerdahl's and Jackendoff's *A Generative Theory of Tonal Music* takes advantage of contemporary linguistic and music-theoretical research to provide a *"formal description of the musical intuitions of a listener who is experienced in a musical idiom,"* 1.

language as an interpreting system, becomes more and more complex.[13]

The foregoing discussion is not meant to devalue the significance of analogy per se. To say that discussions of music in terms of the linguistic model are best left on the level of analogy is to hint at a possible analytical framework that cuts across these two systems. To understand the processes of one system in terms of those of another may prove enlightening. By drawing attention to the limitations of analogy, however, we are made more aware of the need to look within the "purely musical" for an interpretive framework, and, assuming that such a search yields something positive, not only to accord this intramusical framework the highest status in analysis, but also to treat its similarity to other frameworks as fortuitous—or, at best, suggestive.

Viewed from the perspective of post-Saussurean linguistics, the engagement with language in the writings of Rosen, Ratner, and Blume is also an implicit engagement with semiotics. The danger with such a claim, however, is that it may stretch the purview of semiotics so widely that it takes in practically all signifying phenomena. Yet such an enterprise in no way contradicts the fundamental motivation of semiotics, which is a sharper delineation of the ways in which we know things. It is beyond the scope of this study to provide a comprehensive survey of semiotics and music, but I should like to acknowledge those contributions that have left visible traces on the present study.

III

As one of the most significant developments in twentieth-century intellectual history, semiotics has had a liberating influence on disciplines as diverse as linguistics, anthropology, literature (including drama), music, and several others. Umberto Eco's list of "political boundaries" of the "field" of semiotics includes the following categories and subcategories: zoosemiotics, olfactory signs, tactile communication, codes of taste, paralinguistics, medical semiotics, kinesics and proxemics, musical codes, formalized languages, written languages, unknown languages, secret codes, natural languages, visual communication, systems of objects, plot structure, text theory, cultural codes, aesthetic texts, mass communication, and rhetoric![14] The fact that it resists simple definition—is it a field or a discipline?—is perhaps the strongest testimony to its searching and dynamic quality. That no semiotic inquiry completely severs its bonds with traditional modes of thought further testifies to its inert historicism.

"We think only in signs," wrote Charles Sanders Peirce, whose broad aim, according to Émile Benveniste, was to develop "an increasingly complex apparatus of definitions aimed at distributing all of reality, the conceptual, and the experiential into various categories of signs."[15] To contemplate the various ways in which we might distribute the "signs" of music is to gain a sense of the magnitude of the enterprise. First we need to solve, or at least to define more precisely, the problem with which Roman Ingarden and others have grappled—the identity of the work.[16] Then, depending on whether we locate it in a certain notational representation, or in a specific realization, or in   an idealization of that realization, or in the interface of a specific realization and the listener's idealization, or in the composer's idealized realization—we would go on to develop the appropriate definitional

---

[13] On the question of music as a system of communication, see Nattiez, *Musicologie Générale et Sémiologie*, Chapter 1, especially 38–51.

[14] Umberto Eco, *A Theory of Semiotics*, 9–14.

[15] Émile Benveniste, "The Semiology of Language."

[16] Roman Ingarden, *The Work of Music and the Problem of Its Identity*.

apparatus. And even if we narrowed down the enterprise to the notes on paper—as seems convenient for the analyst—we would still need to contend with various lower-level signs and significations including clefs, pitches, and expressive markings, not to mention the conventional parameters of melody, harmony, rhythm, timbre, and others. The mind boggles at the thought of a "universal algebra of [musical] equations!"

Because the attainment of Peirce's ideal has not proved to be an easy task, many scholars have followed the urge to limit realistically their domain of inquiry. In fact the huge and complex edifice that Peirce erected for distributing various kinds of reality has more or less trickled away, leaving in its wake a tripartite division of signs into icons, indices, and symbols. And it is the implication of this state of affairs that motivates Robert Scholes's claim that "the great usefulness of semiotics ... will not be found in its elaborate analytical taxonomies, but rather is to be derived from a small number of its most basic and powerful concepts, ingeniously applied."[17]

What does the field of music semiotics promise? The inevitable point of departure, in light of the foregoing remarks about Peirce, is an attempt to delimit the field in order to focus the analytical enterprise. Robert E. Innis offers the following questions for attending to such an exercise: "What is a sign? Why are there signs? Where do signs come from? How many types and kinds of signs are there? What is the basis for their classification? What are their respective powers? How do they stand to one another? What are the various uses to which they can be put?"[18]

The all-embracing nature of these questions already suggests the magnitude of the methodological problems facing music semioticians. The fact, though, that these are basic questions about the nature of musical communication itself suggests that they may have been considered earlier in the history of musical thought. It should therefore be acknowledged that semiotics, although it has sharpened the formulation of these questions, is not the first discipline to point to them. There is, in fact, an important prehistory of musical semiotics that has been virtually ignored by recent semioticians, a history that dates back to the seventeenth and eighteenth centuries. It would take me too far afield to begin to recount that history here, but suffice it to say that "semiotic awareness"—if that is taken to mean the awareness of music as a sign system or a system of signification—was very much in the minds of eighteenth-century music theorists such as Johann Mattheson, Francesco Galeazzi, Heinrich Koch, and Johann Friedrich Daube. It is difficult to imagine that a great rationalistic age such as the eighteenth century did not consider fundamental questions about music's meaning and capacity for signification.[19]

Out of the wide variety of music-theoretical offerings now claiming a semiotic orientation has emerged two distinct schools of semioticians, one which I shall call the *taxonomic-empiricists* (following Allan Keiler),[20] and the other, which I shall call the *semanticists*. These two groups espouse different gospels both between each other and, to a lesser extent, within each one. There is, however, sufficient consistency of purpose to justify the labels. The taxonomic-empiricist *par excellence* is Jean-Jacques Nattiez, whose numerous publications have come to be regarded as representative of the field of music semiotics. In a comprehensive survey of the field of musical

---

[17] Robert Scholes, *Semiotics and Interpretation*, xi.

[18] Innis, *Semiotics*, vii.

[19] A proper account of the prehistory of music semiotics might take as point of departure the numerous theoretical treatises of the eighteenth century that describe musical grammar, language, and linguistics as well as various referential modes of signification. A synthesis of these findings could then be set against the results of recent linguistic and semiotic research. Although not formulated in explicitly semiotic terms, Ratner's *Classic Music* provides valuable grounds for writing this history.

[20] Keiler, "Two Views of Musical Semiotics," 139.

semiotics published in 1977, Nattiez undermines the efforts of semanticists in order to uphold his own as the more promising semiotic method: "The goal of a musical semiotics is to inventory the types and modalities of symbolic references to which the music gives rise, and to elaborate an appropriate methodology to describe their symbolic functioning."[21]

If the "symbolic" were to play more than a nominal role in Nattiez's semiology there would be, at least potentially, a way of reconciling the enterprise of the taxonomic-empiricists with that of the semanticists. No such synthesis develops, however. Instead, Nattiez single-mindedly pursues a rigorous distributional-analytic method, whose premises are indebted to the work of Nicholas Ruwet and Jean Molino. Among the numerous categories developed, one of the most useful—because of the way it clarifies the analytical enterprise—is the poietic–esthesic–neutral tripartition, which Nattiez borrows from Jean Molino. The poietic describes the production processes of a work, while the esthesic describes its perception processes. But it is the neutral level that holds the most potential for Nattiez. Being "a descriptive level containing the most exhaustive inventory possible of all types of configurations conceivably recognizable in a score,"[22] it satisfies the analyst's instinct to eliminate as many a priori decisions as possible, and to develop an objective, and in some senses a scientific or empirical, analysis of music. We have already come a long way from Nattiez's ideal aspiration to provide an account of the *symbolic* nature of music. It seems that the methodological apparatus has become so involved in its appeal to rigor that Nattiez is not quite able to return the analysis to the level of the music as a symbolic phenomenon. Thus, even in the most impressive of his analyses—the one of Varèse's "Density 21.5," which also typifies the method of the taxonomic-empiricists—the great interest seems to lie precisely in those improvisatory moments at which the technical issues are in conflict and are therefore suspended in order that a symbolic aspect of the music might be elucidated.[23]

For two main reasons this study does not follow the tradition of the taxonomic empiricists: first, although I sympathize with the essential interpretive motivation of Nattiez's work, I find the execution, especially its severe taxonomic framework, profoundly tautological. And although a certain amount of tautology is unavoidable in music analysis, the reluctance of taxonomic-empiricists to transcend those very taxonomies makes their work more interesting with respect to method than to application. Second, the taxonomic-empiricists have had virtually nothing to say about the repertoire that we are considering in this book.

The semanticists, the other group of semioticians, form a much more heterogenous group. It consists of the writers who have, in one way or another, addressed questions of meaning in music

---

[21] Nattiez, "The Contribution of Musical Semiotics to the Semiotic Discussion in General."

[22] Nattiez, "Varèse's 'Density 21.5': A Study in Semiological Analysis," 244.

[23] The best introduction to and critical assessment of Nattiez's ideas is David Lidov's "Nattiez's Semiotics of Music." Nattiez's many writings on musical semiotics pose a serious problem for anyone attempting a quick summary, for the connecting thread is not always clearly visible. Thus, the distributional-analytic framework of *Fondements* and the Varèse analysis yield to what might be described as a metacritical approach in *Musicologie Générale et Sémiologie*. Moreover, a central construct, such as the tripartition, is redefined in the later work—obviously in response to the various attacks on the notion of a neutral level—to include six levels. This process of redefinition, played out vigorously in public, makes it difficult to support a stable view of Nattiez's semiotics. In retaining my references to his earlier, rather than later, works in this book, I am merely pointing to those issues that were discussed at particular stages of semiotic thinking, rather than holding Nattiez to positions that he has since left behind. Numerous and diverse responses to Nattiez's work have touched on, among other things, the nature of analysis, the nature of style, the nature of Varèse's music, and the legitimate scope of music semiotics. See reviews of *Fondements* by Rose Rosengard Subotnik, Robert S. Hatten, Jonathan Dunsby, and Roger Scruton. See also Jonathan Bernard's critique of Nattiez's Varèse analysis in "On 'Densité 21.5': A Response to Nattiez." Nattiez responds to his critics in *Musicologie Générale et Sémiologie*.

by invoking (formally or informally) notions of sign-functioning. They are not theorists so much as interpreters. The following survey makes no attempt at comprehensiveness. Wilson Coker's *Music and Meaning*,[24] committed as it is to Peircean trichotomies on one hand, and a fluid, psychologically based model of musical signification on the other hand, becomes, in the end, an application of semiotic principles to the analysis of music, rather than an analysis of music using semiotic principles as an aid. Particularly fruitful is the distinction between congeneric and extrageneric meaning, which roughly parallels the structural/expressive, introversive/extroversive, and similar oppositions that I shall develop later on. Of more direct relevance to this work are Frits Noske's essays on Mozart and Verdi operas, which rely on conventional or associative signs for forging various readings.[25] Although Noske's methodological premises are not always secure, his willingness to speculate on various types and shades of meaning, even where the exercise contradicts the theoretical stance, is suggestive. It serves further to remind us of the need to keep theory and interpretation in a healthy symbiotic relationship.

David Lidov's essays on various aspects of semiotics seem to me to achieve an enviable balance between theory and interpretation, providing a positive compromise between traditional music theory and the new semiotic literature. His essay on Nattiez, redraws the boundaries of music semiotics in order to show that the theories of Leonard Meyer, for example, are vitally involved with semiotics. Similarly, Lidov's attempt to incorporate Berlioz's hermeneutic reading of the Allegretto of Beethoven's Seventh Symphony into a semiotic interpretation, quite apart from the provocative results that it yields, provides a bridge between the poeticizing analyses of certain nineteenth-century writers on music and the more self-consciously theoretical bent of recent semiotics.[26]

A more significant debt is owed to three writers who do not claim a semiotic orientation, but whose work displays affinities with that of semanticists. Ratner's *Classic Music*, mentioned earlier in this chapter, deciphers meaning from a reading of its signs as both referential and rhetorical. Janet Levy's short study of the opening movement of Haydn's String Quartet Op. 64, No. 3 relies on a particular definition of a specific musical sign—the closing gesture—as a conventional sign; she then shows how Haydn, relying on the competence of his listeners, "plays" in ingenious ways with this sign. In other words, Levy isolates both the physical sign itself and its shifting semantic value throughout the movement.[27] Finally and most importantly, Wye Jamison Allanbrook's study, *Rhythmic Gesture in Mozart*,[28] uses both eighteenth-century theorists' and Ratner's notions of reference to read *Figaro* and *Don Giovanni* with respect to a number of conventionalized signs—in this case, the specific signs stemming from the eighteenth-century dance repertoire.[29]

[24] Wilson Coker, *Music* and *Meaning*.

[25] Frits Noske, *The Signifier and the Signified*.

[26] David Lidov, "Nattiez's Semiotics of Music"; idem, "Musical and Verbal Semantics," and "The Allegretto of Beethoven's Seventh."

[27] Janet M. Levy, "Gesture, Form and Syntax in Haydn's Music." See also her "Texture as a Sign in Classic and Early Romantic Music."

[28] Wye Jamison Allanbrook, *Rhythmic Gesture in Mozart*.

[29] It is an almost thankless job to attempt to summarize all the writings on music that claim a semiotic orientation. The proceedings of the 1973 Belgrade conference, published as *Actes du 1er Congrès Internationale de Sémiotique*, offer a heterogenous collection of essays in semantics, semiotics, and old-fashioned style criticism—all of which point to the extraordinary diversity of the field. Nattiez's outline of the field (cited in Note 21) encompasses a broad bibliography (through 1976). Among recent publications, the following may be cited: Reinhard Schneider's, *Semiotik der Musik*, Vera Mizcnik's "Gesture as Sign," Eero Tarasti's *Myth and Music* [reviewed by Robert S. Hatten in *Semiotica* 30 (1980): 345–58], Patricia Tunstall's "Structuralism and Musicology," David Osmond-Smith's "Music as Communication," Raymond Monelle's "Symbolic Models in Music Aesthetics," Peter Faltin's "Musikalische Syntax," idem, "Musikalische Bedeutung," John Stopford's "Structuralism, Semiotics and Musicology," and Charles Boilès' "Processes of Musical Semiosis."

It is questionable whether the efforts of my semanticists qualify as semiotics. In one sense, this is simply a problem of definition. But since the relationship between semantics and semiotics has sometimes remained obscure, it may be worth our while to clarify the distinction as the final stage in this preliminary discussion.

Benveniste, in the article cited earlier,[30] has aired these issues with particular lucidity, and his words will serve us here too. Although his discussion is concerned with language, a simple substitution of "music" for "language" is, in most cases, sufficient to clarify the distinction between semiotics and semantics, without implying any added levels of equivalence between the processes of the two semiotic systems. First of all, Benveniste notes that these two "modes of meaning" are characteristic of language. This is, of course, true of music, although there are profound disagreements about what the semantic mode denotes. Benveniste goes on to say that "the only question to which a sign gives rise, if it is to be recognized as such, is that of its existence, and the latter is answered by yes or no." He emphasizes this "neutral" aspect of the linguistic sign: "All semiotic research, in the strictest sense, consists of the identification of units, the description of characteristic features, and the discovery of the increasingly fine criteria of their distinctiveness." This reads as a perfect description of Nattiez's efforts, especially as it pertains to the analysis of the neutral level. And so, Benveniste concludes, "Taken in itself, the sign is pure identity itself, totally foreign to all other signs, the signifying foundation of language, the material necessity for statement. It exists when it is recognized as signifier by all members of a linguistic community, and when it calls forth for each individual roughly the same associations and oppositions. Such is the province and the criterion of semiotics."

The semantic mode, on the other hand, is a mode of meaning "generated by discourse." We know that language produces messages, and that it is the semantic mode that makes explicit the nature of those messages. Benveniste puts it like this: "Semantics takes over the majority of referents, while semiotics is in principle cut off and independent of all reference. Semantic order becomes identified with the world of enunciation and with the universe of discourse." Finally, in a direct assertion of the difference between the two modes, an assertion that seems to support music's semiotic properties while casting doubt on its semantic content, Benveniste notes: "Semiotics (the sign) must be recognized; semantics (the discourse) must be understood."

In Benveniste's view, then, the business of semiotics is the linguistic sign, whereas that of semantics is discourse. Nattiez's contribution echoes this fundamentalist definition of semiotics and works within its limits. The group of semanticists, on the other hand, although they are concerned with questions of discourse, have never, so far as I can tell, formulated their questions in this form. But it is clear that we need both modes in order to gain the richest understanding of Classic music. Benveniste in fact goes on to state, at the end of his article, that the semantic domain requires "a new conceptual and definitional apparatus." Musical semantics, too, seems to require "a new conceptual and definitional apparatus." Whatever form this new apparatus takes, however, it will have to show why the present apparatus is inadequate. I should therefore like to explore next some possible applications of key semiotic terms and concepts to music analysis. Implicit in such an exploration is a covert claim that the explanatory potential of these terms is in some senses greater than that of "traditional" music-analytical terminology—this in spite of the considerable overlap in explanatory domains. Since there is as yet no stable set of definitions for music-semiotic terms, I shall adopt a somewhat casual, common-sense approach to the pursuit of analogy, rather than unload various critical debates about the most basic of these terms. In any case, only after

[30] Benveniste, "The Semiology of Language."

the interpretive exercise at the end of this chapter will it be possible to judge the appropriateness or inappropriateness of these terms.[31]

IV

At the heart of Saussure's theory is a distinction between two dimensions of language: *langue*, which refers to the larger system of language, and *parole*, which may be translated as speech, or the individual utterances made by speakers of the language. Langue is social; parole, individual. We might think of the classical style as a langue, and the individual "utterances" of Mozart, Haydn, and their contemporaries as various paroles. This dialectical distinction between the two dimensions of language is not dissimilar to Ratner's idea of a universal eighteenth-century language, of which the various utterances of Haydn and others are "sublanguages." The distinction enables us to posit certain generalizations about eighteenth-century tonality, indeed the sort of generalizations that make possible Rosen's study of the classical style as a self-sufficient and self-regulating system. It is also possible to apply the langue-parole distinction on "lower" interpretive levels—that is, within the larger langue of a single composer's *oeuvre*. The language of Mozart's symphonies may be thought to embody a specific set of utterances, a specific parole, as opposed to the language of his operas, which would embody another parole. And if we admit this generic distinction—which is, of course, limited, as we shall see in Chapter 2—we can then go on to discern "subparoles" on even lower levels, not of genre, but of work, movement, section within movement, and so on.

We could also read the langue-parole distinction chronologically, taking account of another important distinction that structuralism has taught us—that between synchronic and diachronic dimensions. The historical changes represented in the evolution of a composer's language fall under the diachronic dimension. The study of a slice of that system, so to speak, without the props of chronology, encompasses the synchronic dimension. The latter has been an important component of the structuralist enterprise, and it informs the approaches of Rosen and, to a lesser extent, Ratner; it is also invoked in this book. The attempt to explicate the senses in which Classic music means relies on a synchronic view of the classical style, on a view of the style as complete at any given time and therefore capable of study in and of itself. But the actual account of meaning inevitably takes a narrative form, retaining an implicit diachronic dimension.

The synchronic-diachronic distinction permits the formulation of another fundamental structuralist-semiotic concept, the idea that the relationships between units of language are more important than any intrinsic properties of those units. Although we have not yet defined the elementary units of music, it is clear that we shall be dealing fundamentally with a relational system rather than with a substantive one. Musicians are familiar with this concept from the system of functional harmony, for example, by which a given note can take on different meanings depending on the key in which it occurs, and, within that key, the actual chord within which it functions. One subclass of this classificatory scheme, the so-called binary classification, in which the relationships between phenomena are perceived as oppositions, may also be seen in the metaphors that we apply to various dimensional behaviors: pitch and register are conceptualized within a high-low axis, rhythm and duration on a long-short axis, timbre on a dark-bright axis, texture on a thick-thin axis, and so on.

---

[31] For a concise introduction to these terms—to which my own discussion is indebted—see Terence Hawkes, *Structuralism and Semiotics*. Boilès provides a cogent explanation of basic semiotic terms in "Processes of Musical Semiosis."

Another widely used distinction in semiotics is that between paradigmatic relations and syntagmatic ones. The paradigmatic axis mirrors the vertical plane in language, and it takes account of the fact that certain units of language may be substituted for others without violating the essential grammatical structure. The syntagmatic plane, on the other hand, retains language's commitment to the flow of time, and depends on the gradual unfolding of linguistic meaning during the "performance" of a given utterance. These relations are readily understood in reference to any Classic piece. The idea of substitution along a vertical axis is well known to advocates of a theory of harmony that recognizes chords as functional families (as in Riemann). The substitution of a seventh chord for a dominant chord in a given cadential situation, for example, need not violate the actual grammatical construction, however different is the phenomenal experience it generates. A paradigmatic table of harmonic equivalences may therefore be drawn, in which possible substitutes are grouped together. Similarly, on the level of harmony, there are explicit rules in Classic music for the horizontal unfolding of chords. These laws, which we know today as abstractions from various theoretical writings, were followed explicitly by Classic composers and at the same time violated in the spirit of artistic license. The conjunction IV–V, for example, may be understood in particular contexts as an intensification toward the cadence. As in language, meaning is secured only when the entire chain has passed.[32]

Perhaps the most basic semiotic term, and one with the least stable meaning, is the sign. Peirce defined it as "something which stands to somebody for something in some respect or capacity." This definition depends on three constructs: an object, its interpretant, and its ground. For Saussure, the sign is a double entity, consisting of the union of the signifier and the signified. The signfier is the actual acoustic or sound image, a physical phenomenon. The signified is the concept embodied in a particular signifier. It is the "indissoluble union of the two components" that constitutes the linguistic sign. In attempting to define the musical sign or the elementary units of music, we face problems. For one thing, if we treat the individual note as the elementary unit, we run into the immediate problem that not only does a single note have no meaning except in relation to others, but also the note is, for all practical purposes, a very small unit indeed. The sheer labor involved in developing an analysis of a piano sonata, symphony, or opera, with the unfettered note as sign, is considerable, and speaks against such a premise. (It is not surprising that the most rigorous demonstrations of the taxonomic-empiricist method have been of monodies.) This is surely an indication that the elementary units of music are best defined at a level greater than the single note, and therefore that they embody a relationship as primitive.

There cannot be a single definition for "sign" in music, for each of a work's dimensions displays a unique mode of signification. Signs denoting tempo or expressive effect may be given in language as short phrases or words. Signs denoting "structural melody" will be understood only within a specified theory of diminution and displayed graphically (as often happens in Schenkerian analysis). And signs denoting topic are significant only within a cultural context that recognizes the conventional associations of certain kinds of musical material. To insist on a single and stable definition of musical sign is, to my mind, to falsify the semiotic enterprise even before it has begun.

[32] For further discussion of the syntagmatic-paradigmatic axis in music as it applies to the harmonic domain, see Lidov, "Nattiez's Semiotics of Music," 37–39 and Jonathan Dunsby, "A Hitch-Hiker's Guide to Semiotic Music Analysis." For a provocative application, see Dunsby's Schenkerian/semiotic (and, one might add, Jakobsonian) analysis of Beethoven in "A Bagatelle on Beethoven's WoO. 60," which "interprets WoO. 60 roughly as a projection of the paradigmatic axis onto the syntagmatic axis," (68).

V

So much for background and terminology. These simple definitions of terms and generalizations about their possible application, useful though they may be as points of orientation for later discussion, must ultimately yield to a consideration of actual music, since it is only in the deployment of the terms that their usefulness can be assessed. I should now like to close this chapter with another reference to Mozart—not to his words, with which we began this chapter, but to his music—the first sixteen measures of the Symphony No. 38 in D Major, K. 504, which dates from 1786 (see Example1.1).

The aim of the following sample analysis is to outline an interpretive framework for Classic music in which the two central concerns of this book, expression and structure, engage with each other. With the aid of the notion of "topic" (elaborated upon in Chapter 2) a reading of the surface of Classic music as historically and socioculturally specific is first developed. Topics, however, are defined by specific dimensional behaviors. Procedurally, this requires an engagement with the supremely relational pitch structure, followed by a playing off of the referential surface against the apparently nonreferential tonal structure. I hope to show that, in its historicism, the nonteleological topical discourse contains the seeds of its own destruction, so to speak, and that

Example 1.1. Rhetoric and structure in Mozart's Symphony No. 38 in D Major ("Prague") K. 504—
First movement, measures 1–16

Example 1.1. (*cont.*)

its validation requires the background of an intramusical discourse (formulated after Schenker). The latter, on the other hand, is best understood against the processes of topical signification although it can be (and often is) discussed independently. I shall conclude that it is within the confines of this *play* between the two modes that we may apprehend the rich meanings that underlie this far-from-"classical" music.

First, the elements of expression: Since I shall deal more fully with the notion of topic in Chapter 2, I will mention here only that topics are subjects of musical discourse, and that they provide a framework for discussing various kinds and levels of associative signification in eighteenth- century music. Example 1.1 shows Ratner's topical analysis of the first sixteen measures of the "Prague."[33] The analyst's aim is to distribute the reality of the piece into two broad classes of signs—the sequence of topical or referential signs given in the top layer of annotations, and the more heterogenous set of what might be called "formal" signs (here, the application of certain rhetorical categories to music), given below (I shall return to this second set of labels later). The list of referential signs, drawn from eighteenth-century historiography, is as follows: French overture, coups d'archet, sensibility, singing style, learned style, fanfare, sensibility (again), fanfare (again), and ombra (supernatural). The argument here is that we hear this texturally fragmented musical surface not as a sequence of value-free signs, but as a set of references to various historically-situated styles and types of music current in the eighteenth-century.

How are we to evaluate Ratner's analysis? I suggest, following Roman Jakobson, that we insist on two things: first, that the analysis have intuitive adequacy, and second, that it display descriptive adequacy. On the first count, this analysis has much to recommend it. Why? Because Ratner's topics form part of the listening environment of composers and listeners alike, so that an analysis that takes this condition as its point of departure satisfies the empiricist's demand for a verifiable point of departure. We might even invoke the notion of implicit contractual values between composer and audience in order to argue not only that a topical approach is intuitively adequate, but also that it constitutes a necessary—but equivocally implicative—analytical preliminary. Moreover, although each topic takes its cue from a specific historical moment, its phenomenal "generalizability" encourages a broadly intertextual perspective, providing the analyst with a tool for engaging several levels of comparison: that between the slow introduction and the rest of the movement (from which it emerges that most of the topics played out in the Allegro section are already present in these introductory measures), that between this movement and others (such as the first movement of the Symphony No. 39 in Eb Major, K. 543, whose slow introduction shares the "Prague" Symphony's topics but not its mode of utterance), and that between this movement and works in other genres, such as opera, allowing an effective description of the "operatic" element in the movement.

To what extent is the analysis descriptively adequate? Here, I think we need to anticipate the kind of response we expect from such a question. Ratner's topics, culled from various eighteenth-century sources, are for the most part conventional signs. This of course says nothing about their explanatory power. The problem arises in moving from an abstract conception of a particular topical class to its specific realization in a given musical context. Some critics would maintain that any discourse that is sustained by notions of "pointing to," "suggesting," or "referring to," instead of one that answers positively or negatively to the question "is it or is it not?" is doomed to failure because it is based on shaky premises. To argue in this fashion, however, is to fail to appreciate the vitality of a critical stance that, by acknowledging that there is no such thing as "topic" outside its particular manifestation in a given musical context, retains a dialectical interplay between the conceptual or archetypal and its idiosyncratic realization. It is therefore not that the objections of Ratner's critics are invalid, but rather that they are irrelevant—the answers that they seek are likely to freeze the discussion instead of encouraging mobility.

Perhaps the most fundamental limitation of any topical analysis is its lack of consequence after

---

[33] Ratner, *Classic Music*, 104–5.

the "initial, over-arching characterization."[34] While topics can provide clues to what is being "discussed" in a piece of music—thus making them authentic semiotic objects—they do not seem able to sustain an independent and self-regulating account of a piece; they point to the expressive domain, but they have no syntax.[35] Nothing in Ratner's scheme tells us *why* the singing style should come after the outbursts of sensibility, or why fanfare is used toward the conclusion of the period. At best, we may propose what might be called "marriages of convenience," by arguing that certain topics are more appropriate for certain points in the musical discourse than others are. Thus, the clarifying function of the cadence is underlined by a descending arpeggio in the form of a fanfare, while the requirement of a clear and unambiguous beginning is met by the use of the coups d'archet. The instability and inquiring nature of sensibility conversely suggest the middle of a discourse, although nothing prevents such a sign from appearing at the beginning. The crucial point is that we impose these contextual attributes on this particular sequence of topics; there is no general scheme—except perhaps the possibility of generating a compositional plot—for making such decisions.

If expression has no syntax, then topics are ultimately dependent signs. However suggestive the notion of a fluid topical discourse is, however attractive the possibility of constructing a plot for this movement is, and however implicative the notion of topic is for negotiating that tricky transition from artistic work to real life, the fact remains that the ultimate allegiance of musical structure is to a contrapuntal process that preserves its utter temporality—to invoke a tautology for the sake of emphasis. It is to this second interpretive domain that we must turn.

A good place to begin studying notions of structure is with the succession of rhetorical terms given in Example 1.1 (listed below the sequence of topics). These show that the span of the piece is framed by an exordium on one hand and a peroratio on the other, while the events of its journey utilize devices such as antithesis, gradatio, anadiplosis, dubitatio, and so on—devices that point more explicitly to the temporal dimension of music. We need to do more than merely label the parts of a formal structure, however. Beneath the music quoted in Example 1.1, I have simplified the temporal scheme by reinterpreting the passage within a two-voice framework, the assumption here being that this contrapuntal framework forms the structural basis of all Classic music. It is, however, not the counterpoint per se, but rather the functions implicit in the succession that matter. To make these functions explicit, we need to redistribute contrapuntal reality into a set of conventional signs—a beginning, middle, and end (discussed more fully in Chapter 3)—labels that denote not necessarily the temporal occurrence of particular passages, but their function. To recognize the signifying functions implicit in this paradigm is to recognize the possibility of playing with them. And it is well known that one of the sources of great excitement in listening to Classic music is the constant rereading of these signs.[36]

As much as it captures the temporal quality of this sixteen-measure passage as a closed harmonic progression (ignoring for the moment the hierarchic inferiority of the closing D minor to the opening D major), the two-voice contrapuntal progression outlined in Example 1.1 is somewhat primitive, and requires further corroboration within an interpretive framework that gives pride of place to the various levels of dynamic temporal signification in Mozart's music. Example 1.2 offers such

---

[34] Arnold Whittall, "Analysis as Performance."

[35] For an empirical study of the syntax of expression, see Eric Clarke, "Structure and Expression in Rhythmic Performance."

[36] Discussions of this phenomenon may be found in Levy, "Gesture, Form and Syntax in Haydn's Music," in Leonard Meyer, *Explaining Music*, 242–68, and throughout Rosen, *The Classical Style*.

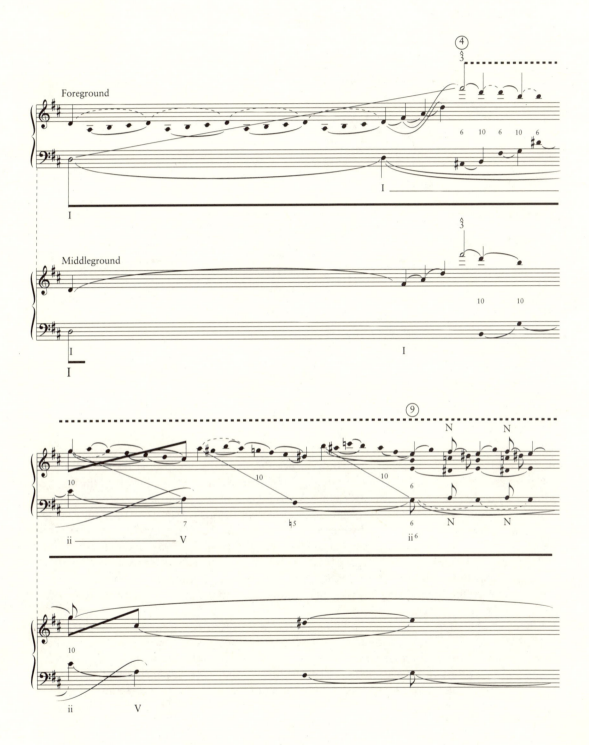

Example 1.2. Voice-leading graph of Mozart's "Prague" Symphony—First Movement, measures 1–16

Example 1.2 (cont.)

an interpretation. It is a Schenkerian voice-leading graph on two structural levels, the foreground and the middleground.[37] Without going into the details of various interpretive decisions, I might mention a few salient features of this arhythmic graph. The overall melodic profile of the passage (considered within the confines of this discussion as a "complete" piece), is a descent from $\hat{3}$ to $\hat{1}$ with its accompanying I–V–I bass arpeggiation (both progressions are shown in open noteheads). Scale degree $\hat{3}$ is set up in measure 4 by means of an arpeggiation, led down to a preliminary $\hat{1}$ in measures 11–12 (note here that the structural melody is in the inner voices), and then brought to final closure in measures 15–16. The space between the first and the second $\hat{3}$ is prolonged by means of unfoldings within an essentially dominant orbit. The foreground graph shows how the elements of the middleground are prolonged by means of familiar diminutions, including passing notes, neighbor-notes and arpeggiations.

What sort of reading is enshrined in Example 1.2? Just as Ratner's analysis was evaluated for both intuitive and descriptive adequacy, so the Schenkerian analysis is to be judged. There is little doubt that an interpretation that maintains at all levels the temporal extent of any piece of tonal music, and that offers various levels on which the life of tones may be heard, satisfies the most native instincts of musicians. At the risk of overstating the case for a Schenkerian interpretation, I might say that its greatest achievement is not only providing an account of, but celebrating the fundamental temporality of tonal music within a structuralist framework. The implicit process of

[37] In this and subsequent examples, I have adapted the notational practice codified by Allen Forte and Steven Gilbert in *Introduction to Schenkerian Analysis.*

semiosis prescribes a way of hearing each event in relation to others in an ordered temporal structure. The explanation it provides for the logic of certain foreground events serves to show both the coherence that derives from the background, and the liberty or play in which Mozart indulges in the foreground. For example, the surprising harmonization of the high F♯ in measure 4 is shown to result from a temporal displacement of melodic 3̂ from harmonic I on the foreground (the diagonal line linking the two functions argues for a conceptual simultaneity on a deeper level); the singsong figure in measure 4 results from the prolongation of a neighbor-note, G, which delays the arrival of the structural dominant; and the onset of the tonic minor at the end, although it marks off a sixteen-measure period, is unstable enough to initiate further dynamic activity.

Is the analysis descriptively adequate? Here I think the answer is not only "yes" but a less reluctant yes than the one given earlier in connection with Ratner's analysis. Whereas topical signs are given in and through language, a Schenkerian interpretation assumes a metalinguistic form, using music as both object-language and (with some verbal mediation) as metalanguage. Although words are not thereby eliminated from this analytical representation, the fact that there exists an iconic relationship between object-language and metalanguage offers rich possibilities for creating "artistic statements, in music, about music."[38]

We have now heard the opening bars of the "Prague" in two ways—first, as a set (rather than an ordered sequence) of expressive gestures culled from an eighteenth-century topical universe, and second, as a composing out of an archetypal contrapuntal structure. What sort of synthesis is possible between these two modes of "musical thought"?

It will have emerged from this preliminary discussion that these are not two disjunct modes of musical thought, but rather two (potentially) intersecting perspectives. My aim is not so much to effect a reconciliation between structure and the morphology of expression as to present a semiotic framework that not only accommodates but insists on the mutual interaction between the two. It is in the interaction between topical signs and structural signs, a notion that might be described in terms of play, that the essence of my theory lies.

To establish this model, we need to introduce one more critical term deriving from Roman Jakobson: this is the distinction between "introversive semiosis" and "extroversive semiosis," the argument being that in music the former predominates over the latter.[39] By introversive semiosis, Jakobson means "the reference of each sonic element to the other elements to come" (and presumably to those that have come before), while "extroversive semiosis" denotes "the referential link with the exterior world." Whether or not the hierarchy implied by Jakobson exists for all music is open to question. What is not open to question, at least for the music of the Classic era, is the mutual presence of qualities that are analyzable with respect to the two processes of semiosis. Applying Jakobson's terms to the analysis carried out here, one might conclude that topical signs represent the world of extroversive semiosis whereas intramusical signs, such as those enshrined in the Schenkerian graph, depict the world of introversive semiosis.[40]

---

[38] William Benjamin, "Schenker's Theory and the Future of Music," 160. On the metalinguistic properties of Schenker's graphs, see Allan Keiler, "On Some Properties of Schenker's Pitch Derivations" and my "Schenkerian Notation in Concept and Practice."

[39] Roman Jakobson, "Language in Relation to Other Communication Systems," 704–5; quoted in Nattiez, "The Contribution of Musical Semiosis," 125.

[40] The interpretation of the domains of introversive and extroversive semiosis used in this book stems from a simplification, if not a distortion, of Jakobson's meaning. Obviously, internal and external references can be found in all dimensions of a Classic piece. For example, a V–I progression may be said to "refer" to other V–I progressions (including embellished or prolonged ones, such as IV–V–I, V–VI–V–I, and so on. On the level of harmony, therefore, we can speak

The problem with this distinction, which is manifest in many other dichotomies current in music criticism—intramusical versus extramusical, inner versus outer, referential versus nonreferential, structuralist versus expressionist, congeneric versus extrageneric—is that it is ultimately false. The elements of extroversive semiosis (such as fanfare) are presented in and through a particular configuration of notes, so that their action can be described in purely musical terms. It is precisely this coherent fluidity that enables an easy progression from a multileveled diminutional play to a historical style such as sensibility, thus obliterating the distinction between "structuralist" and "referentialist" accounts. To put the matter directly: extroversive and introversive semioses are linearly related, lying at opposite ends of a single continuum.

By way of elaboration, consider the following representation of this dichotomy in which notions of topic and harmony are categorized under extroversive and introversive semiosis respectively.

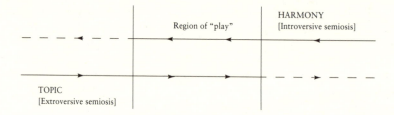

Figure 1. A model for the interplay between introversive and extroversive semioses

Moving from left to right (the lower of the two parallel horizontal lines), the direction of the arrow charts a simplifying process—the aim of the exercise being to investigate what results from systematically stripping topics of referentiality. What, then, are the essences of topics? It soon emerges that because of the essentially arbitrary (in the Saussurian sense) relationship between the name of a topic and its music-defining qualities, and because topics are not necessarily fixed with respect to dimensional behavior, there are discontinuities among various topical essences, a limitation conveyed through the broken line. The reductive process must ultimately assume an intramusical form. Reading from right to left (the upper line), on the other hand, mirrors the conceptual journey from a relational deep structure (Schenker's Ursatz) to a manifestly expressive surface. While it can approach the foreground through systematic diminution, this analytical process cannot generate an explicit, historically specific musical surface. Now, observe that the functional domains of the two lines (the solid parts) overlap significantly before reaching the threshold of a potentially discontinuous section. It is this overlap alone that guarantees a semiotic integration of the two modes of musical thought. What takes place in that region, and how it takes place, are what I call "play."

The point of a semiotic analysis, then, is to provide an account of a piece, in which the domains of expression (extroversive semiosis) are integrated with those of structure (introversive semiosis). It is not always the case that both modes yield equally significant results. Part of the analyst's task

of extroversive semiosis as well as introversive semiosis. I have, however, restricted the use of the term "extroversive" to the domain of topical signification for the simple reason that the explicit and most readily accessible engagement between classic "texts" is to be found in this dimension. The ways in which topics refer to one another are, in my view, more significant than the ways in which one V–I progression "refers" to another.

is to assign the appropriate values to these explanatory modes. It needs to be said, however, that analytical models that do not provide for both modes of inquiry are limited in significant ways. For example, a search for topics, although it provides one kind of account of a work, cannot be an end in itself, given the dependent status of topical signs. Similarly, the dismissal (in Schenkerian circles, especially) of the necessarily referential aspects of the musical surface is equally limiting. It is the dialectical interplay between manifest surface and structural background that should guide the analysis. And it is only within such a framework that we can appropriately acknowledge the rich and subtle meanings that underlie the deceptively simple and familiar music of the Classic era.

TWO

EXTROVERSIVE SEMIOSIS: TOPICS AS SIGNS

I

IN CHAPTER 1, the concept of topic was introduced by a quotation from a letter of Mozart's to his father, which included references to "Turkish music." Later, we cited Ratner's analysis of the introduction to the "Prague" Symphony, which included references to "singing style," "sensibility," "fanfare," "ombra," and several other referential signs. I suggested at that point that it might be better to grasp the broad outlines of Ratner's analysis than to worry about the particular labels that he applies to those changes of musical texture. In this chapter, I should like to embrace the notion of topic head-on, and attempt a more comprehensive definition as well as an evaluation of its structural potential. What is a topic? How are topics perceived? Does every piece of Classic music have a topic? How many topics can a single work sustain? How are topics presented—do they unfold singly or can they unfold simultaneously Are topics hierarchically organized? What role do topics play in Classic music? Some evidence from eighteenth-century writings on topic will first be outlined, followed by a consideration of more recent discussions of the phenomenon. Then, five pieces by Mozart, Haydn, and Beethoven will be analyzed from the viewpoint of their topical content. A concluding section assesses the theoretical and analytical significance of this concept.

II

Practically every major writer on music in the eighteenth century referred to notions of topic, or subjects of musical discourse. These references take different forms, ranging from a discussion of the strategies for good performance or "delivery" to methods for composing effective sonatas; they also vary in depth of discussion. Although none of the writers develops the notion of topic into a system—in contrast to the numerous "how to" systems devised by theorists like Mattheson, Kirnberger, and Koch for composing everything from a simple dance tune to a full-fledged symphony—it is worthwhile to recall some of their comments here in order to provide a point of departure for our own attempt to systematize the concept for the purposes of analysis. If the quotations from eighteenth-century sources appear to be vague sometimes, it is not because the subject is unimportant, but rather because notions of expression, feeling, and emotion are inherently ambiguous, requiring careful delimitation in context.[1]

One of the most important sources of unity in eighteenth-century music is the character of a work—the word "character" taking on a variety of meanings. Character, of course, is an aspect of expression, created and judged by notions of "good taste" and by the degree of unity

---

[1] For a survey of notions of expression in music, see Nancy Baker and Roger Scruton, "Expression," *The New Grove Dictionary of Music and Musicians*. See also Scruton, *The Aesthetic Understanding*, 34–100 for a wide-ranging discussion of the dimensions of musical expression. Among recent treatments of the subject, Peter Kivy's *The Corded Shell* has attracted wide attention. Anthony Newcomb summarizes a large number of aesthetic and critical writings on musical meaning in "Sound and Feeling."

attained by the work's elements. Johann Georg Sulzer, for example, stresses the foundational role of "character" in the compositional process:

> Every piece of music must have a definite character and evoke emotions of a specific kind. This is so both of instrumental and vocal music. Any composer would be misguided if he started work before deciding on the character of his piece. He must know whether the language he is to use is that of a man who is proud or humble, bold or timid, violent or gentle. He must know if the character is a supplicant or one in authority. Even if he comes upon his theme by accident, he should still examine it carefully if he is to sustain its character throughout the piece.[2]

Similarly, Daniel Gottlob Türk contrasts "compositions of a spirited, happy, lively, sublime, magnificent, proud, daring, courageous, serious, fiery, wild, and furious character" to those of a "gentle, innocent, naive, pleading, tender, moving, sad, melancholy...character," but not without noting the illusive nature of notions of expression: "certain subtleties of expression cannot really be described; they must be heard."[3]

These overarching characterizations are made possible by purposeful variety within the work. Quantz claims that "the agreeableness of music lies not in uniformity or similarity, but in diversity," referring in this instance to intermovement, rather than intramovement, variety.[4] Similarly, Koch, speaking of "larger compositions," refers to the symphony's three [sic] movements as being "of different character."[5] It is in characterizing the nature of that variety that some writers invoke notions of topic. Georg Joseph Vogler, for example, writes about thematic contrast within a sonata-allegro movement in ways that respond to surface character, and although he does not attribute this character to preexistent dance music, it would not be hard to draw up paradigms from the dance repertoire for his "strong" and "gentle" themes: "In the symphony there are usually two main themes, the first being the stronger, which supplies the material for development ["Ausführung"], the second being the gentler, which relieves the heated commotion and bolsters the ear with a pleasing contrast."[6]

Francesco Galeazzi echoes Vogler's distinction with the claim that certain parts of a sonata-allegro movement have specific character: "The characteristic Passage or Intermediate Passage is a new idea, which is introduced, for the sake of greater beauty, toward the middle of the first part. This must be gentle, expressive, and tender in almost all kinds of compositions, and must be presented in the same key to which the modulation was made."[7]

It is but a small step from here to the converse notion that ideas of a certain character are suitable for certain moments in the musical discourse. Galeazzi's location of what will be referred to as the "brilliant style" has evidently been borne out by the practice of many composers: "If the voice or instrument has shown its gentleness [and] expression in the Characteristic Passage, it shall display animation and skill, with agility of voice or hand.... Consequently, in

---

[2] Johann Georg Sulzer, *Allgemeine Theorie der schönen Künste*, Vol. 1, (Leipzig, 1792–1794), 355; trans. in Peter le Huray and James Day, eds., *Music and Aesthetics*, 126.

[3] Daniel Gottlob Türk, *School of Clavier Playing*, 337, 339, 337.

[4] Johann Joachim Quantz, *On Playing the Flute*, 295.

[5] Heinrich Christoph Koch, *Introductory Essay on Composition*, 197. In the annotations to her translation of Koch, Nancy Baker describes Koch's reference to a three- rather than a four-movement symphonic plan as "reactionary."

[6] Georg Jospeh Vogler, *Mannheimer Tonschule*, Vol. 2, 62; quoted and trans. in Newman, *The Sonata in the Classic Era*, 34. The entire second chapter of Newman's book contains numerous citations of direct and indirect references to notions of contrast and, by implication, topic in Classic music.

[7] Francesco Galeazzi, *Elementi teorico-pratici di musica*, Vol. 2, 256; trans. in Churgin, "Sonata Form," 193.

this period in vocal music, one especially places passages and brilliant passagework, and in instrumental music the most difficult passages, which then close with a final cadence."[8]

The most direct references to topic occur in the context of discussions of style. Style attaches easily to a wide variety of contexts, including national styles (the "French," "German," or "Italian" styles), chamber styles, socially based styles (low and high styles), and so on. Thus Charles Burney typifies the eighteenth-century connoisseur's concern with identifying specific character traits, in this case among Italian composers: "Jommelli's works are full of great and noble ideas, treated with taste and learning; Galuppi's abound in fancy, fire, and feeling; Piccini has far surpassed all his contemporaries in the comic style; and Sacchini seems the most promising composer in the serious."[9]

William Crotch also identifies various styles of music in an attempt to define the nature of musical expression. He speaks of "the military, or the pastoral, or the pianoforte style," and goes on to consider the timbral transferability of these various styles. "On the pianoforte," writes Crotch, "though all styles are not equally calculated to suit its peculiar expression, all may be distinctly heard, the sacred, the military, the pastoral, the concert, the opera and its own appropriate style." He is therefore able to dismiss the idea that "the style depend[s] upon the instrument alone," and to argue for a more flexible notion of style. So, although Crotch does not speak of "topics" as such, his implicit claim that styles possess invariant characteristics that are genre-blind introduces an important attribute of topic.[10]

Quantz also recognizes the transferability of styles. He speaks of arias played on an instrument—but, for him, the process by which meaning is generated is a one-way flow from vocal music to instrumental music, not vice versa:

> Vocal music has some advantages that instrumental music must forgo. In the former the words and the human voice are a great advantage to the composer, both with regard to invention and effect. Experience makes this obvious when, lacking a voice, an aria is heard played on an instrument. Yet instrumental music, without words and human voices, ought to express certain emotions, and should transport the listeners from one emotion to another just as well as vocal music does.[11]

In his *Dictionnaire de musique moderne*, Francois Hénri Joseph Castil-Blaze makes a distinction between expression and effect (*effet*). Expression is the umbrella category that encompasses ideas and sentiments that the musician wishes to "express," while "effet" refers to those foreground effects that are products of, or in turn generate, styles—and therefore topics. For example, "trumpets, trombones, kettledrums [and] bells, which have too often been misused, are, for the composer, a great source of tragic and brilliant effects." Castil-Blaze notes that such effects "are to music what figures [of speech] are to oratorical discourse," and he goes on to caution that these be handled carefully and without excess.[12]

Castil-Blaze's remarks point to one of the most distinctive features of Classic music—its

---

[8] Ibid.

[9] Charles Burney, *The Present State of Music in France and Italy*, 307.

[10] William Crotch, *Substance of Several Courses of Lectures on Music*, 62. In the wide-ranging third chapter, "On Musical Expression," from which these quotations are taken, Crotch distinguishes between the descriptive power of music (citing the opening of Haydn's *Creation*) and its associative power. He seems to be suggesting that while styles are fixed and definable, instrumental associations are not.

[11] Quantz, *On Playing the Flute*, 310.

[12] François Henri Joseph Castil-Blaze, *Dictionnaire de musique moderne*, s.v. "Expression" and "Effect," 226–31 and 209–12 respectively. The quotation appears on 211.

use of mixed styles. The conjunction of styles is never considered an end in itself, but it plays an important role in characterizing the surface of many Classic pieces. Haydn, Beethoven, and their contemporaries all explored, in varying degrees, the mixed style—but perhaps its greatest exponent was Mozart.[13]

Quantz's discussion of "mixtures of contrasted ideas" might seem to be value-laden—mixture is one of the "characteristic signs of the excellence of a piece"—but the assignment of higher value to mixed styles is not necessarily shared by all theorists: "Mixture of different ideas is necessary not only in solos, but in every type of musical composition. If a composer knows how to manage this matter successfully, and by this means to inspire the passions of the listener, it may justly be said that he has achieved a high degree of good taste, and that he has, so to speak, found the musical philosopher's stone."[14]

Johann Friedrich Daube's *Anleitung zur Erfindung der Melodie und ihrer Fortsetzung* (1798, 2 vols.) refers to the central role of "figures" in melodic construction. Daube distinguishes between a "*singbar*" figure, a "*Rauschend*" [or "Brilliant figure"], and the "*Vermischt*," which is a mixture of the two. So, even in this characteristically modest context—Daube is writing for amateurs, not for the sophisticated master—the composer is encouraged to explore the alternation between styles.[15]

Heinrich Koch also writes about mixture of styles—but, unlike Quantz, Koch appears ambivalent about the significance of this historical development. Thus, Koch blames the decline of the overture on the emergence of this particular compositional device: "[This decline] may be because the strict fugue is too austere nourishment for the fashionable taste of our time, which likes fugal composition and double counterpoint in an instrumental work only when it is combined with comic ornaments in one and the same movement to provoke laughter. Now so many amateurs of the art wish to have such compositions, many composers, indeed, serve them up."[16] Among the composers who "serve them up" is Mozart, whose "Haydn" Quartets are singled out by Koch "on account of their special mixture of the strict and free styles and the treatment of harmony." One consequence of the juxtaposition of styles is the creation of secondary topics, as Koch makes clear during a discussion of phrase connection: "In the performance of compositions an idea contained in a phrase is often immediately carried further and the phrase thereby extended. This immediate continuation of an idea contained in a phrase can occur...through undefined and mixed figures of notes."[17] Koch thus acknowledges a deeper level "narrative line" that defers to surface contrast. Significantly, his musical example at this point, like Daube's illustration of mixed styles, reveals a threefold succession of topics: alla zoppa–fanfare–brilliant style.

Finally, Türk invokes the principle of "mixed style" to explain the superlative position occupied by the keyboard sonata in the eighteenth century:

> Among compositions written for the keyboard, the sonata probably has the greatest claim for being in the first place.... What is understood as an ode in the art of poetry is apparently that which in

---

[13] On the mixed style, see Newman, *The Sonata in the Classic Era*, 39.

[14] Quantz, *On Playing the Flute*, 319.

[15] Johann Friedrich Daube, *Anleitung zur Erfindung der Melodie und ihrer Forsetzung*, Vol. 1, 19–20. For further discussion of Daube's illustrations, see George J. Buelow, "The Concept of 'Melodielehre'," 182–95 and Ratner, *Classic Music*, 96–97.

[16] Koch, *Introductory Essay*, 197.

[17] Ibid, 52.

music is the proper and true sonata.... Just as the subjects of the ode are uncommonly diverse and treated at quite different lengths, so is this true of the sonata. The composer is therefore in no instrumental composition less restricted—as far as character [is] concerned—than in the sonata, for every emotion and passion can be expressed in it. For the more expressive a sonata is, the more the composer can be heard, as it were, to speak; the more the composer avoids the commonplace, the more excellent is the sonata.[18]

From this brief sampling, it is clear that notions of expression, and by implication, topic were central to theoretical and aesthetic discussions in the eighteenth century.[19] At the same time, there is no settled *modus operandi* for the analysis of expression; what is considered "expressive" varies from writer to writer. Moreover, if everything in a composition is assumed to be at least potentially expressive, then our division between structure and expression must seem, at best, fragile.[20]

Our theorizing instincts are, however, fed by the foregoing quotations in one specific way. We can draw up a list of topics, being the sum total of topics found in the works analyzed in this book.

1. alla breve	15. Mannheim rocket
2. alla zoppa	16. march
3. amoroso	17. minuet
4. aria	18. musette
5. bourrée	19. ombra
6. brilliant style	20. opera buffa
7. cadenza	21. pastoral
8. sensibility (Empfindsamkeit)	22. recitative
9. fanfare	23. sarabande
10. fantasy	24. sigh motif (Seufzer)
11. French overture	25. singing style
12. gavotte	26. Sturm und Drang
13. hunt style	27. Turkish music
14. learned style	

Figure 2. The Universe of Topic

This list, given as Figure 2, will be referred to as a provisional universe of topic—its provisional status necessitated first by the high degree of selectivity exercised in the choice of works to analyze (hence the dozens of topics found elsewhere in Classic music that are, however, non-occurrent in this book's repertoire), and second, by the fact that as later research uncovers more topics, the universe will expand accordingly. The idea of expression is therefore limited to the particular notion of topic and to the limits of this universe.[21]

[18] Türk, *School of Clavier Playing,* 383.

[19] Newman, *The Sonata in the Classic Era,* Ratner, *Classic Music,* and Allanbrook, *Rhythmic Gesture in Mozart* all include extensive quotations on this subject from various eighteenth-century sources. See also Alexander L. Ringer, "The Chasse as a Musical Topic of the 18th Century" and David Charlton, "Orchestra and Image in the Late 18th Century" for further discussion of mimesis in eighteenth-century music.

[20] On the distinction between structure and expression, see Newcomb, "Sound and Feeling."

[21] The present universe of topic, culled from various sources, is less comprehensive than that found throughout Ratner,

III

So much for the eighteenth-century view. Just as we examined certain characteristic descriptions of Classic music in Chapter 1 in order to show the nature and extent of the linguistic analogy, so we will now turn to recent descriptions of Classic music that allude to notions of topic. It must be said, however, that these writings have not, for the most part, advanced much beyond the eighteenth–century discussions of expression from which we have already quoted. The fact, that no sensitive writer on Classic music can avoid engaging with such issues is, however, enough justification for taking the subject seriously.

In Chapter 26 of his book *The Age of Mozart and Beethoven*, Giorgio Pestelli prefaces his discussion of Mozart's music with a summary of "stylistic opportunities of the musical world around 1770,"[22] the idea being to show what was available to Mozart by way of a compositional code, and then to assess his exploitation of this set of norms. Although Pestelli does not actually use the term "topic," the domain covered by his list significantly overlaps that covered by our universe. According to Pestelli, devices such as "singende allegro" and "Alberti bass" depict the "extrovert side" of the galant style. The empfindsam style is another topic, one that describes the "serious side" of the galant style. Pestelli distinguishes between a "stile osservato"— counterpoint as an academic exercise—and a "secular" counterpoint, and between a comic style and a comic vernacular; he also refers to the frequent use of dance rhythms and popular melodies in serious instrumental music. It is within this historically specific code that Mozart and other Classic composers worked, and they reacted both positively and negatively to these opportunities. Pestelli does not go on to tell us whether there were any models of stylistic succession in Classic music, or how they might have been exploited by Mozart; he leaves us only with the thought that these elements of style provide a clue to music's structural and expressive content.

Notions of topic also permeate a good deal of Charles Rosen's writing about Classic music, and the extent of this permeation is indicative of the difficulty of separating not only linguistic analogy but also notions of expression from discussions of later eighteenth-century music. Rosen's ultimate concerns are with musical dramatic structure as manifest in various aspects of temporal ordering, so that references to topic become incidental, though not inorganic, aspects of his discourse. When he refers to a "blending of genres" in the finale of Mozart's Piano Sonata in B♭ Major, K. 333, to the invocation of a "concerto style" in the first movement of the same sonata (measures 56–59), to "marchlike flourishes" in the opening movement of the C Major symphony, K. 338, to an "orchestral fanfare" and "alla breve" in the opening movement of the E♭ Major piano concerto, K. 271, and to "military allegros" in the opening movement of the G Major piano concerto, K. 453, Rosen is alluding to topics. That is, the topic of discussion in K. 333, for example, is a genre—the concerto. Similarly, within the more fundamental argument of K. 338, a paradigmatic march is incorporated, just as allusions are made to the commonplace "fanfare" in the introductory movement of K. 271. These elements are simply identified by Rosen, who raises no basic questions about the status of the paradigms from which they are drawn. Commenting on the Eroica symphony, for example, he notes that "the opening theme...is essentially a horn-call, but the horn is never allowed to play it solo until the

---

Classic Music and Allanbrook, *Rhythmic Gesture in Mozart*. To avoid falling even deeper into the trap of nominalism, I have listed only those topics that actively shape the pieces discussed in this book. Perhaps a later researcher, less concerned with interpreting particular pieces, will be able to offer a more comprehensive list of eighteenth-century topics.

[22] Pestelli, *The Age of Mozart and Beethoven*, 136.

recapitulation is under way."[23] Such an apparently suggestive description raises important questions about the identity of Rosen's topic, the horn-call. Here, one might ask just what musical parameters define the horn-call, especially when the topic apparently retains its identity even outside the domain of timbral specificity. (Recall the comments of William Crotch, quoted earlier, on the transferability of styles between instruments.)

Joseph Kerman is another writer who often refers to topical elements in his writings on Classic music. In *The Beethoven Quartets*, Kerman identifies a "prefatory fanfare" in the Scherzo of Op. 127, and a "folklike tune" in the finale of the same piece. Unless "fanfare" is being used metaphorically, it must be seen within the class of musical fanfares that other writers identify. In discussing Op. 132, for example—a work to which we shall return in Chapter 6—Kerman identifies, among other things, a "cantus firmus," a "marchlike melody," a "scream," a "fanfare on B♭," an "orthodox fugal exposition," and a "slack Italian aria."[24] These descriptives (with the possible exception of the category "scream"), like Pestelli's "stylistic opportunities," point to the incorporation of certain characteristic styles into Classic music. How, for example, is it possible to hear an Italian aria in a string quartet—especially when the latter uses no words? Is this merely an invocation of aria style, or is there a larger generic allusion to aria, or are these actually metaphorical "arias on instruments," as Quantz might say? Is the "fanfare on B♭" equivalent to the fanfare at the opening of Op. 74? Is the melody a march, or is it merely marchlike—and what are the minimum conditions for producing a marchlike topic? These are some of the questions that we need to answer in order to provide theoretic support for the notion of expression.

The first modern recognition of topic as an independent category, rather than as an adjunct to structural description, is to be found in Ratner's *Classic Music*, whose opening chapter offers a preliminary definition and classification of "topic," as well as several analytical applications of it. Ratner proceeds from the assumption that all eighteenth-century music is nominally referential, although the strategies for expressing that referentiality differ within the various phases of stylistic evolution. Topics are forms of associative signification that may be grouped under two broad categories: the first consists of musical types, and includes various dances, such as minuet (itself assuming a wide variety of expressive forms), passepied, sarabande, polonaise, bourrée, contredanse, gavotte, gigue, siciliano, and march. Classic music inherited these stylized dances from the earlier part of the eighteenth-century, and not only used them as individual musical types, but also incorporated them into other works. For example, a minuet may occur as a movement in a string quartet or symphony, but the minuet style could also be invoked in another movement.

The second broad category consists of styles of music, under which Ratner lists a heterogenous collection of references to military and hunt music, fanfares, horn-calls, singing style, brilliant style, French overture, musette/pastorale, Turkish music, Sturm und Drang, sensibility or Empfindsamkeit, the strict or learned style, and fantasia. These styles are again similar, perhaps even equivalent, to Pestelli's "stylistic opportunities," and they are incorporated into Classic music rather than structured by it. Thus, Ratner argues, topics mirror certain expressive stances, but they never assume the role of fundamentally structuring Classic music.[25]

[23] Rosen, *The Classical Style*, 78.

[24] Kerman, *The Beethoven Quartets*, 244–45.

[25] Charles Rosen makes a not-dissimilar point when he describes the difference between Baroque and classical aesthetics in terms of "a basic shift in musical aesthetics, away from the hallowed notion of music as the imitation of sentiment toward the conception of music as an independent system that conveyed its own significance in terms that were

The rationale for hearing a topical discourse in Classic music rests partly on the observation that topics were part of a musical vernacular current in the eighteeenth century, which formed the listening environment of composers and listeners alike. Wye Jamison Allanbrook, speaking specifically of Mozart's operas, states:

"[Composers were] in possession of something we can call an expressive vocabulary, a collection in music of what in the theory of rhetoric are called *topoi*, or topics for formal discourse. [They] held it in common with [their] audience, and used it... with the skill of a master craftsman. This vocabulary, when captured and categorized, provides a tool for analysis which can mediate between the [works] and our individual responses to them, supplying independent information about the expressive content of the arias and ensembles.... [Each] musical *topos* has associations both natural and historical, which can be expressed in words, and which were tacitly shared by the 18th century audience.... An acquaintance with these *topoi* frees the writer from the dilemma he would otherwise face when trying to explicate a given passage: that he can at the one extreme do no more than detail the mere facts and figures of its tonal architecture, or at the other merely anatomize his private reactions to a work. By recognizing a characteristic style, he can identify a configuration of notes and rhythms as having a particular expressive stance, modified and clarified, of course, by its role in its movement and by the uses made of it earlier in the piece. In short, he can articulate within certain limits the shared response a particular passage will evoke.[26]

Allanbrook's statement effectively represents the critical tradition from which this sort of discourse stems, showing it to be not a single tradition, but, rather, numerous traditions fused together. The statement points to two crucial facets of a topical analysis. First, competence is assumed on the part of the listener, enabling the composer to enter into a contract with his audience. If something is commonplace, then it is meant to be understood by all competent listeners. There is nothing natural about this ability; it is acquired by learning. Second, the "natural" and "historical" associations of topic point to an irreducible conventional specificity. In some cases, the combination of topical sequences and essences enables the analyst to construct a plot for the work or movement. By "plot," I mean a coherent verbal narrative that is offered as an analogy or metaphor for the piece at hand. It may be based on specific historical events, it may yield interesting and persuasive analogies with social situations, or it may be suggestive of a more generalized discourse. These are not programs in the sense in which the *Symphonie Fantastique*, for example, has a program; nor are they necessarily literal representations of

---

not properly translatable" (*Sonata Forms*, 11). While I agree that structure is not "properly translatable" into other media, I find problematic the claim that later eighteenth-century music could form an "independent system." This popular notion which includes an attendant claim for autonomy in Classic music, needs to be undermined in view of at least the referential content of Classic music. If "independence" is invoked freely, however, then there is no reason why it should not apply equally well to both Baroque and, later, Romantic music.

[26] Allanbrook, *Rhythmic Gesture in Mozart*, 2–3. Topos-research has a longer and more distinguished past in literary studies than in musicology. For example, Ernst Robert Curtius's seminal work, *European Literature and the Latin Middle Ages* not only devotes an entire chapter to *topoi* but includes frequent references to these commonplaces of medieval literature. Curtius's list includes topics of consolatory oratory and affected modesty, historical topics, topics of exordium, topics of conclusion, and invocation of nature. While there are obvious points of contact between the topics of literature and those of music, the analogy between music and language encounters a conceptual block with respect to a possible semantic content for music. For a comprehensive listing of rhetorical devices, see Hans Heinrich Unger, *Die Beziehungen zwischen Musik und Rhetorik*. See also Seymour Chatman, "How Do We Establish New Codes of Verisimilitude"?

extramusical events. Plots arise as a result of sheer indulgence: they are the historically minded analyst's engagement with one aspect of a work's possible meaning.

The creation of a plot, however, remains perhaps an optional rather than an obligatory stage in the analysis, since this step depends on the analyst's erudition. The more positivistically oriented analyst may wish to pursue the morphology of individual topics, arriving at a summary structural rhythm mirroring the flow of a work, but not tied to a single dimension. Additionally, topical identification enables a comparison of the "content" of different works, and the discovery of works that may be said to have similar discourses.

Topics, then, are points of departure, but never "total identities." In the fictional context of a work's "total identity," even their most explicit presentation remains on the allusive level. They are therefore suggestive, but not exhaustive—which, of course, says nothing about their significance. And they dynamically shape our response to Classic music, without necessarily determining its limits.

IV

It is time to turn to some actual music and consider the status of these various generalizations. I shall discharge two tasks in the rest of this chapter. First, using the Universe of Topic (Figure 2) as point of reference, I shall identify and comment upon topics in a number of excerpts from works by Mozart, Haydn, and Beethoven. Although this is strictly a process of identification, it is a necessary first step in this method of analysis. Second, I shall redefine in semiotic terms the notion of topics as signs, thus enabling an assessment of their structural potential.

Mozart, Piano Concerto in C Major, K. 467—First Movement, Measures 1–68

The conventional explanation for the events in the opening ritornello of the Classic concerto is that the composer acquaints listeners with the ideas—mainly, but not exclusively, thematic—that are to be discussed in the course of the movement. The genre is also flexible enough to accommodate various departures, such as the appearance of a new thematic idea later in the movement, or the "premature" entry of the soloist during the initial ritornello. This confers on the opening ritornello a dual synoptic, as well as expository, function. These functions, together with the necessary gestural obligations of the genre, explain why the concerto relies a great deal on topical interplay. Some of the richest examples in Classic music of referential structuring are to be found in the opening movements of concertos. The first movement of Mozart's Piano Concerto in C Major, K. 467, for example, is no exception, offering within its first sixty-eight measures a remarkable drama of topical interplay. Koch's claim that the concerto "can assume every mood which music is capable of expressing"[27] is, although it may strike some as an exaggeration, in many ways borne out by the strategy of this movement.

Perhaps the most important clue to topical identity lies in surface texture. The interplay of topics is so clearly dramatized by Mozart that there is often little doubt about their compositional origins and points of termination. The first four measures may be described as a march, establishing a link with the hundreds of marches that Mozart knew and wrote. The articulation calls the theatre to mind—especially the short, pithy figures of opera buffa. One can almost

---

[27] Koch, *Introductory Essay*, 208.

hear Leporello lurking behind the scenes. The four-measure phrase is followed for two measures by a melody and accompaniment that suggest the singing style. The melody is, of course, in the first violins, while the rest of the orchestra provides a conventional accompaniment. At the beginning of measure 7, a new topic takes over from the singing style, refusing to allow the first violin's melody to define itself clearly. This topic is march, now presented with greater timbral specificity as a proper wind-band march (measures 7 and 8). But this, too, is short-lived, as the singing style returns in the middle of measure 8 and continues until the beginning of measure 11, at which point the march for wind band returns. Measures 1–12 may therefore be described with reference to a binary opposition between march and singing style. Several assumptions underlie a description such as this. First, we have assumed a process of intertextuality: these measures (and the rest of the movement) comprise gestures that are common stock in the later eighteenth century, and to which the listener can relate as paradigms. The term intertextuality is used in the present context "to signify the multiple ways in which any one [musical] text echoes, or is inescapably linked to, other texts, whether by open or covert citations and allusions, or by the assimilation of the features of the earlier text by the later text, or simply by participation in a common stock of [musical] codes and conventions."[28] The point may be framed alternatively in the language of reception theory:

> Even where a [musical] creation negates or surpasses all expectations, it still presupposes a preliminary information and a trajectory of expectations *[Erwartungsrichtung]* against which to register the originality and novelty. This horizon of the expectable is constituted for the [listener] from out of a tradition or series of previously known works, and from a specific attitude, mediated by one (or more) genres and dissolved through new works. Just as there is no act of [musical] communication that is not related to a general, socially or situationally conditioned norm or convention, it is also unimaginable that a [musical] work set itself into an informational vacuum, without indicating a specific situation of understanding. To this extent, every work belongs to a genre.... [F]or each work a preconstituted horizon of expectations must be ready at hand...to orient the [listener's]... understanding and to enable a qualifying reception.[29]

In both Abrams's and Jauss's statements, the implication is that practically every feature of the piece—harmonic progressions, rhythmic patterns, motivic interplay—may be heard intertextually, so that it becomes necessary to restrict the domain to which the process is applicable. My concern here is with the set of referential topical signs. Each sign is a member of a larger topical class that is defined by certain invariant characteristics whose presence alone guarantees the topic's identity. That is, a given topic may assume a variety of forms, depending on the context of its exposition, without losing its identity. A case in point is the topic of march. That measures 7–8 and 11–12 belong to the classification "march" seems clear enough. What is not so clear is the degree of "marchness" in measures 1–4. Here, we come upon one of the most fundamental conditions for the perception of topic—that a topic assumes its identity by the force of contextual factors, which include the presence or purposeful absence of certain procedures, or elements, or both. In the case of measures 1–4, perceptual structuring owes more to a retrospective view than to a prospective one; these measures assume clear

---

[28] M. H. Abrams, *A Glossary of Literary Terms*, 200. The word "musical" has been substituted for "literary" in this quotation.

[29] Hans Robert Jauss, *Toward an Aesthetic of Reception*, 79. Here, too, the quotation has been adapted for the present context by a substitution of "musical" for "literary" where appropriate.

topical identity only after one has heard the more explicit march in measures 7–8. That is, by a process of retrospective deduction, the identity of measures 7–8 is projected onto that of measures 1–4, since the former lack an explicit topical characterization when they are first heard. Their apparent neutrality is undermined as they are shown to be compatible with march topic.

Last, by identifying an interplay of topics, one sets up the possibility of a fluid topical discourse in this movement. The fact of succession alone, enhanced perceptually by varying degrees of foregrounding, suggests a discourse, possibly a narration. To say that there are clear pointers to a possible narrative is, however, not to underplay the difficulty of determining precisely what is being discussed, or, for that matter, why it is being discussed.[30]

So much for measures 1–12. At the start of measure 12, the opening material returns—now texturally transformed and temporally extended. Its orchestration has been altered—or enhanced—and the original four measures are extended for another four. Segmenting by topical identity only, measures 1–4 are equivalent to measures 12–20 (the actual parallelism is between measures 1–4 and 12–15, although 16–20 are obviously inseparable from 12–15). It would be simplistic to assume, however, that the return of familiar material carries the same expressive connotations as at its original appearance. Topics retain a contextually defined fluidity, which puts their virtual identity on a different level from functional identities, such as keys and chord relations. For, in this case, measure 12 initiates a much more impassioned discourse, here achieved by the addition of a counter melody (flute and first violins) above the original material, and the use of tremolo effects in the upper strings. Two other topics are suggested by these transformations: the rapid string figuration suggests the brilliant style, while the give-and-take between the lower and upper strings is an allusion to the learned style—a style that emerges more fully later in the opening ritornello.

To describe measures 12–19 as containing at least three topics is to indicate the possibility of simultaneous topical unfolding in Classic music. Although topics usually appear singly, they can also appear together, with one superimposed on the other(s). So, by considering musical texture as a sort of compound sign, one can discern various levels of sign structuring. Topics are hierarchically organized with respect both to synchrony and diachrony.

So far, then, we have heard a confrontation between march and singing style—the reasons for their compatibility will emerge later—followed by an intensification of march, during which process the learned and brilliant styles are alluded to. Beginning in measure 20, a new topic is introduced by virtue of the dominant pedal that appears in the lower instruments. This topic shares with the musette both a pedal point (brass and lower strings) and a "naive" melody (upper strings and flute). At the culmination of this passage in measures 24–25, the melody becomes more emphatic (aided by the sequential process), alluding in the process to the Baroque *Seufzer*, or sigh figure. The tension thus generated is diffused in measures 26 and 27, leading to the return of march in measure 28, further modified.

The fact that some of my description begins to give priority to "allusions" rather than explicit statements is consistent with the musical process itself, for one expects that the argument of a piece will contrast significant and explicit assertions to no less significant but implicit allusions or hints. If the topical process becomes accordingly vague, the reason is that such

---

[30] It has not so far been shown that music has the capacity to narrate in any but the most trivial sense. Yet recent musicological encounters with literary theory seem to encourage further speculation along these lines. See, for example, Newcomb, "Schumann and Late Eighteenth-Century Narrative Strategies," Fred Maus, "Music as Drama," and Carolyn Abbate, "What the Sorcerer Said."

defamiliarization is, broadly speaking, inevitable as the movement unfolds. The implication is not that topics are stated clearly only at the beginning of a piece: on the contrary, topics can assume a clear statement anywhere in the work. What is important is to recognize how the musical process itself subsumes the topical discourse in a higher level rhythm.

The binary rhetorical gesture of measures 28–36 recalls that of measures 1–12, and the two passages are related further by the presence, indeed the persistence, of march. Although the sigh gesture mentioned in connection with measures 24–25 is retained in measures 28 and 32, and glossed in 30–31 and 34–35, the unifying topic throughout this passage is march, which assumes varying degrees of perceptual prominence. It moves in and out of focus, persisting, so to speak, on a fluid background-foreground continuum.

Beginning in measure 36, we have another example of simultaneous unfolding of topics: the march is now given in learned style, its first measure used as the subject of close imitation for eight measures. Both topics are present, although it is the learned style that is perceptually dominant. In measure 44, another topic appears—the Sturm und Drang, whose archetypal features include an agitated microrhythmic texture, modal coloration, and a summary intensity of utterance. This passage may be heard as the high point of the oration thus far. A formal close follows on the downbeat of measure 52, and is subsequently echoed in measures 52–56 and 56–64, the peroratio of the opening ritornello. Measures 64–68 provide a culminating rhetorical gesture appropriate to the sense of an ending. The march is in full force, as are the attendant military elements. A conventional closing gesture (measures 67–68) finally signifies, with equal force, the completion of this synopsis. We await the soloist's entrance and subsequent elaboration on these ideas.

Any description of tonal music that does not include reference to harmonic functions runs the risk of overlooking what many consider to be its most important parameter. The foregoing identification of topics has largely avoided the harmonic issue in order to throw into relief the nature and limits of topical discourse. Were we to value the defining parameters of each topic, however, we would discover inherent hierarchies, a number of them privileging harmony. Musette, for example, defines harmonic and rhythmic stasis, while Sturm und Drang embodies harmonic instability. Mozart's choice of these topics is sure to have been influenced by these "structural" attributes.

Three main constraints affect the structural potential of topic. First, not everything in the preceding passage falls neatly under a single topical umbrella. Although I have pointed to the clearest references, it would be foolish to deny that there are also grey areas in which, if pressed, one would have to conclude that their identity arises by default; that is, identity is imposed on it by contiguity on either side of its temporal extension, or, in a few instances, by noncontiguous cross-reference. What this means in terms of an analytical model is that topics, by themselves, have no pronounced teleological obligation; nor is their physical extent normally delimited. They constitute, in the final analysis, a dependent parameter, which needs to be invoked in conjunction with another parameter, usually harmony. Second, topics possess, however, an inert dynamism that ensures that their definition requires a much more fluid framework than one that locates them in virtual time and space. To say that a given passage is a reference to Sturm und Drang, for example, is to argue that Sturm und Drang is, perceptually speaking, the dominant element of reference. As mentioned earlier, there are hierarchies in our perception of topical interplay, so that Sturm und Drang may override, say, the learned style. We therefore need a mechanism for establishing these hierarchies objectively. Third, topical classes are so broad that they seem to admit practically everything, or nothing. In this analysis alone, I have mentioned a genre (opera buffa), a procedure (learned style, peroratio), a dance (musette), and variously historically-located styles (Sturm und Drang, sensibility). The advantage of this flexibility is to allow many more features of the music to be described in order to capture the sociohistorical moment that this concerto embodies, while its disadvantage is to encourage discussion at a very primitive level of reference—reference without consequence.

A brief discussion of the musical attributes of some of the topics encountered in the Mozart concerto will reveal the complexity of the issue of a diachronically based topical model, and will also show why I have deferred theoretically to the much more fluid notion of a structural rhythm. March embodies, fundamentally, a basic meter (duple). Although this meter can assume a variety of notational forms, it forms the conceptual point of departure for identifying that particular topic.[31] There are secondary features that enhance this basic metric gesture, such as the presence of dotted or double-dotted rhythms, and the predominant use of primary harmonies—tonic, dominant, and subdominant. But these are, properly speaking, secondary features whose interaction with the primary feature creates the particular topic. There are other associative factors that enhance the sense of march. One such factor is key, here C major, whose paradigmatic or associative properties are entirely compatible with march. Timbral qualities are not irrelevant, but they are not fundamental, either. For when I said earlier that the wind-band march in measures 7–8 was a clearer topical reference than the opening buffalike figures, I was invoking a further level of association in the appropriateness of wind bands for playing military marches, a role that strings perform only self-consciously (recall Rosen's description of the opening of the Eroica as a horn-call, a horn-call played by strings). To identify a march topic is therefore to invoke a complex interaction of parameters informed by contextual hierarchies.

The singing style that follows march takes its name from the "singing" nature of the melodic line. Here is a lyrical melody constructed within a modest compass, and unfolding at a deliberate pace. Its primary parameter is melody, and its defining attributes are interval, tempo, and, to some extent, rhythm. Unlike march, singing style is completely neutral with regard to meter, making it adaptable to a variety of contexts. Singing style suggests a fundamental fusion of topics by leaving open the question of which dance rhythm is used to express this style. It is irreducibly mixed.

An assessment of the structural potential of topics in the first twelve measures of Mozart's concerto would have to take into account both the presence and the absence of certain parameters, and the possibility or lack thereof for transition between topics. In these twelve measures, rhythm (including meter) holds the fort. It is, for one thing, the dominant parameter of the opening march. When the singing style emerges as a melody-biased topic, it does so as an additional layer superimposed on the march. Thus, there are, in fact, two topics being unfolded in measures 5 and 6—singing style and march—the former in the foreground and the latter in the background. Now notice the various levels of dynamic transition between these two topics. Meter is present in march, but not absent in singing style; this makes it possible, perhaps necessary, for meter to remain perceptible when the music moves from march to singing style. Similarly, melody is not primary in march, but rather in singing style; this makes the emergence of melody in measure 5 both significant—by way of contrast—and consequential—by the absence of any structural conflicts. An analysis of topical process in this movement would therefore be based on these dynamic transitions between individual parameters or groups of

---

[31] On the defining features of march as topic, see Allanbrook, *Rhythmic Gesture in Mozart*, 45–49.

parameters. It is the discourse mapped out by such a process, moving in and out of topics, that I have described as a *structural rhythm*.[32]

The idea of a structural rhythm, while conceding a certain lack of concreteness, seems to me to offer distinct theoretical advantages over interpretations that privilege a single dimension right from the start. This is not to take issue with the long-held view that melody, rhythm, and harmony are the primary parameters of tonal music while texture, timbre, and register function in a subsidiary capacity; rather, I wish to urge a more flexible treatment of that assumption, to argue that even if melody, rhythm, and harmony form the reliable frameworks for such analysis, they should be allowed to emerge contextually from a work's structure, rather than be imposed on it as a premise. Mozart's concerto is, of course, concerned with these so-called primary parameters. But it is concerned with more than that. The piece unfolds a meaningful discourse that, while locating its fundamental coherence in these dimensional processes, also allows for various kinds of play of dimensions. This opens up the possibility for both an inevitable and a characteristic function, the latter hinting at the rhetoric of structure. By conjoining these processes into a summary structural rhythm, we are, in effect, proceeding from a manifest foreground to a latent background, from a referential foreground to a structural background, thereby challenging the conceptual and perceptual distinction between structure and expression.

We can now recast this discussion in semiotic terms by describing topics as musical signs. Each sign, following Saussure, is the indissoluble union of a signifier and a signified. The signifier of a topic is itself comprised of a set of signifiers, the action of various parameters. The musical signifier therefore embodies, even at this primitive level, a dynamic relation. The signified is more elusive. As Nattiez puts it, "Insofar as the only way to find out how the semantic content of music is perceived is to proceed with verbalization, the musical signified, as such, can never be pinpointed accurately."[33] In any case, what is signified by a given topic remains implicit in the historically appropriate label invoked—singing style, Sturm und Drang, learned style, and so on. Furthermore, just as low-level signs can combine to form higher-level ones, so topics in a particular local function can combine to form topics on a higher level. And so we have—theoretically, at least—a process of infinite semiotic linkage with regard to topic, reaching beyond the individual phrase, section, or movement to the work as a whole, and beyond.

---

[32] For the idea of a "structural rhythm," I am indebted to Lawrence Kramer, *Music and Poetry*, 9–11. Kramer explains that "the constituents of that rhythm cannot be determined in advance; they may be images, tropes, levels of style—any rhetorical construct whatever." My adaptation of Kramer's term retains this nonspecificity with regard to dimension, thus reducing the term "rhythm" to no more than a temporal sequence. Something of that larger rhythmic motion may be traced back to seventeenth and eighteenth-century discussions of the affections and passions. For example, there appears to be a fundamental principle of *mouvement* that results from the confluence of referential and pure signs, discussed by Marmontel in *Élémens de littérature*, s.v. "Mouvement du style." Here we read that "[i]n the passionate style, when one enters into the illusion and abandons oneself to nature, the movements vary of their own accord; the 'figures' [topics or tropes], so cold when one has deliberately sought them out, of repetition, gradation, accumulation, and so forth, then offer themselves naturally with all the warmth of the passion which has produced them. The gift of using them aptly is thus no more than the gift of entering into the emotions which one is expressing." Topics, in this view, when stripped down to their essences, produce a rhythmic flow or structural rhythm that is not without significance for the emotional response elicited by the music. (I am grateful to Philip Weller for bringing this passage to my attention.)

[33] Nattiez, "The Contribution of Musical Semiotics," 124.

Haydn, String Quartet in B♭ Major, Op. 64, No. 3 — Minuet

When a movement is labeled "Minuet," we cannot assume a fixed generic identity; only an inspection of the actual music will reveal whether title and contents are congruent, whether the title simply formed a point of departure for the process of composing, or whether the title is an after-the-fact rationalization of a compositional process or product that entertained or entertains concerns other than the specific activity of minuet-writing. These distinctions are important, because they place topic in an objectified category, free of personal or biographical concerns, thereby contrasting it with titles and epithets that may be laden with private signification. In this movement, Haydn retains a number of the procedural premises of minuet. The formal succession Minuet–Trio–Minuet is used; within the Minuet itself—which is all we are concerned with here—the normative triple meter provides the point of departure. Internal repeat signs separate its two parts. All these factors corroborate the normative status of the minuet as a topical type.

The most striking element of topical discourse occurs in measures 11–14 (and subsequently). Within the basic minuet topic emerges a set of horn fifths signaling, perhaps, the hunt style. Horn fifths are normally associated with announcements and opening gestures, so their appearance in this context may seem odd at first. But Haydn has not confined their role to a closing gesture— for by appearing at the end of a repeated fourteen-measure phrase, the topic acquires an opening signification with the repeat. This adaptation of associative properties for different, sometimes contradictory, contexts illustrates one facet of Haydn's play with conventional signs. Note that the horn fifths here gain a certain amount of their expressive impact from being preceded by a normal minuet. Since the primary dimensions of minuet include meter and rhythm, one can hear in the first four measures unequivocal confirmation of that primariness—Haydn leaves no doubt about the identity of this topic. In the second half of the phrase (from measure 5 onward), however, there is some play with meter, mainly through the withdrawal of accompanying instruments in measures 6 and 7. So, although a stock cadential progression (measures 10–12) serves to restore stability to the end of this section, there are already hints of a play in topic.

The fact that the presence of horn fifths has consequence for the structure of the movement as a whole becomes clear from subsequent treatment. As indicated earlier, horn fifths are introduced in measures 11–14, and are extended through 15–16. Then they seem to disappear for some time, until measure 43. But they "seem to" only because one aspect of their syntactic function is retained in the intervening measures. The defining dimensions of this topic include intervallic disposition—specifically, the alternation between vertically disposed fifth and sixth— and an attendant voice-leading, $\hat{2}$ –$\hat{1}$ accompanied by $\hat{5}$ –$\hat{3}$. This weighting of the dimensions of horn fifths contrasts significantly with that of the metrically-based minuet. This is not to say that horn fifths do not have metrical potential. In the present context, because the figure has two elements, a tendency toward duple articulation is evident. The definition of this topic further calls for repetition, for an alternation between the two simultaneities. A single and initial appearance of a vertical fifth followed by a sixth would be necessary, but not sufficient, to define horn fifths; only through repetition is the topic's identity firmly established, unless of course there is a clarifying factor such as timbre present.

Two aspects of the sign are exploited in this Minuet. First, the alternation between fifth and sixth, because it defines a normative dominant-tonic progression, is made compatible with the prevailing harmonic process. Thus, between measures 11 and 12, the topic is first introduced as part of a strongly defined perfect cadence. The subsequent repetition of the fifth–sixth intervallic pattern in measures 12–16 gains from this contextual harmony; it retains an identical harmonic association, thereby adding some rhetorical weight to the sense of closure in the phrase as a whole. Second, while adding to this sense of closure, the phrase's metric tendency challenges the triple grouping already evident in the phrase, by offering a duple articulation that cuts across the triple meter. The hemiola effects do not disrupt so much as strengthen—in the long run—the sense of triple meter. The point, then, is that Haydn has adapted the syntactic properties of the horn topic to the prevailing harmonic process.[34]

After the first double bar, the horn fifths are heard in the two lower instruments, and then they disappear until measure 42. But observe here that the upbeat pattern of the phrasing is retained throughout. Now since the disposition of the horn fifths is compatible with the upbeat pattern, the implicit reference to hunt is absorbed by the prevailing minuet. When the horn fifths return in measure 43, they appear initially as before, and are then transformed harmonically in measures 46–48. This transformation leaves us in no doubt that it is the same hunt topic we are hearing, only now defamiliarized. The minuet proper returns in measure 49 for four measures, and is superseded by an area of relatively "neutral" topical activity (measures 53–56) before returning for the final cadence.

This process of moving in and out of topics is crucial for evaluating the role of topics. In this Minuet, the basic topic is minuet, which shapes our experience of the piece. Minuet is, however, subject to both explicit and implicit definition. When it is defined explicitly—as at the opening of the movement—there is, so to speak, a balance between foreground and background. Where it is defined implicitly—as in measures 11–16—it occupies only a background position, while another topic is foregrounded. Topical discourse in the minuet is therefore not confined to the world of minuet, but is expanded to take in other topical worlds.

Earlier reference to the syntactic property of topic continues to underscore the fact that, although topics retain an associative element that locates them in a specific historical discourse, their syntactic significance or structural potential is equally important, and no less implicative for the establishment of historical identity. Nor are the two aspects discontinuous with one another, as is sometimes held. The analytical method advocated here is one that proceeds from the specific stylistic context to a search for what the background might yield in the way of a structural rhythm. A so-called "purely musical" analysis—one that takes as premise the extraordinary motivic coherence of the minuet, for example—may seem to offer insights that the topic-based analysis lacks. What the topic-based approach advocates, however, is a much broader set of premises, that eventually includes the motivic elements, but that is not restricted to them. In short, once we have established the play of topic and defined the syntactic property of each topic, we can advance an explanation for the particular contextual contiguity of various topics. So, what is often disparaged as the extramusical is no more extramusical than Roman numerals. In the Classic style, topics are not extramusical in the sense of having nothing to offer a syntactic reading of the piece. On the contrary, they are able to account in part for a work's historic specificity, which ultimately locates its syntax in the same historical continuum. The idea that syntax exists in a timeless, synchronic dimension seems unduly facile.

---

[34] On the syntactic properties of the "Lebewohl" topic, see Meyer's analysis of Beethoven's Piano Sonata Op. 81a ("Les Adieux") in *Explaining Music*, 242–68. For a broader discussion of referential as well as structural aspects of certain characteristic textures in Classic and early Romantic music, see Levy, "Texture as a Sign."

Haydn, String Quartet in D Major, Op. 20, No. 4— Minuet

Although this movement (Example 2.1) is labeled "Minuet," its "minuetness" is not straightforwardly felt. Some of this ambiguity characterizes the Minuet of Op. 64, No. 3, but it is not as extreme as in this movement. Haydn, of course, is well known for performing rhythmic and metric "tricks" of this kind, but the point is not always evident that these tricks either result in, or are caused by, the play of topics. The basic confrontation in this piece is between a normative minuet (which finds its most unambiguous definition in the Trio), an implicit gavotte, and the Gypsy style that inspired Haydn's indication to the performer, "Menuet alla Zingarese." If we frame this insight in terms of a foreground-background axis, we can say that the minuet and Gypsy style occupy a background level while the gavotte occupies the foreground. The gavotte, however, tends toward a deeper level than just the foreground. Its articulation is so stable that it assumes a primacy that is not merely deferential to minuet. In this sense, the present movement differs from the one analyzed previously, in which one hears the horn fifths over a still-perceptible minuet, not in place of it. Here, the minuet is barely perceptible at the beginning; only gradually does it establish its identity, and only in the Trio is this identity unequivocal.

The source of much of the dynamism in this minuet is the series of accents that challenge the articulation of the basic triple meter. In each of the four string parts, *sforzando* markings occur in counterpoint and consistently on beats two and three of each measure, so that the triple meter achieves its primacy virtually by grouping rather than by articulation. The play with meter is not restricted to secondary accents, but includes tonal rhythm as well—the harmonic procedures make this clear. For example, in measures 6–8, the alternation of tonic and dominant confers a duple grouping on the music (hence the gavotte feel)—a grouping that further frustrates the listener's expectation of metric resolution at this cadence point. This tug-of-war continues unchanged through the second half of the Minuet, and is heightened by the reenacting of this drama not in the dominant, as before, but in the tonic. Since the dominant represents a harmonic dissonance in the first eight measures, its acceptance of metric dissonance constitutes a heightening of tension. The fact, however, that the same metric dissonance is retained even when harmonic resolution has been achieved (in the second phrase) contributes to the perception of a gavotte topic. This Minuet may be regarded not simply as a movement in and out of triple meter, but as a "trimetric" compound structure involving two dance topics, gavotte and minuet, overseen by an umbrella Gypsy style.

Beethoven, Piano Sonata in C Minor, Op. 13— First Movement, Measures 1–11

Much of the expressive drama in this movement (Example 2.2) derives from Beethoven's strategic exploitation of topical contrast—although, as we shall see later, such contrasts begin to suggest departures from an objectified topical structuring toward a personal, idiosyncratic retreat into private codes. At least three topics are introduced in the opening measures, of the movement: sensibility, cadenza, and French overture. The broken rhetoric of the opening measures, together with the emphasis on diminished-seventh harmony, recalls C.P.E. Bach specifically, or the sensibility style in general. The soloistic display on the last beat of measure 4 may be heard as a mini-cadenza, and therefore as an allusion to the concerto style. The allusion gains perceptive force later on in the introduction (measures 10–11), when the same gesture, this time complete with the conventional precadenza syntax (a six-four chord prolonging the dominant), secures closure for the introduction and launches the Allegro section of the movement. The sense of an

Menuet alla Zingarese
Allegretto

Example 2.1. Haydn, String Quartet in D Major, Op. 20, No. 4—Minuet

Example 2.1. (*cont.*)

overture is conveyed by the "Grave" tempo indication, the ordinal position of the passage, and the characteristic dotted rhythms.

Beginning in measure 5, we hear a songlike melody that appears to be an aria, complete with a throbbing accompaniment. But this aria is not allowed to sing through. Rather, it is interrupted by a diminished seventh-laden gesture that not only recalls the opening of the movement (note also the registral parallel), but also suggests—in the confluent action of register, dynamics, and triadic types—another topic, Sturm und Drang. Measures 5–8 are dominated by this alternation between Sturm und Drang and aria, and it is not until the beginning of measure 9 that the interplay ceases, replaced by allusions to the delicate aspects of the sensibility style. Then follows the cadenza leading to a final resolution on the downbeat of measure 11.

The fact that there is a topical discourse at work here seems evident from the foregoing description, but there are important differences between the practice of Beethoven and those of Haydn and Mozart. The emphasis on Sturm und Drang adds fuel to the fire of those who wish to hear in Beethoven the beginnings of musical Romanticism. Of course, such precursors of Romantic tendency may be heard in C.P.E. Bach, Gluck, Haydn, and Mozart, among others, so there is nothing unusual about this movement. But the topic Sturm und Drang, defined more by absence rather than by presence, admits ambiguity both on the level of substance and within the context of other topics. When a composer prefers ambiguously defined topics to precisely defined ones–such as dances–the "romantic" tendency becomes quite pronounced in his music. But the evidence of eleven measures of music must not be exaggerated; what I am getting at is a larger historical point—that along with the nineteenth century comes an emphasis on topics that are increasingly less concerned with stylized identity and that therefore take one aspect of a work's discourse out of the public realm into a composer's private world. This is not, however, a claim that there are no public codes in nineteenth-century music, or, conversely, that private codes are missing from late eighteenth-century music. There is, rather, a shift in emphasis from public meanings to private, perhaps even self-evident ones.

Mozart, Piano Sonata in F Major, K. 332—First Movement, Measures 1–93

One of the most remarkable of Mozart's essays in topical interplay is the first movement of the F major piano sonata, K. 332. Within the broad sonata-form trajectory, a topical discourse of immense proportion and subtlety unfolds, enhancing, contradicting, predicting, or simply highlighting the harmonic points being made. An analyst who sees only the sonata form outline will be baffled by the wealth of thematic invention. And it would be an evasion of the issue to explain this away simply as another "active" sonata movement. The movement, in fact, epitomizes the "mixed style" spoken of by Quantz, Koch, and Crotch. An analyst who dispenses with the referential nature of the surface by invoking the neutral notion of design will miss the uniquely historicist nature of Mozart's discourse. Only by means of topic can we adequately explain the unique drama of this movement on both surface and deeper levels of structure.[35]

Proceedings begin with an aria accompanied by an Albertilike bass. There may be a suppressed musette here as a result of the piece's refusal to act harmonically, or, rather, its refusal to make explicit its potential harmonic activity (the inclusion of E♭ in measure 2 is a false sign). In measures 5–9, the learned style is hinted at in the form of two-part imitative counterpoint between treble and bass. How different this gesture is from that of the first five measures—the earlier "song" has disappeared, and is replaced by a decidedly unsingable melody. Allanbrook suggests an element of parody in these measures, implying that not only is the learned style the immediate topic, but that a larger topic, counterpoint, is being treated in some ironic fashion.[36] The jaggedness of this counterpoint, the melodic skips, and the hemiola effects contribute to this sense of parody. At the conclusion of the opening phrase (measures 9–12), the learned style is abandoned, and almost as if by default, the main topic of the movement, a minuet, emerges, leading to the first perfect cadence of the piece, in measure 12. The minuet emerges "by default" because it has, to some extent, been present all along, although its presence, like that of the Minuet in Haydn's Op. 20, No. 4 discussed previously, has been in the background. Even this stepping forward into the foreground is to be superseded later in the movement (from measure 41 onward), so that what we are dealing with here are varying degrees of foregrounding. The strategy of the first twelve measures, then, involves a "backgrounded" minuet that is dramatized by aria, musette, and learned style. Note, again, that such symbiosis is possible because of the individual attributes of the topics. Aria, musette, and learned style are adaptable to various metric situations, so that minuet, which is invariant with respect to meter, can shape these topics (or, conversely, be shaped by them) without losing its ultimate identity.

The second period of the movement begins in measure 12, and presents a set of hunt-calls, complete with a simulation of what Koch calls a "horn duet."[37] Here, as before, the minuet remains operative in the background, but it is, in fact, so much more present than it was at the beginning of the first period that we might refer not to a layered "minuet and hunt style," but, rather, to a fused "minuet in hunt style." The continuity between the two topics results from the fact that the horn duet's intervallic pattern is entirely compatible with the meter-invariant minuet. Repetition of this intervallic sequence is also necessary, hence the division of the phrase into two similar halves (measures 12–16 and 16–20). The fact that the articulation of hunt demands local repetition may now be seen to influence the emphasis on closure at the end of this period (measures 19–22). This is basically a rhetorical gesture, but one that takes advantage of—or is necessitated by—a structural element of its topic. It is this adaptation of topical material to structural articulation—a process that can also be conceptualized the other way

---

[35] Writers who have taken note of the textural changes in this sonata, but who have not read these changes referentially, include Wilton Mason, "Melodic Unity in Mozart's Piano Sonata K. 332," Wallace Berry, *Structural Functions in Music*, 41–45 and Alan Walker, *An Anatomy of Music Criticism*, 60–63.

[36] Allanbrook, *Rhythmic Gesture in Mozart*, 6.

[37] Koch, *Musikalisches Lexikon*, 554.

Example 2.2. Beethoven, Piano Sonata in C Minor, Op. 13 ("Pathetique")—
First Movement, measures 1–11

around—that lends weight to an interpretive approach rooted in topic. It might even be argued that without the notion of topic, it becomes difficult to find a convincing *raison d'etre* for the juxtaposition at the beginning of a sonata of two periods, both composing out a progression in F major, and both having similar middleground structures. Tonal redundancy may result. To call it a surface discourse is to miss the point, since it, and not the tonal process (insofar as the separation is possible), carries the dynamic sense of the piece so far.

The plunge into D minor in measure 22 ushers in a style reminiscent of C.P.E. Bach. Two not-unrelated topics, Sturm und Drang and fantasia, are implied here. The increased microrhythmic activity, the use of the minor mode, the emphasis on diminished harmonies, and the impassioned style of declamation—all these are the archetypal features of musical Sturm und Drang. But there is something of the fantasia here, too. It is ultimately a moot point whether the music beginning in measure 22 is Sturm und Drang or fantasia, given that the defining elements of both topics overlap significantly. More important is the structural potential of these topics. The passage from measures 22 to 40 is a transitional one, taking us from the tonic area of F major to its dominant. Since transitions are inherently unstable, composers are likely to employ in those sections topics that are themselves inherently unstable. Both fantasia and Sturm und Drang are united in being characterized by the absence of stability, and this alone makes their appearance in the present context appropriate.

It is worth stressing that although certain topics are appropriate at certain points of the musical discourse—as in the sonata-form work that we are considering—a composer is just as likely to use an "inappropriate" topic and, by so doing, draw attention to compositional procedure by playing with the listener's expectations. At the beginning of the so-called "Dissonance" Quartet, K. 465, for example, Mozart uses a fantasia topic to call into question the formal or rhetorical premise of a clear and unambiguous opening in a Classic work. But there is a further level of topical signification, for by calling into question one of the norms of the classical style, Mozart transforms tonality itself into a topic. The fantasia thus provides the procedural means by which a larger topic, tonality, is discussed.[38]

To say that a tonal work is "about" tonality may sound tautological since, given the premise of tonality, all tonal works compose out an archetypal contrapuntal progression. But just as poems can be about poems, films about films, and novels about novels, so music can be about itself, and tonality about itself, too. There is, in fact, no shortage of works whose discourses are in some respect metamusical, whether these be variation sets of eighteenth- and nineteenth-century composers, or the deliberate use of pre-existing material by twentieth-century composers such as Mahler, Stravinsky, Berio, Crumb, and Rochberg. Compared to the "Dissonance" Quartet, however, the F major sonata at which we are looking does not exploit the topicality of tonality to quite the same extent, except in the transhistorical sense in which all tonal music is about tonality. A related phenomenon in this discussion is the idea of structural premises with invariable attributes. In describing the "Dissonance" Quartet, I had to postulate an initial premise of clarity. This is something we shall come to in the next chapter when we discuss beginning, middle, and ending gestures, and consider what sorts of normative constraints are imposed on various forms. It is these that will clarify the evident self-referentiality of the "Dissonance" Quartet. But let us return to the F major sonata.

[38] Another example of this kind of process occurs in the first movement of Beethoven's String Quartet in C Major, Op. 59, No. 3, in which fantasy elements confer on the opening of the work a self-referential mode of discourse; only at the beginning of the Allegro is this self-referentiality—the discussion of tonality—abandoned, or rather, taken for granted.

The transitional passage, from measure 22 onward, is also characterized by an active arpeggio figuration that suggests the topic fanfare. But there is an important twist here, for fanfares are archetypically major-mode invariant—so that to call this particular celebration fanfare is to extend significantly the domain encompassed by that term. Measures 33–34, however, offer the proper modal version of fanfare, so that one might argue that the earlier minor-mode version is retrospectively restructured. But then, what about the return to minor in measure 31, and the arpeggiation of the German sixth chord in measure 35? A fanfare is essentially a rhythmicized arpeggio, which makes it a particularly mobile topic. Now, given that the motivic history of the piece so far has included a large number of arpeggios, their perception as fanfares in this transitional passage is not as disjunct with the prevailing motivic process as the heretical term "minor-mode fanfare" might lead one to suspect.

The topic at the beginning of the second key area (measure 41) is unequivocally minuet. Although this topic has been present all along, and even defined by default in measures 8–12, only here is it foregrounded. The rhythmic-metric situation gives prominence to the triple grouping, while the left-hand articulation of downbeats in measures 41 and 42 further emphasizes the sense of minuet. This topic continues to dominate the proceedings in the following measures, allowing a fleeting amoroso sentiment in the stroking two-against-three rhythm of measures 49–50. Sturm und Drang returns in measure 56, featuring some of the same flatted harmonies of its earlier occurrence, and is followed by a musettelike stasis in measure 67. In measure 71 the topic is minuet once again, and this leads to a brief Sturm und Drang in measure 82. Finally, as is appropriate to the tonicization of the second key, a flourish in the form of brilliant style (measures 86–90) confirms the priority of C major. The final four measures of the exposition show no explicit topical commitment, although fanfare is implicit while the ubiquitous minuet is now heard only on a distant horizon.

There is no need to discuss further the succession of topics in the rest of the movement since no new topics are introduced; the development section "develops" both minuet and Sturm und Drang, while the recapitulation restates the topics of the exposition in the same order and with the appropriate tonal adjustments.

Allanbrook has described this exposition as a "miniature theater of human gestures and actions," thereby seeking to persuade us that Classic music is "pervasively mimetic, not of Nature itself but of our natures—of the world of men, their habits and actions."[39] Certainly the description offered here supports the suggestion that a topical discourse conveys part of the drama of the movement. The human dimension of this drama is also implicitly supported by this analysis, but the subject is a complex one, and cannot adequately be dealt with within the scope of this book. Suffice it to say that by empirically locating the content of Mozart's sonata in an eighteenth-century sound environment, we have provided a point of departure for making sense of that eloquent and richly diversified drama.

IV

The critical exercise in which I have just engaged has been an exercise in interpretation, in perceiving potential meanings in a number of classic works within the deliberately restricted framework of their topical structure. Many of the theoretical assumptions that I have made are

[39] Allanbrook, *Rhythmic Gesture in Mozart*, 3.

implicit in what has been said, but it is necessary, in this final part of the chapter, to make them explicit. Let us return to the set of questions posed at the beginning of this chapter, answering them directly, and allowing a certain amount of generalization.

1. What is a topic?

Topics are musical signs. They consist of a signifier (a certain disposition of musical dimensions) and a signified (a conventional stylistic unit, often but not always referential in quality). Signifiers are identified as a relational unit within the dimensions of melody, harmony, meter, rhythm, and so on, while the signified is designated by conventional labels drawn mostly from eighteenth-century historiography (Sturm und Drang, fanfare, learned style, sensibility, and so on). The world of topic, like its parent world of the sign, is potentially open, so that one cannot—and need not—specify the total number of topics current in the eighteenth century. At the same time, it is analytically expedient to limit the domain of topic empirically—hence my adoption of a provisional universe (Figure 2). The identity of a topic is least dependent on the name of that topic. What matters, following the structuralist idea of relationality, is the difference between various topics. It is possible to work from the pure acoustical phenomenon, through its representation in notation, to its disposition as sound in motion, and finally, to the meaning that it assumes for the listener. This means, following Barthes, that topics may be read or heard as at least second-order semiotic systems, since they take a musical sign (or set of musical signs), drain it of signification, and then refill it with meaning.

2. How are topics perceived?

The primary condition for the perception of topic is listener-competence. In order to be able to locate a given piece within the class of contemporary eighteenth-century discourses, the listener needs to be schooled in the idiom of the eighteenth century. To be schooled in eighteenth-century stylistic devices is to have in one's memory a series of paradigmatic classes from which one can draw in order to produce meaning from the sequence of gestures in a given work. This is not so much a linguistic ability as it is an ability to recall a certain vocabulary. Although, with the benefit of hindsight, it is possible for a twentieth-century listener to acquire competence in an eighteenth-century idiom, the primary epistemological appeal of a topical analysis is to a contemporary eighteenth-century view. Both that view and a twentieth-century one are ultimately united in a listener-oriented dialectic, and it is the strength of this analytical model that it provides a framework for integrating into a twentieth-century listener's response to classic music aspects of this music that originate from the eighteenth century.

3. Does every piece of music have a topic?

Theoretically yes, but let us not forget that the substantial domain of topics, like that of language, remains open, allowing for the possibility of discovering more topics. In the examples considered in this chapter, references to an area of "neutral" topical activity indicate not necessarily the absence of topic but, rather, the absence of an appropriate label within the restricted domain of our topical universe. All Classic music, then, is conceptually laden with topical signification—although the extent to which that signification is made perceptually evident varies from context to context.

4. How many topics can a single work sustain?

Like the previous answer, this one remains unspecified with respect to domain. A work can theoretically sustain any number of topics from the full series of topics. However, there are practical or stylistic constraints on the number of topics that a work can meaningfully sustain. If a topic, taken at its literal meaning, is a subject to be discussed, then it is clear that this can only take place in time, so that a certain temporal commitment becomes necessary. Just as a modulation requires both the presence of a certain harmonic syntax and a commitment in time to inform the listener of its occurrence, so the unfolding of successive topics requires a temporal dimension that depends, among other things, on generic as well as strategic constraints. Slow introductions to symphonies, expositions of concerto movements, sonata-form movements, minuet movements, overtures—all these have generic constraints that affect the number of topics that can be meaningfully exposed. Of course, these are only normative guides subject to a considerable amount of play.

5. How are topics presented—do they unfold singly or can they be combined?

Topics unfold with respect to a syntagmatic axis while achieving their contextual identity with respect to a paradigmatic one. The syntagmatic axis is also a compound axis, allowing for further combinations of topics. Thus, in a given piece of music, topics can assume the disposition Topic 1–Topic 2–Topic 3–Topic 4, these being virtual and nonoverlapping identities. I would call this the "model of topical succession." But there is an extremely wide range of transformations of this model. First, adjacent elements in the model may overlap. Although one can often tell where a given topic ceases and another takes over, it is generally the case that adjacent topics merge into one another. I have described part of this continuity on the level of the "background" with respect to a structural rhythm. Second, the members of the model may be presented simultaneously. We have seen instances in which Topic 1 is introduced initially and prolonged in the background while Topics 2, 3, and 4 are foregrounded.

6. Are topics hierarchically organized?

The supreme source of hierarchy in tonal music is, of course, the tonal-harmonic structure, which we have not yet considered. So it is difficult to discuss the hierarchic organization of topic without reference to this more naturally hierarchic framework. If topical hierarchy is considered within a syntagmatic axis in which proportion is the chief determinant, then there is a natural hierarchy— or, rather, the hierarchy is possible to the extent that the individual topics are isolatable. But to discuss hierarchy meaningfully, we need to attach topic to a harmonic framework, since the dictates of that framework determine considerably the nature of an intratopical hierarchy.

As semiotic objects, then, topics provide important clues to the meaning of a Classic work, whether this meaning be structural-syntactical, or broadly expressive. Although I have refrained from assigning fixed signification to topics—believing that this is very much a contextual matter—I hope to have shown the senses in which this music is far from pure, autonomous, or abstract, and is as concerned as ever with sociocultural norms that structure its discourse. It is also clear by now that to discuss the topical content of a work without reference to other dimensions is to present a partial picture of that work. In order, therefore, to assess fully the role of topical signs in Classic music, we need to confront a second class of signs, which is more often regarded as mirroring the primary framework of Classic music: its tonal-harmonic structure.

THREE

INTROVERSIVE SEMIOSIS:

THE BEGINNING–MIDDLE–END PARADIGM

I

IN THE PREVIOUS chapter, I argued that Classic music is nominally referential, and that referential signs, far from being merely surface elements, do in fact sustain structural procedures on a deeper level. I suggested that a fluid structural rhythm is operative in the background, and that a succession of individual topical essences results in a scenario whose coordinates can be accommodated along the axis of this rhythm. Referential signs, however, form only one class of signs in Classic music. There is another class consisting of what we might call "pure" signs, signs that provide important clues to musical organization through conventional use, but not necessarily by referential or extramusical association. The purpose of this chapter is to elucidate this second class of signs.

The most powerful framework for analyzing pure signs is one that gives pride of place to the dynamic quality of Classic music, to the sense of directed motion. Schenker's theory conveys this quality especially lucidly, and it will serve as a guide in the analyses to follow. But this cannot be a fundamentalist application of Schenkerian principles, which, because of their organicist bias, will be adapted to the elucidation of the more local levels of musical structure rather than that of the global ones. Classic music depends as much on contrast, conflict, and the juxtaposition of ideas as on organic continuity and articulation. Specifically, then, I shall discuss local dynamism within the framework of a Schenkerian Ursatz, in which is enshrined the archetypically dynamic nature of tonal motion. Rather than extract various *Ursätze* from the pieces to be analyzed, however, I shall concentrate on the rhetorical strategy enshrined in the Ursatz. This means framing the discussion in terms of a beginning–middle–ending paradigm, the argument being that there are specific attitudes to a work's beginning, its middle, and its ending, and that these strategies are an important clue to the dramatic character of Classic music. The chapter falls into three parts: First, I shall show how the idea of dynamic totality has been dealt with by both eighteenth-century writers (Mattheson) and their twentieth-century counterparts (Fischer, Schenker, and Ratner). Then, I shall isolate the three constituent elements of our beginning–middle–ending paradigm and discuss each with reference to a number of examples drawn from the music of Haydn, Beethoven, and Mozart. The third part of the chapter reconstitutes the paradigm and introduces the theoretical notion of playing with signs. Here, too, a single example illustrates ways in which Classic composers "play" with pure musical signs. It is this notion of play that provides the key to meaning in Classic music.

II

In *Der vollkommene Capellmeister* (1739), Johann Mattheson, proceeding from the premise that "a good composition should have the same form as a good speech," offers practical advice to composers about how they can construct "good" pieces.[1] It is Mattheson's belief that the rhetorical strength of a composer's musical ideas be given in a particular order, the strongest arguments at the beginning, the weaker ones in the middle, and stronger ones at the end. What is of interest here is not merely the rhetorical ploy, but the implicit recognition of a whole structure shaped by three constituent parts. In fact, when Mattheson goes on to discuss his own compositional process—he is careful not to prescribe this for every composer—he says that he worries most about the end of an oratorio. "I usually begin at the end," he writes, although he never loses sight of "the rest of the work." And he does this because "listeners have always been so moved at the end, where it matters most, that they remembered a great deal of it." These are radically modern-sounding words from a theorist in whose generation the attitude to a work's ending often followed explicit conventions.

Mattheson is concerned with more than the end, however. "A good beginning is half the job," he writes, and proceeds to give advice on how this can be achieved. It is worth stressing that for Mattheson, a work's rhetorical strategy is essentially melodic, that a "good melody" will reveal all the relevant rhetorical parts. Two broad categories of rhetorical organization are indicated. The first involves a set of analogies between grammatical punctuation and musical punctuation. The aim is to show varying degrees of closure, and also to prescribe particular degrees for particular moments in the musical discourse. Mattheson's model is a sixteen-measure minuet, a *paragraphus*, which is articulated by periods, colons, semicolons and commas. The second category, also the more relevant one for the present purposes, is a structural model borrowed from rhetoric, and valid for an entire (vocal) composition.

Exordium–Narratio–Propositio–Confutatio–Confirmatio–Peroratio.[2]

Two things matter here: the actual contents of the model, and the sequence of functions. The actual contents, according to Mattheson, may vary from piece to piece. Although he does not specify which ones are indispensable, it is clear that Peroratio, for example, is an invariant element of the model. Exordium, too, must be present in order to introduce the work, as well as to provide a foretaste of what is to follow. Narratio is specific to a vocal work, marking the entrance of the vocal part and hence the exposition of the verbal meaning of the work. Propositio describes process, the working out of a previously exposed idea. Confirmatio nails down the principal subject or premise, while Confutatio provides a much-needed challenge to the status quo—leaving Peroratio to conclude the oration.

The importance of Mattheson's model lies, first, in its recognition of the idea of wholeness, an implicit anticipation of the organic orientation that dominates music-theoretical thought in the nineteenth century. Then there is the distinction between what might be described as "statement" and "elaboration," between the exposition of an idea (as in Exordium) and its subsequent elaboration (as in Propositio). Third, there is an implicit awareness of the rhetorical functions of constituent parts, an insight that I shall later concretize with respect to a beginning–middle–ending paradigm. Thus, although it may seem farfetched to suggest that Mattheson's model in one way anticipates Schenker's, the proposition is not without corroboration from some of the functions outlined in the preceding.

---

[1] Johann Mattheson, *Der vollkommene Capellmeister*. This and subsequent quotations are taken from Hans Lenneberg's translation, "Johann Mattheson on Rhetoric and Affect." A complete English translation by Ernest Harriss was published by UMI in 1981.

[2] This model, or variants of it, was widely discussed by theorists during the sixteenth–eighteenth centuries as part of the prehistory of musical form. For a recent digest, with an emphasis on Burmeister and Mattheson, see Bent, *Analysis*, 6–8.

The same concern for the piece of music as a dynamic totality is at the heart of Schenker's theory—but where Mattheson offers only a schematic outline, Schenker details the actual musical elements that are embodied in that outline. There is, to be sure, no explicit concern with a beginning–middle–ending paradigm in Schenkerian theory (some intriguing remarks about endings in *Der freie Satz* notwithstanding[3]) but various voice-leading procedures strongly suggest such an orientation. The Ursatz, or fundamental structure (as distinct from background), is a two-voice contrapuntal structure that provides the conceptual frame for a piece of tonal music (Example 3.1).

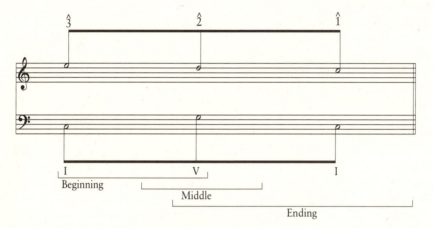

Example 3.1. Schenker's *Ursatz*

We might interpret its three sonorities as overlapping instances of beginning (I–V), middle (V), and ending (V–I) respectively. Nominally, the Ursatz enshrines a progression from stability through instability back to stability; that is, the first member provides a stable point of departure (beginning), is undermined (middle), and is returned to the initial point of stability (ending). But this is very much an abstraction, a level far beneath the surface of the piece. In an actual composition, this structure is subject to various kinds and degrees of prolongation. Each of its members functions as the focal point, the contrapuntally superior moment, in a given passage. The beginning, for example, may be preceded by a preludial ascent (Schenker's *Anstieg*), or an arpeggiation. The initial member may also represent an entire tonic area of the piece, an area of motion in which the tonic is defined by means of a progression involving the dominant. Or, it may represent the bulk of a given piece, yielding to its dominant only at the last minute.

Schenker's Ursatz has no prescribed internal proportions; all it asserts is that a piece will begin in the tonic, move to the dominant, and return to the tonic, and that this key-defining progression is the essence of a tonal piece. There are, to be sure, "defective" *Ursätze*, but those can always be measured against normative ones.[4] Indeed, one of the principal differences between eighteenth- and nineteenth-century music centers on this notion of defective structures—the argument being that open or incomplete structures become more and more normative in the nineteenth century.

The second member of the Ursatz, the middle, is also the most nebulous. To designate something

---

[3] See Schenker's remarks on "the definitive close of a composition" in *Free Composition*, 129.

[4] For an example of a "defective" Ursatz, see Schenker's analysis of Chopin's A Minor Prelude, Op. 28, No. 2 in *Free Composition*, Figure 110, a3. See also Harald Krebs, "Alternatives to Monotonality," for a fuller discussion of such open tonal structures.

a "middle " is to risk being attacked for not specifying where that middle begins, or where it ends. Yet, in terms of function, the middle both undermines and prolongs the beginning. It undermines the beginning by departing from it, generating tension in the process. It prolongs it in the sense that the beginning finds its ultimate definition only through the middle and ending. Both beginning and ending functions therefore necessitate a middle.

And finally, the ending, the third member of the paradigm, serves to close the structure. It signifies a return to stability, thereby completing the linear definition of tonality. But it also differs significantly from the beginning: as the voice-leading model shows, the top voice is now a $\hat{1}$ instead of the initial $\hat{3}$, meaning that it is in a more complete state of rest than at the beginning. And the fact that it is approached through a descent strengthens its status as the goal of the global progression. The lower voice, on the other hand, completes the *Bassbrechung* (bass arpeggiation). It confirms the hierarchical supremacy of the initial member by virtue of harmonic identity—but, because it is arrived at through a linear process, it serves to complete something that was previously incomplete.

Although Schenker's Ursatz has by now guided a large number of analyses, it has rarely been understood rhetorically. As a highly abstract structure, it seem's to go beyond rhetoric to structure—but I want to argue that this ultimate structure is necessarily an instance of a rhetorical strategy. The Ursatz is subject to a variety of realizations on background, middleground, and foreground, as well as on several sublevels of these three levels. And insofar as each realization is dialectically linked with an abstract, underlying pattern, the latter may be said to participate fully in the rhetorical life of the piece.

What Mattheson offered in terms of a set of functions within the syntagmatic chain, Schenker concretizes in the form of a contrapuntal structure. There are two other approaches to this pheno-menon that we must consider before moving on to specific examples—one deriving from the work of Wilhelm Fischer, and the other from the work of Ratner. In a recent reformulation of Fischer, Laurence Dreyfus has drawn attention to the harmonic functions implicit in a Bach ritornello.[5] Although the repertoire is different from that we are considering in this book, the issues are significantly close. Fischer, searching for the origins of the Classic style in pre-Classic music, arrived at the functions implicit in Bach's ritornello structure. Proceeding from the premise that the ritornello is tonally closed, Fischer went on to designate its invariable features as *Vordersatz–Fortspinnung–Epilog*. As Dreyfus explains, the Vordersatz "defines the tonic chord by reference to its dominant"—a I–V progression, in other words. The Fortspinnung is "premised on the absence of a defined tonic," exhibiting sequential voice-leading patterns. The Epilog signifies the "formal cadence in the tonic," closing melodically on $\hat{1}$ and harmonically on I. This scheme is nothing but the beginning–middle–ending paradigm, applied on a small scale to an ideal ritornello. Like Schenker's *Ursatz*, its members "display complementary tonal features," by which Dreyfus means that only as a totality is their ultimate meaning secured.

Operating outside the Schenkerian tradition, Ratner has attempted to concretize the idea of a harmonic rhetoric for Classic music in terms that strongly resemble Schenker's. Harmony, for Ratner, is "the broadest theater of action" in Classic music. "Whatever may take place in the course of a movement, it must begin and end in the same key. Events are planned so that the harmony follows an unbroken path from beginning to end."[6] Note that Ratner is already concerned explicitly with beginnings and endings, and implicitly with middles. For the Classic composer,

---

[5] See Wilhelm Fischer, "Zur Entwicklungsgeschichte des Wiener klassichen Stils" and Laurence Dreyfus, "J. S. Bach's Concerto Ritornellos and the Question of Invention."

[6] Ratner, *Classic Music,* 48

Example 3.2. Ratner's model for harmonic function in Classic music, with three realizations

then, monotonality was a way of life; so, what mattered was the strategy by which that monotonal structure was individualized in a given composition. Ratner argues that cadences hold the key to tonal expression, and that the linking of beginning to middle to ending is chiefly a matter of cadential action. His model of harmonic functions given in Example 3.2 describes these cadential functions. $\hat{1}$ is a stable point of departure, $\hat{4}$ "moves away from $\hat{1}$," and $\hat{7}$ "pulls back towards $\hat{1}$... thus reversing the action." Finally, $\hat{1}$ forms a point of arrival, or a new point of departure.

There are significant parallels between Ratner's model and Schenker's Ursatz, although the differences are also noticeable. Both models are concerned with the expression of tonality as a closed structure. For Ratner, like Mattheson, this is very much a melodic process, although the fact that the discussion occurs in a chapter on harmony—and the fact that there is constant reference to harmonic functions—suggests that melody may be only the clearest manifestation of the rhetorical strategy. Ratner's $\hat{4}$ and $\hat{7}$ are functionally equivalent to Schenker's $\hat{2}$; the difference lies in Ratner's willingness to accommodate, even on this level, a supertonic or subdominant function (see the second and third realizations of the model in Example 3.2). Schenker's model prescribes voice-leading, whereas Ratner's is less insistent on it; in fact, the disjunction implicit in $\hat{4}$ not finding resolution to $\hat{3}$ in Ratner's model is noticeable, although the third realization in Example 3.2 shows how this is corrected. But, perhaps most significantly, whereas Ratner's model is operative on a local level of structure—the model was devised primarily to explain the action within individual periods—Schenker's is a global model that often finds replications on local levels.

What Ratner adds to this musical reduction, however, is a verbal description of aspects of its strategy. Following closely the eighteenth-century idea that a piece of music must follow "the course taken in rhetorical argument," Ratner offers, as a global strategy, a three-phase model: to present an idea or thesis, to explore and develop it, and then to confirm it. Translated into the terms of key definition within a single period of the composition, this means, first, an indication of key, second, an establishment of key, and third, a confirmation of that key. It is a pity that this model is not given a specifically musical or contrapuntal representation, but only a set of suggestive verbal designations. This reduces its explanatory potential significantly, because it does not include the parameters by which such values can be assigned. Ratner also includes other aspects of harmonic rhetoric that rest on the beginning–middle–ending paradigm. For example, he isolates a number of progressions that "appear in the course of a period"—meaning, in our terms, that they are middle progressions. He also notes that pedal points on the tonic "represent statement and conclusion"—

implying beginning and ending respectively—whereas those on the dominant "build cadential drive," implying middle.[7]

Mattheson, Schenker, and Ratner are thus united in providing explanatory models for eighteenth-century music in which the beginning–middle–ending conjunction functions fundamentally—Mattheson's in the form of a string of verbal symbols, Schenker's in the form of a two-voice contrapuntal structure, and Ratner's in the form of a melodic–cadential progression. What we need to do now is to consider the constituent elements of this global mechanism within the functions outlined earlier. I have assembled a number of excerpts for this purpose, and I shall discuss them under three headings. It should perhaps be said that, although the three elements together form a whole, and although none of them has meaning without the others, there is a hierarchical formation in the attitudes enshrined in the model. That is, the concerns of a beginning, for example, because they are chronologically superior, often assume greater importance than those of a middle, just as the celebration of an ending (Mattheson's words notwithstanding) can sometimes assume ultranormative forms—various repeated cadential progressions. The most extensive discussion will be of beginnings, followed by that of endings, then middles.

III

Edward Said writes about the beginnings of literary works in ways adaptable to those of musical works. "We can regard a beginning as the point at which, in a given work, the writer departs from all other works; a beginning immediately establishes relationships with works already existing, relationships of either continuity or antagonism, or some mixture of both."[8] We might describe this as the paradox of beginning. When a composer sets out to write a string quartet, he is under obligation to locate the discourse of that quartet within certain norms; at the same time, the fact that he has chosen to write another string quartet implies that he is under obligation to establish relationships of difference between this and previous string quartets. Said's point is that it is the beginning that makes this paradox most apparent. "Beginning," Said continues, "is the first step towards the intentional production of meaning." As the initial element in a finite structure, a beginning establishes certain premises or points of reference, and our perception of subsequent events in that structure is inevitably informed by beginning processes.

Whatever relationships of difference and antagonism that are established by beginnings assume "precedence and priority" in the work. It is here that the premise of clarity in the presentation of subjects becomes important. It is, of course possible to premise a beginning on ambiguity instead of clarity, but that strategy is much more characteristic of nineteenth-century music than of eighteenth-century music.[9] Said notes further that a beginning is "an activity which ultimately

---

[7] Carl Dahlhaus also argues implicitly for a beginning–middle–ending paradigm in Classic music when he writes: "The meaning of any sequence of chords must depend on where, formally, it occurs. The widespread theory that in classical music all harmonic relationships can be seen as expansions or modifications of the cadence is thoroughly mistaken. It is necessary to distinguish between closing sections, whose harmony constitutes a cadence, and opening and middle sections. The astonishing harmony at the beginning of Beethoven's Waldstein Sonata Op. 53, for example, would be out of place at the end of a movement: its effect as a beginning is compelling and forward-looking. And harmonic sequences characteristic of development sections cannot convincingly be traced to the cadence; nor could they be used as beginnings or endings" ("Harmony," *The New Grove Dictionary of Music and Musicians*)

[8] Edward Said, *Beginning: Intention and Method*; subsequent quotations are taken from the opening two chapters.

[9] On the use of ambiguity as premise, see David Epstein, *Beyond Orpheus*, 161–77. Although it is possible to cite some

implies return and repetition rather than simple linear accomplishment." This places certain constraints on the nature of that beginning—constraints that demand, for example, that it be identifiable, that it have a life of its own, so that its return can also be easily identified. Beginnings often have a sort of "detachable abstraction"; they constitute a "formal appetite imposing a severe discipline on the mind that wants to think every turn of its thoughts from the start."

How does this apply to music? Consider the first thirteen measures of Beethoven's Op.12, No.1, quoted in Example 3.3. The passage may be described, following eighteenth-century theorists, as constituting a period, because the processes are secured by a perfect cadence in measures 12–13.[10]

Example 3.3. Beethoven, Sonata for Violin and Piano in D Major, Op.12, No.1—
First Movement, measures 1–13

of Haydn's "nervous" openings as instances of ambiguous premises, the mere introduction of a chromatic element in order to hint at a forthcoming modulation does not alter the tonal allegiance of that opening. Contrast this practice with that of work such as the Prelude to *Tristan und Isolde*, in which a genuine ambiguity as premise is played out subsequently.

[10] A concise summary of eighteenth-century discussions of periodicity may be found in Ratner, *Classic Music,* 33–47. See also Elaine Sisman, "Small and Expanded Forms," for a detailed discussion and application of Heinrich Koch's models of periodic organization to Haydn's music.

In terms of Said's paradox, the relationships of difference reside in the specific disposition of notes, clothed in this particular key, this meter, these rhythms, this tempo, these articulations, this instrumentation, these dynamics, and so on. It is hard to mistake this work for another, partly because the sample space is itself not that big, but also because the nature of musical composition is not at all likely to breed the sort of replicas that would result in rewriting a single work. Of course, there are works that sound similar, but that only confers on them membership of a particular generic or stylistic class.

This opening period has a twofold strategy. Its first five measures, harmonically speaking, offer nothing but the tonic chord in various arpeggiations. This is equivalent to establishing the tonic area as an acoustical phenomenon. These measures are, in that sense, gestural rather than structural. It is in the second half of the period that beginning, as an activity, actually commences. The main melodic idea is introduced by the violin (measure 5), while the piano accompanies mainly with scalelike figures. This polarization is maintained until approximately measure 11, in which the melodic and accompanimental roles are merged, leading to the close of the period.

More important than the establishment of generic identity is the process of musical definition that accounts here for the period as a structural unit. Beginning in measure 5, Beethoven composes out a progression in D, which serves to establish the priority of that key as a point of departure as well as premise. Low-level arpeggiations in measures 1–4 are followed by a $\hat{5}$–$\hat{4}$–$\hat{3}$–$\hat{2}$–$\hat{1}$ descent in the top voice and its I–V–I bass counterpart. The entire gesture comes off as a single, indivisible one, despite the presence of a very local close in measures 8–9.

Two important characteristics of Classic beginnings emerge from this account. First, the beginning provides a complete definition of the periodic activity in the piece. That is, a beginning contains or comprises a period that provides, in miniature, the structural process of the piece as a whole, a sort of piece within a piece. The features of the smaller piece are then mapped onto that of the larger one. Second and consequently, beginning has a life of its own, a "detachable abstraction," as Said describes it. It is also evident that the actual definition of key requires not merely an emphasis on the tonic of the key, but a progression involving the dominant.

The argument that the beginning is detachable suggests that beginning *itself* has a beginning and an end. That it has a beginning, there is no doubt—since, after all, a piece of music must begin somewhere, the beginning being the point at which ontological time is replaced by musical time.[11] But there is a more interesting question to be asked: Where is the "real beginning" of a piece? Even in the foregoing example, I have implied that the music up to the downbeat of measure 5 is preludial to the "real beginning" of the piece. This judgment derives from an invocation of structural procedure as prescribed by Schenker, which sees neither a harmonic progression nor a defined structural melody in the opening measures. Such effects are not uncommon in Classic music, and we can get at them by asking, "When is a beginning not a beginning?" The idea of diminutions as determinants of structure offers a good explanation for this sort of activity, and helps to disentangle a proper beginning from its gestural prelude.[12]

The opening period of the first movement of Haydn's String Quartet in D Major, Op. 64 ,No.5

[11] Cf. the discussion of musical beginnings in Edward T. Cone, *Musical Form and Musical Performance*, 22–25. Also of interest are Lewis Rowell, "The Creation of Audible Time," Jonathan D. Kramer, "Beginnings and Endings in Western Art Music," and Judith Schwartz, "Opening Themes in Opera Overtures of Johann Adolf Hasse."

[12] László Somfai explains some of the opening strategies in the Op. 71–74 string quartets of Haydn with respect to the constraints posed by Haydn's London audiences. Thus Somfai speaks of "noise-killer effects" and distinguishes between "integral" and "non-integral" openings. None of these "external" factors, however, replaces the constraints posed by a purely musical logic. See Somfai, "The London Revision of Haydn's Instrumental Style."

Example 3.4. Haydn, String Quartet in D Major, Op. 64, No. 5—
First Movement, measures 1–8

provides another example of beginning premises, although its details differ from those enshrined in the Beethoven violin sonata (see Example 3.4). One of the two popular subtitles of the movement, "Hornpipe" derives from the topical reference in the opening measures. (The other, "The Lark," a descriptive title, need not concern us here, since its musical definition falls outside the opening period.) Horn signals have a dual, somewhat paradoxical signification in eighteenth-century music. Although they are often heard as signifiers of beginnings or as curtain-raisers, they also function frequently as parting signals—that is, as signifiers of ending. A famous example is the opening movement of Beethoven's Op. 81a, in which the *Lebewohl* motif depends for its effect on a reading of an opening sign as a closing one. This dual signification is dramatized in the opening of Haydn's movement, as well: the work is announced in terms of a horn duet—now simulated by strings—while at the same time carrying a strong and persuasive sense of closure. When a composer begins a piece with a closing gesture, he may well be hinting at an aspect of its rhetorical structure that is to be subsequently played with. This period, then, begins and ends with an ending sign, the former hierarchically dependent on the latter.

Not all opening periods are saturated with closure, but all opening periods must have a close. Said's idea that a beginning implies return and repetition is true of music, because what the opening period offers in microcosm is often what is played out throughout the rest of the piece, a beginning–middle–ending paradigm on a grand scale. Haydn's Sonata in C Major, Hob. XVI: 35 (Example 3.5) begins with a detachable period whose structural procedure, like that of the opening of the Quartet Op. 64, No. 5, is spread across the eight-measure span. The period is articulated in two halves, a four-measure phrase moving from tonic to dominant, and another four-measure phrase returning to the tonic. Phrase structure and voice-leading do not share the same surface articulation, however. Cutting across the 4 + 4 articulation is a $\hat{5} - \hat{4} - \hat{3} - \hat{2} - \hat{1}$ structural descent, whose $\hat{5}$ controls the first four measures, and whose $\hat{4} - \hat{3} - \hat{2} - \hat{1}$ control the second four. This is, of course, the normal proportioning of such descents—giving the most compositional space to the initial member of the line. Note, however, that between measures 5 and 6, a weakly supported $\hat{3} - \hat{2} - \hat{1}$ close functions as a mini-ending within a larger beginning (the eight-measure phrase), whose own beginning and ending occur elsewhere. In Examples 3.4 and 3.5, then, we have instances of endings nested within beginnings, thus pointing to the reciprocal functions between beginnings and endings.

Example 3.5. Haydn, Piano Sonata in C Major, Hob. XVI: 35—
First Movement, measures 1–8

It is not always the case that a beginning asserts, rather than passively acknowledges, the principal tonality, but even in circumstances where such clarity is underplayed, the shadow of an essential I–V–I progression is never out of view. The opening of Haydn's String Quartet in G Major, Op. 76, No. 1 (Example 3.6) is an example of a work that begins by asserting closure, and then proceeds to offer a monophonic opening period whose gestural sense, although dwarfed by that of the opening two measures, is subsidiary to its structural sense, which outdoes the opening two-measure gesture. What I am calling a closing gesture is a I–V–I cadential progression, whose closing sense is challenged, but not negated, by an ascending, rather than a descending, melodic profile— $\hat{1}$–$\hat{2}$ –$\hat{3}$ (measures 1–2). This opening therefore enshrines a tension that is only gradually diffused as the movement unfolds. What immediately follows this contradictory gesture is a period that is subdivisible into four and four—the first four moving to the dominant, and the next four answering

Example 3.6. Haydn, String Quartet in G Major, Op. 76, No. 1—
First Movement, measures 1–10

that move with a close on the tonic. It is these eight measures, therefore, that fulfill the normal conditions of a beginning period—but, because of their textural disposition and the weight of the preceding *forte* gesture, their meaning remains far from straightforward. We could hear measures 3–10 as a harmonic expansion of measures 1–2 and speak of not one but two beginnings. Unlike the two previous examples, Example 3.6 is not a larger beginning that nests a smaller one; rather, it comprises two successive beginnings.

There are situations, notably in Beethoven, in which the structural functions of an opening period are under threat from a play in the temporal dimension, but these functions are never overthrown. The opening of the Rondo of the D Major Piano Sonata, Op. 10, No. 3 (Example 3.7) has all the ingredients of a beginning, despite its erratic outbursts. The downbeat of measure 9 secures closure for the opening period, but this is a hard-won battle, rhetorically speaking. Structural $\hat{3}$ is announced at the beginning of the period (upbeat to measure 1), transferred up the octave in measure 3, brought back down at the end of measure 4, and carried through $\hat{2}$ and $\hat{1}$ in measures 8 and 9, (not without a deceptive turn to $\hat{1}$ in measure 7, much like the Haydn opening cited in Example 3.5). Harmonically, measures 1–4 form an open unit, describing a movement from tonic to a tonicized dominant, before resuming in the tonic and closing eventually in the tonic. This reading suggests an overall interrupted structure. There is much internal expansion in the second part of the period, including secondary dominants to VI (measure 5) and ii (measure 8), but the main outlines are

Example 3.7. Beethoven, Piano Sonata in D Major, Op. 10, No. 3—
Third Movement, measures 1–9

held intact. It is worth stressing that in spite of these disintegrative tendencies—rests, shifts of register, stops and starts, dynamic contrasts—there is no threat to the basic security of the sense of beginning in Classic music. This contrasts with the practice of later composers such as Chopin, Schumann, and Liszt, in whose music the idea of a stable and internally coherent beginning no longer forms a necessary procedural premise.

Beginnings, then, are beginnings because they possess certain invariant characteristics. The most important of these in Classic music is that of a beginning as a detachable and internally complete abstraction, with a life of its own. I have suggested that every beginning contains or comprises a period in which is enshrined an expression of tonality evident in certain voice-leading patterns. There are other kinds of beginnings, such as slow introductions to larger movements, which we have not touched upon; nor have we considered the distinction between an introduction and a beginning. The latter need not concern us here since such ambiguities are not really central to the Classic repertoire. But one important issue to consider before moving on to the next element of the paradigm, middles, is that of the end of the beginning, for by stressing the presence of a self-contained period at the beginning of Classic works, I may have left the impression that the beginning ends with the perfect cadence at the end of the period, followed immediately by the middle. The situation is a bit more fluid than that. The normal course of a movement, after its beginning, is to head for an alternative tonal center. The scale of this move varies from piece to piece and from genre to genre, but it is invariably present. If we must locate the beginning of a middle, it would occur at the beginning of the transitional passage to the next key. But I shall argue, following Dreyfus,[13] that although a beginning's functions follow a preconceived pattern, its virtual extension is ultimately unimportant—just as the least important aspect of a middle is where it begins and ends.

IV

A middle, or transitional sign, is one whose dependent status is uppermost. A middle is what is neither a beginning nor an ending, and is characterized by the absence of the crucial features of either beginning or ending. In practice, the middle is open at both ends—unlike the beginning, which is partially open at its end, or the ending, which is partially open at its beginning. The middle foregrounds process as opposed to statement; hence its inherent instability. Although, strictly speaking, a middle has harmonic allegiances—all middles are, on the deepest level, dominant prolongations—these reside beneath the surface. What is most palpably obvious is the feature of instability, of simulated motion, be it directional or circular.

Consider the example from the slow movement of Mozart's Piano Sonata in A minor, K. 310 (Example 3.8). On the largest level, the passage may be heard as a prolongation of C, the dominant of the home key. The chord of C, in its minor color, forms the point of departure, while the major color acts as goal of the progression. How is this prolongation brought to life rhetorically? The passage begins with a iv–V–i progression in G minor that sets up an expectation for a sequential continuation. But the expectation is thwarted when the next iv–V–i (in D minor) is replaced by iv–V–VI, a deceptive resolution (measures 39–41). Sequence now yields to a set of linear intervallic patterns involving 2–3 suspensions, first circling D minor (measures 43–47) then moving on to a pedal point on C, this last prolonged by upper and lower chromatic neighbor-notes. Embedded

---

[13] Dreyfus, "J. S. Bach's Concerto Ritornellos."

Example 3.8. Mozart, Piano Sonata in A Minor, K. 310—
Second Movement, measures 37–53

Example 3.8. (*cont.*)

in the second half of the progression is an elaborate motion through the circle of fifths motion (measures 43–47), which functions as "regulator" of the entire prolongation: A–D–G–C–F–B–[E–A]–D–G–C (the bracketed notes do not occur). Although the passage has an overall profile, nothing in it points to the exposition of a stable idea; it comes off most readily as a commentary on previously exposed thematic ideas. The contents of this middle, to the extent that they can be isolated, are arpeggiations, octave leaps, and descending lines; that is, those relatively neutral commonplaces of the tonal system that are hard to perceive apart from their specific presentational modes. And although commonplaces can be used characteristically as principal ideas—Beethoven's triadic themes are a case in point—they are not given such a treatment in this context. The passage foregrounds process. And it performs this function by eschewing the dominating strategies of its adjacent portions, beginning and ending.

A second example of middle is from the opening movement of Mozart's Piano Sonata in F Major, K. 280 (Example 3.9). Although the passage progresses from I to V, thus expressing something of a normative beginning, its use of sequence as premise, coupled with the absence of a well-defined idea, confirm that it can only be a middle in a larger structure, and not a beginning. The passage begins with two statements of a two-measure model whereby the harmonic progression I–V^7–I (measures 13–14) is answered by V^7–I–V^7 (measures 15–16). This is followed by a line descending chromatically in parallel tenths between the outer voices (measures 17–22). Then comes an elaboration of the precadential ii^6 chord, simulating the effect of a cadenza, and pointing to the half-cadence that signifies the end of the middle (measure 26).

It is unlikely that this fourteen-measure passage would comprise a beginning in Classic music, since it is characterized more by process than by exposition. This is not to deny that process, too, may be offered as a premise, but whenever this happens, process is articulated in such a way as to draw attention to itself—to assume, in other words, the profile of a musical idea. In this passage, however, we have spoken of not one but three local processes.

A third example of middle is drawn from the first movement of Haydn's Piano Sonata in C Major, Hob. XVI:3.5 (Example 3.10), and further illustrates the foregrounding of process. Broadly, the passage begins in F major, moves through a number of subsidiary keys of varying degrees of

Example 3.9. Mozart, Piano Sonata in F Major, K. 280—
First Movement, measures 13–26

strength, and arrives at the dominant of A minor, or V of vi, the point farthest removed from a C major tonic. Then, with the aid of a circle-of-fifths progression, harmonic orientation is redirected via V/ii to ii, and then to V[7], and finally to I for the recapitulation. The overall progression falls into two parts—the first ascending mainly chromatically, and the second descending partly diatonically and partly chromatically. Cutting across this larger surface ascent/descent pattern is the aforementioned progression through the circle of fifths (see circled notes in Example 3.10). One would not speak of an idea being exposed, but, rather, elaborated upon.

The argument that there are specific attitudes toward middles in Classic music harbors a contradiction that now needs to be made explicit. To say that the identity of the middle is its foregrounding of process is to argue that the device of foregrounding is sufficiently articulated to make it evident without implying that such processes are confined to the middle. That is, particular progressions that I am calling "process" are available for all portions of the syntagmatic chain (beginnings, middles, and endings), but it is in middles that they play a decisive characterizing role. Thus, the progressions such as chromatic or diatonic ascents and descents, especially those that occur in the bass, pedal points, and sequences are archetypically "middle" progressions. The material differences between beginnings, middles, and endings therefore rest partly on differences of extent. But one should not underplay their significance in view of the fact that the Classic repertoire depends fundamentally on effective rhetorical strategies.

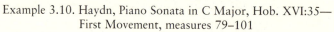

Example 3.10. Haydn, Piano Sonata in C Major, Hob. XVI:35—
First Movement, measures 79–101

V

The primary obligation of an ending is to secure closure for the entire structure. As a sign, the ending has two components—a syntactic component and a rhetorical one. The syntactic component is the melodic-harmonic event that closes the overall structure, usually a $\hat{2}$–$\hat{1}$ (or functionally equivalent) melodic progression supported by a V–I harmonic progression. The rhetorical component, on the other hand, is the set of devices that emphasize the close—notably, repetition in various dimensions and on various temporal levels. Both are necessary for the structure to be complete, but attitudes toward the second component vary from genre to genre.

Like a beginning, the ending is open at one end (its beginning), but whereas the beginning has an obligatory opening period that therefore confers on it a nominal end, the ending takes over from the middle and is only retrospectively perceived as having begun. Consider the ending of the

Example 3.11. Elements of closure in Mozart's String Quintet in C Minor, K. 406—
First Movement, measures 66–94

exposition in the first movement of Mozart's C Minor String Quintet, K.406. The beginning of the end may be located in measure 66, where the fundamental line reaches $\hat{3}$ over III or, more locally, $\hat{1}$ over I in E♭ major. The following twenty-eight measures are therefore, strictly speaking, confirmatory, providing the rhetorical component to the previously executed syntactic function. But it is in the latter passage that we can most clearly observe some of the features of ending. Example 3.11 presents, in paradigmatic form, the entire melodic substance of the ending, making explicit what Koch calls the "multiplication of ending formulas."[14] Seven paradigms are shown, although Paradigm G, is, technically, not a paradigm since it occurs only once and clearly grows out of Paradigms E and F. Repetition plays a crucial role here: note the twofold repetition of Paradigms A, D, and F, the threefold statement of Paradigm E and the fourfold statement of Paradigms B and C. Repetition is both varied and exact, and it occurs on a variety of temporal levels (the beat level, the bar level, and the phrase level).

The harmonic implications of these elements are equally significant. In Paradigm B, for instance, the introduction of the pitch D♭ (♭$\hat{7}$ in the key of E♭ major) is an explicit signifier of ending. It points immediately to the subdominant chord, thereby serving to flatten the harmonic orientation of the progression, giving it a homegoing quality. The second and third elements of Paradigm C also depart from the precedent set by the first element in avoiding a cadence on the tonic; this serves to heighten expectation of closure. The avoidance of closure is subsequently prolonged by a circle-of-fifths motion in Paradigm D. It comes as no surprise, therefore, that a vigorous, five-measure celebration of this hard-won battle follows, first on a pedal point (Paradigm E), then with a unison fanfare (Paradigm F), and finally with a pair of block chords supporting $\hat{3}$ and $\hat{1}$ (Paradigm G).

One important consequence of what appears to be a stylized attitude toward closure in this music points to an important difference between eighteenth- and nineteenth-century music. In many of the smaller forms of nineteenth-century music, closure, as I have argued elsewhere,[15] becomes a subject for discussion, and in that discussion the subject need not be revered. Its validity may even be questioned—hence some of the incomplete closes that give Romantic music its explicitly "poetic" sense. In the later eighteenth century, on the other hand, the end is often left intact, with few attempts to challenge the premise of a rhetorically satisfying ending (one thinks, to use a famous example, of Haydn's Symphony No. 45, the so-called "Farewell"). The passage at which we have just looked, from a work in sonata form, shows this closing norm clearly—but we must not forget that this is not even the end of the piece, only the end of the exposition. Of course, there is a dialectical process at work by which E♭ major, having undermined C minor, needs to proclaim its victory in loud and clear terms, since the victory is a temporary one. Where such a generic requirement is absent, closure may be understated, but its defining components are never absent.[16]

Consider an analogous situation from the slow movement of Mozart's Piano Sonata in C Minor K. 457. A beginning period in the tonic (measures 1–7) is followed immediately by a passage in the dominant, with no transition. With the upbeat to measure 10 comes a well-defined melody, an aria, perhaps, that is prolonged through a deceptive close in measure 11 before attaining full

[14] Koch, *Introductory Essay*, 47–48.

[15] See my "Concepts of Closure and Chopin's Opus 28."

[16] This interpretation of the role of repetition at the end of the exposition may be challenged on the grounds that the end of the recapitulation uses a similar rhetorical strategy, but carries a permanent, not temporary status. My claim that the second key area needs a strong rhetorical presentation is of course ad hoc, but it would be wrong to suppose that repetition must mean the same thing wherever it occurs. Surely we rationalize repetition differently depending on context, so that, in the case of the end of the exposition, we may speak of a temporary celebration, whereas in the case of the end of the recapitulation, we may speak of a permanent triumph.

closure in measure 13. At this point, the syntactical obligation of closure has been met, but not the rhetorical one, whose extent may be rationalized in retrospect as necessitated by the apparent absence of transition between the two harmonic areas.

Example 3.12 presents a synopsis of measures 10–16 in paradigmatic form on eight successive levels in order to show how the ending is executed. Level 1 describes an explicit move toward the tonic of B♭, ending, however, in a deceptive cadence. Level 2 then "corrects" the cadence, substituting a tonic for the previous submediant chord. This is already repetition on the two-measure level. Following this, the terminal cadence of Level 2 is isolated and repeated six times in different registers and with different note-values, dynamics, and melodic profiles (Levels 3–8). There is

Example 3.12. Elements of closure in Mozart's Piano Sonata in C Minor, K. 457—
Second Movement, measures 9–16

little doubt that a point is being made of closure in these measures. And only after these repetitions does Mozart reinterpret B♭ as the dominant of E♭, returning us to the primary register of the piece, and to the restatement of the opening material (measure 16). Here, too, we are not led gently by a transition.

The next two examples provide further illustration of the function of the structural and rhetorical components of endings. The last seven measures of the exposition of the first movement of Haydn's C♯ minor Piano Sonata Hob.XVI:36 offer an archetypal closing passage. The synoptic and paradigmatic presentation (Example 3.13) shows, first, that a goal-oriented motion (Level 1) is

Example 3.13. Elements of closure in Haydn's Piano Sonata in C♯ Minor, Hob. XVI:36—
First Movement, measures 27–33

thwarted, the top voice failing to descend to î. A second attempt (Level 2) bypasses the tonic through a deceptive cadence before arriving at the crucial î (Level 3). For Haydn, as for Mozart in the two previous excerpts, or indeed for the Classic composer in general the arrival of î over I is an occasion for celebration, and Haydn follows this with a fivefold reiteration of the cadence (Levels 4–8).

A similar strategy is evident in the first movement of Haydn's D Major Sonata (Example 3–14). The exposition closes with a gavottelike figure that is repeated with melodic but not harmonic variation (Level 2). Then its terminal elements are given a twofold repetition (Levels 3 and 4). The remarkable similarity between this and the three closing strategies discussed earlier provides ample evidence for the normative significance of endings in Classic music.[17]

Example 3.14. Elements of closure in Haydn's Piano Sonata in D Major, Hob. XVI:37—First Movement, measures 35–40

It is unlikely that any of the passages cited in Examples 3.11, 3.12, 3.13, and 3.14 would open a movement in a Classic piece. The degree of repetition is such that for a piece to begin with confirmatory chords, it would have to presuppose a previously exposed problem; this, however, is logically impossible. At the same time, this description of endings points to important connections between endings and beginnings. Because, as I have argued previously, a beginning constitutes or includes a period, it exploits the same closural functions as an ending. The difference between the two is therefore not only structural, but rhetorical. Thus, the ending proper makes a point of its ending precisely because it is the completion of the global utterance—whereas the beginning necessarily understates its ending, since there are no competing claims as yet.

The examples discussed so far lend weight to the argument that in the Classic period,

---

[17] The pattern of cadential reiteration in Examples 3.11–3.14 could help answer one question about the syntax of rhetoric: What determines the specific number of reiterations? It is probably merely coincidental that Examples 3.12 and 3.13 are shown to comprise exactly eight levels each. However, the larger pattern of rhythmic diminution—that is, a progression from longer to shorter note values—is constant. It is not clear whether the process follows an arithmetic procedure, as does the rate of harmonic change within a typical Classic period—but, on the surface, this pattern seems to involve a halving of rhythmic values.

beginnings are beginnings, middles are middles, and endings are endings, that there are specific attitudes to these three interrelated and interdependent segments of the syntagmatic chain, and that although they share certain features, they are, on the whole, not interchangeable. To recognize these functions is, paradoxically, to recognize their potential interchangeability, the possibility of playing with them, of reinterpreting them or working against their normative prescriptions—in short, of using them creatively.

VI

Now that we have discussed the two broad classes of topical or referential signs and pure signs, we are in a position to develop a semiotic interpretation of Classic music that draws on the two modes of explanation and follows the method outlined at the close of Chapter 1. The rest of this chapter is devoted to a discussion of the phenomenon of playing with signs in Classic music. The single example chosen is the first twelve measures of the Allegro of Mozart's D Major String Quintet, K. 593 (Example 3.15). Again, this is an excerpt from a larger piece, which, for the sake of analysis, is treated as a complete piece.

There is something jerky about the utterance of this piece. Ratner ascribes this to comic rhetoric, wit and humor, while Alfred Einstein notes a "groping, combinative character" in what he calls "a very unusual movement."[18] Although the aim of my analysis is neither to confirm nor to reject these descriptions, it will be seen that in making explicit both the functioning of topical signs and that of pure signs, we can understand more clearly the sources of the work's character. I shall proceed in three stages: first, I provide a voice-leading analysis of the piece to show its inner workings. This graph is then reinterpreted in reference to the beginning–middle–ending paradigm

Example 3.15. Mozart, String Quintet in D Major, K. 593—
First Movement, measures 21–33

[18] Ratner, *Classic Music*, 387–89, and Alfred Einstein, *Mozart*, 193.

Example 3.15. (cont.)

and supplemented by other demonstrations of organic coherence in the piece. Then, I consider the nature of topical structuring that, in this instance, yields a plot. Finally, I examine points of contact between the two kinds of utterance, arguing that it is the continuing dialectic between both types of sign structuring that offers the richest interpretation of the piece.

Example 3.16, Line 1, is a middleground graph of these twelve measures. The implicit background (open noteheads) shows an overall $\hat{3}$–$\hat{2}$–$\hat{1}$ melodic progression over a I–V–I bass arpeggiation covering the first eight measures, and then a twofold repetition of the final cadence, descending not from $\hat{3}$ but from $\hat{5}$. The content of the background is prolonged in the middleground principally by means of unfoldings—that is, by the horizontalization of a previously or subsequently verticalized interval.[19] Unfoldings serve to focus the harmonic allegiances of particular passages, and thus point to their underlying hierarchies. For example, in measure 1, the melodic rise from F♯ to A is interpreted as an unfolding, suggesting that the first four quarter notes of the excerpt involve a prolongation of the D major triad. This initial prolongation is followed by a preliminary descent down to the tonic, $\hat{3}$–$\hat{2}$–$\hat{1}$. Another unfolding begins on the upbeat to measure 5, and involves the tritone-related pitches C and F♯, which in turn form part of a local V[7] harmony. The C–F♯ unfolding, presented in two distinct registers, resolves to a G–B unfolding (unfoldings often come in pairs), part of the precadential subdominant harmony. Finally, the second of the postcadential echoes includes a G-C♯ unfolding (measures 11–12).

We may contrast Line 1 of example 3.16 with two other demonstrations of organic coherence in the passage. Line 2 is Rosen's demonstration of a chain of descending thirds.[20] These thirds do not necessarily coincide with the changing surface patterns. Line 3 is Ratner's two-voice reduction of the passage, based, as in the "Prague" analysis at the end of the first chapter, on the assumption that such contrapuntal progressions lie at the basis of Classic music.[21] Lines 1, 2, and 3 are not three mutually exclusive readings of the passage, but rather three intersecting

---

[19] For further discussion of unfoldings—Schenker's term is *Ausfaltung*—see Schenker, *Free Composition*, 50–51.
[20] Rosen, *The Classical Style*, 283.
[21] Ratner, *Classic Music*, 389.

demonstrations of structural coherence, each emphasizing a different feature of the piece and betraying a particular authorial view of syntax. Rosen's thirds, for example, reveal an element of continuity that overrides the jerky surface, while the Schenkerian connections encompass not only adjacent but distantly placed events. And Ratner's "structural line" sits on the middleground between Rosen's and Schenker's graphs, retaining the former's commitment to local connections and the latter's reductive impetus.

Descending thirds, arpeggiations, stepwise motion, unfoldings—all these show the remarkable extent to which the music's inner processes are beautifully integrated. But were we to attempt to infer Mozart's foreground from these reductions, we would have great difficulty. This is not to claim that Mozart's is merely a surface drama, but rather to suggest that if the analysis does not reach the level of the surface where a great deal happens (or, as some might say, where it all happens), if there is no attempt to make sense of what is hardly a value-free musical surface, then one is missing something that is not only significant but fundamental to the piece.

One way of approaching this surface drama is to reinterpret the Schenkerian analysis in light of the beginning–middle–ending paradigm in order to show the ways in which specific attitudes to these three related aspects of the piece are embodied in specific syntactical procedures. Ratner's two-voice reduction provides a valuable framework for this exercise (see Example 3.16, Line 4). To facilitate reference, I have given each dyad an ordinal number from 1 to 14, including a supplementary 6a and 6b that do not actually occur but that form part of the conceptual background to the progression.

Items 1–4 cover beginning. The $\hat{3} - \hat{2} - \hat{1}$ descent (also shown in Line 1) shows again that one of the invariant characteristics of beginning is a composing of the global progression in miniature. There are details in this opening, however, that are of rhetorical significance. First, the goal, $\hat{1}$, is supported by a first inversion, rather than a root position, tonic chord, so that its strength is undercut somewhat. This amplifies a point made earlier about the ending of the beginning as opposed to the ending of the ending, the former being necessarily weaker than the latter. Another feature of this beginning is the $\hat{2} - \hat{3}$ melodic progression at the beginning that, because it is supported by a V–I progression, assumes the normative status of a cadence. The cadence is in the first instance a resolution of the unresolved dominant chord from the end of the preceding Larghetto, so it needs to be heard in a larger context for its proper significance to be grasped. But even if the piece had begun with a cadence, the rising melodic profile, $\hat{2} - \hat{3}$, would have detracted from the sense of closure by implying motion outward, not motion toward a point of rest. In a fundamental sense, therefore, this beginning (items 1–4 of Line 4) is as concerned with ending as it is with beginning. The beginning begins and ends, so to speak, with an ending.

The middle is represented by items 5–9. Here the question of segmentation is both relevant and irrelevant. It is relevant simply as an indication of the fluidity of a middle, which, as I argued earlier, is much less concerned with a specific proportional representation than it is with the foregrounding of procedure. One might dispute, therefore, the interpretation of item 5 as the beginning of the middle, for this item clearly grows out of item 4. Similarly, one might ask whether the end of middle is not item 8, since items 9 and 10 obviously belong together (note that the Schenkerian interpretation conflates items 8 and 9 into a single event). Although these are legitimate questions, they are ultimately irrelevant insofar as the crucial thing about this middle is the sequential progression by which it prolongs the beginning. This sequence is most clearly perceived in the ascending bass fourths, A–D, B–E, D–G and E–A, the whole describing a dominant prolongation. Were the sequence to cover each step in its span, it would include the notes labeled

6a and 6b. Those notes are, however, non–occurrent. This middle, then, shows the course followed by the beginning, while avoiding any sense of the former's stability.

The ending is not just a resolution, but an amplification of that resolution. Items 8–14 (sixty percent of the passage) cover this ending, which begins with a strong IV–V–I cadence (items 8–10). The last four items are heard in pairs, 11–12 and 13–14, confirming the cadence. There are differences in the structural significance of the three cadences, however. Items 8–10 are clearly the most important of the three, for they provide the resolution to the activity in the period so far. What follows is an echo of that cadence. Yet, when we turn to the topical process, we find that Mozart uses this apparent structural redundancy to introduce a strategic gesture that must be counted as "structural" in the final analysis.

In short, while Lines 1, 2, and 3 of Example 3.16 demonstrate some of the ways in which this piece operates below the surface, the beginning–middle–ending structure (Line 4) reveals ways in which that subsurface activity is given rhetorical representation. All demonstrations argue for a cogent, connected, and coherent piece.

In the domain of topical structuring, however, we encounter an erratic surface that does not merely give profile to the harmonic process, but plays against it and with it. Because of this, it is difficult, indeed, undesirable—to separate out the two types of signifying processes.

Ratner has identified the major topics of this piece as shown in the annotations above Line 1 of Example 3.16. What is most significant about the identification is that there is no longer a hard and fast distinction between the apparently secure world of topic and that of metaphor, between a public code and a more specific private one. Ratner concludes that the process of these twelve measures suggests Mozart imitating an episode from a *commedia dell'arte*, thereby providing a plot that subsumes the individual topical gestures.[22]

What are these topics and how do they generate such a plot? The opening suggests bourrée/march, a dual topic defined by both meter and articulation. Horn fifths are present in measure 2, where they constitute the cadence with which beginning ends. Military overtones may be heard in the opening two measures, and these are strengthened by the fanfares that underlie the music. Succeeding the military supertopic in the first two bars is an unspecified peasant topic. Ratner refers to "heavy-footed cadential figures." This is followed by an expanded ornament, a "fanciful roulade," that suggests both brilliant style and cadenza, as well as an unnamed brusque topic. The cadential figure in measures 7–8 is neutral with respect to topic (on the surface of the surface, so to speak, since topics are already on the surface), although one might wish to historicize Ratner's "hammer strokes." With the cadence—and presumably the completion of the essential structural procedure in the piece—comes the singing style, which "smiles" at the previous cadence. A hint of fanfare and military may be heard in measure 10, followed by a repetition of that singing figure.

For a twelve-measure piece, this is quite a few topics, and certainly one of the sources of drama in this piece resides in their rapid succession. The argument that they add up to a dramatic scenario such as an episode from a *commedia dell' arte* rests on the makeshift nature of Mozart's rhetoric. Stock characters, recognizable by both connoisseurs and amateurs, fill a harmonic frame with shapes that do not easily blend into one another, thus giving the whole something of a comic profile. The theatricality of the piece is, however, not restricted to the succession of topical gestures, but extends to the peculiar interaction between surface and background, between structure and expression. The distinction is artifical, of course. Structure shades into topic, topic into structure, and this is the "music."

[22] Ibid.

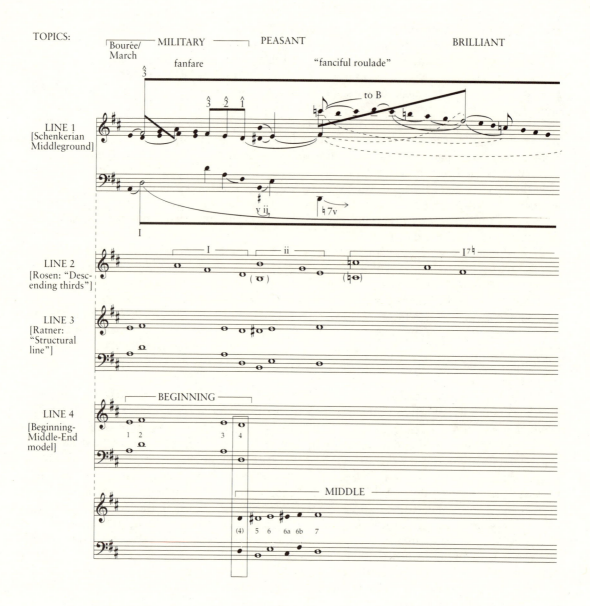

Example 3.16. Structural and expressive elements of Mozart's String Quintet in D Major, K. 593—
First Movement, measures 21–33

Example 3.16. (*cont.*)

Consider some aspects of this symbiotic play. The adaptation of horn fifths to a closing gesture in measure 2 is a relationship of parallelism. Mozart uses a topic with conventional (paradoxical) associations in ways in which those associations are kept intact. The "heavy-footed cadential figures" in measures 2–4, however, find minimal representation in our voice-leading graph, although both the disposition of dynamics and the resultant play with meter are central to the effect of the passage. Surely, Ratner's scenario, complete with overtones of peasants dancing, owes a great deal to this prolonged cadence on E; to reduce it away is to minimize a salient feature of the piece. But perhaps the most striking aspect of this erratic succession of topics occurs after the cadence in measure 8, in which the singing style appears after the completion of what matters most in a Schenkerian interpretation. Where the improvisatory nature of Mozart's rhetoric allows only a nominal disjunction between the "hammer strokes" and the singing style, the voice-leading graph articulates a clear separation of structural process. It is difficult to transfer the principles of a hierarchy of topic to a hierarchy of structure, but it is precisely in the attempt to effect such a transfer that we encounter what is most fundamental about the piece—the uneasy interaction between individual hierarchies.

The notion of playing with signs therefore defines, in the most general sense, mutual interaction among separate or separable processes. In the spirit of the eighteenth-century *ars combinatoria*, playing is the composer's business. But it is also the listener's business to follow the progress of this play. Although it may be theoretically desirable to concretize this notion by offering a dimensional or interdimensional equation, such concretization must not be allowed to obscure the inherent and irreducible ambiguity of the process. Hans-Georg Nägeli, writing in 1826, invokes a concept of play in order to undermine the view that music has a specifiable content. For him, the real essence of music is play itself. In our terms, there is introversive semiosis, but not extroversive semiosis. In the following statement, Nägeli simply asserts play but does not explain or defend it:

> The term "play" has always assumed a role of the greatest significance in the language of art and in the theory behind it; and this could and should have been grasped long ago. As play is music's real essence, it "plays away" any random elements that move us momentarily. In doing so, it plays itself into their place. Its essence is play, through and through; nothing else. It has no content of any kind that men have tried to adduce from and give to it. It simply comprises forms, regulated combinations of sounds and sequences of sounds. [23]

It is precisely the refusal of the musical object to stand still and be pinned down, so to speak, that makes Nägeli's conception of play attractive. One need not endorse Nägeli's impatience with the matter of musical "content" in order to find suggestive his description of play. More recently, Lawrence Kramer has invoked notions of play in ways that retain the fluidity of Nägeli's definition. Writing about the connotative and combinatory features of music and poetry, features that roughly parallel our extroversive and introversive dimensions respectively, Kramer states:

> In both [music and poetry], the alliance of connotative and combinatory features becomes significant in two ways: intertextually, through allusion, generic affiliation, and the play of stylistic codes; and intratextually, through rhythmic design and the play of likeness and difference among particulars. Even by omission, these elements are always interlaced with each other, and what I call "play"—their suppleness, inventiveness, balletic energy—joins the sensuous and emotional satisfactions of music and poetry to the play of critical intelligence. To say this is to reject the formalist equation of pure music with pure

[23] Hans-Georg Nägeli, *Vorlesungen über Musik mit Berücksichtigung der Dilettanten*, 29–34, trans. in Peter le Huray and James Day, *Music and Aesthetics*, 398.

form, if only because any listener who responds emotionally to a composition is implicitly investing it with connotative content. [24]

Mozart's play with signs in the first twelve measures of the Allegro of his String Quintet in D Major, K. 593 is a play that is first and foremost dramatic, and it is the elucidation of that drama that should form the highest goal of an analysis. My argument has been that both the purely musical signs discussed in this chapter and the topical signs discussed in the previous chapter contribute equally to the articulation of this drama. I mean, therefore, to challenge the supremacy accorded structuralist interpretations of Classic music (and tonal music in general), and to argue for a more expanded interpretive framework. I have not, however, proposed a verbal narrative for this piece, although Ratner's scenario retains a bounded temporality. The reason is that such narratives usually trivialize the complex play of temporal forms by privileging a single one of those forms—the flow of events comparable to those of a story or drama. There is, of course, nothing wrong with individual listeners resorting to such discourse, so long as its claims are not stretched unduly. To say this is to register an implicit confession that certain aspects of the musical experience are beyond analysis. An analysis works best if it proceeds in a two-way stream, making explicit some of the listener's intuitions (a confirmatory function) while at the same time firing the imagination that contemplates the music (an exploratory function).

In order to hear Classic music in a rewarding way, then, one needs to apprehend the continuing dialectic between a referential surface loaded with signification and the inevitable contrapuntal background without which that surface cannot exist. It is my aim, in the following three chapters, to demonstrate further this continuing dialectic in three relatively extended movements.

[24] Kramer, *Music and Poetry*, 5.

FOUR

A SEMIOTIC INTERPRETATION OF THE FIRST MOVEMENT OF

MOZART'S STRING QUINTET IN C MAJOR, K. 515

I

THE AIM of this chapter is to provide an interpretation of the first movement of Mozart's C Major Quintet, K. 515, drawing on the interpretive strategies and analytic tools introduced in preceding chapters. What formal constraints regulate the basic utterance of the piece? Is the musical surface value-free or is it laden with signification? In what terms is the tonal argument conducted, and what is the nature of the relationship between this argument and the signifying processes of the musical surface? How, in short, does the movement mean?

The formal argument of this movement is conducted within the constraints of sonata form. Recent writing on sonata form continues to underscore the fact that it was not a set form into which material was poured, but rather a way of organizing material, a flexible dramatic structure, a feeling for proportion.[1] The most important defining element of sonata form, its fundamental imperative, is a harmonic scheme in which a polarized I–V relationship is conducted within a set of rhetorical norms to yield a closed and balanced tonal argument. The view of structure projected by this definition is one in which indispensable elements are given the highest premium.

To argue for harmonic primacy, however, is not necessarily to prescribe a way of attending to the drama inherent in any sonata-form piece. If the major achievement of sonata form is "a dramatized clarity"[2] in the presentation of the composer's ideas, then it is with the variety of ways in which that drama is enacted that an analysis should be concerned. In its ideal form, such an *explication de texte* would require a mastery of various dimensional processes, and an account that goes back and forth between dimensions. It would, in other words, shift its referential grounds according to what is deemed most significant at any given moment in the unfolding of the piece.

Without attempting to analyze each of the work's dimensions in all the detail called for as a preliminary to providing an account of meaning, I will try, in this chapter, to "think through" the movement three times, in three distinct but overlapping and complementary ways. I begin with an informal description of the movement as a whole. This enables a view of the signifying modes in sonata form. Then, I consider the operation of topical signs both within the syntagmatic chain and on a paradigmatic axis, invoking the world of Mozart's string quintets as the intertextual limits of this particular argument. This yields a view of the movement's extroversive semiosis. A third section considers the nature of the tonal argument, concentrating on matters of harmonic rhetoric enshrined in the beginning–middle–ending model, thus hinting

---

[1] The view of sonata form developed in this and succeeding chapters has been culled from diverse sources including Donald Tovey, "Some Aspects of Beethoven's Art Forms," James Webster, "Sonata Form," in *The New Grove Dictionary of Music and Musicians,* Charles Rosen, *Sonata Forms,* and Leonard Ratner, *Classic Music,* 217–47.

[2] Rosen, *Sonata Forms,* 12.

at a pattern of introversive semiosis. A brief concluding section assesses the limitations of these perspectives.

II

First, then, we will embark on an informal diachronic account of the movement as a whole. (From this point on the reader should refer to a copy of the score in order to follow the description.) An extraordinarily long period opens this work. Lasting a total of fifty-seven measures, it is one of the longest expositions that Mozart ever wrote. The initial dialogue between the outer instruments, cello and first violin, points to a binary segmentation that is operative throughout the movement and manifest in a number of oppositions involving register (high/low), dynamics (soft/loud), rhythm (active/static), mode (major/minor), and what might be called "phrase sense" (question/answer). The exchange is heard three times in five-measure groups, and, as is usual in Classic rhetoric, the third becomes the occasion for change. Measure 15 is the first point of culmination for the ensemble as a whole, the point at which the ensemble defines itself texturally. This leads to a half cadence in measure 19, whose effect is heightened by a subsequent measure rest.

The normative effect of a half cadence is both to stress the incomplete nature of an event, and to point to its eventual completion. The listener therefore awaits the resumption of the process of these first nineteen measures, and anticipates a full close. The process just interrupted resumes in measure 21. Although it employs the same musical ideas as the beginning of the movement, it is marked by two changes: a striking modal change from tonic major to tonic minor, and a textural inversion in which the initial dialogue between first violin and cello is reversed. The full implications of this shift of mode will emerge when we consider the details of the harmonic argument, but it is worth pointing out that the change ushers in darker, more mysterious, and less stable harmonies. Thus, the major chord in measures 1–3 becomes a minor chord in measures 21–23, and is intensified further into a diminished chord in measures 26–28, the latter repeated in transposed form in measures 31–33. A preliminary winding down begins with the set of imitations initiated by the cello in measure 34. This leads to an intermediate resting point in measures 38–41, at which the twofold plagal cadence provides some reassurance of the tonic. But because it does not include the dominant, this cadence is incapable of resolving the tension built up within the period thus far.

An explicit preparation for closure is thwarted in measures 45–46 by the discovery that this is only a deceptive cadence. We must try again, but not before another extensive harmonic episode (measures 47–54), which now brings to a high point the expectation for closure that has been mounting throughout the period. In measures 55–57 the familiar cadential six-four chord is followed by a perfect cadence, the first perfect cadence in the movement. This completes the opening period.

The extraordinarily long wait for this cadence leaves an indelible mark on the listener's perception of what follows. For one thing, the single cadence in measures 56–57, while fulfilling a syntactical obligation, does not carry sufficient rhetorical weight to provide an effective balance for the period as a whole. The event necessitates a complementary confirmation—hence measures 57–60, which constitute a prolonged cadence, a summing up, in fact, of the process of the entire fifty-seven-measure period (this point will become clearer when we consider aspects of its voice-leading).

Thus far, then, the initial obligation of a sonata-form piece has not only been fulfilled, but fulfilled in style. That is, an opening set of ideas has been conducted within the framework of a single, extended period and brought to a satisfactory conclusion. This conclusion has been confirmed. The next major event is the establishment of an alternative tonal premise. This begins in measure 60 with the previous closing material, and leads via a self-consciously sequential passage to the dominant of the next key (measure 69). Instead of moving directly to the next key, however, Mozart stops to savor his opening arpeggios one more time. The inverted form of the dialogue (recall measures 21–33) begins in measure 69 and is repeated only once this time. The gesture of measure 77 seems to be an implicit protest against the dominance of the outer voices—why not involve everyone in this?—and so each of the five instruments gets a turn at the answering phrase of the opening dialogue, moving from the lowest- to the highest-sounding instrument in the ensemble. In measure 82 the first violin, after completing the set of imitations, leads the way directly to the second key, a gesture that is significant for reasons of theme, register, and pulse. In fact, measures 84–85 virtually adumbrate the profile theme of the second key area.

The alternative tonal premise of this movement is G major, the dominant of the home key. Its purpose is to undermine the key of C, and thereby set up a polarized tension that will be prolonged in the development section. The formal proceedings of the second key area begin in measure 86 over a tonic pedal—a significant contrast, rhetorically speaking, to the beginning of the first key area. Coupled with the singsong figure in the first violin and the tonic-dominant alternation in the middle voices, the impression left by this passage is of a refusal to act, of suspension or stasis. G major is apparently quite satisfied to be at center stage now. When this brief moment of restraint ends, the music reaches—as in the opening period—a half-cadence (measures 92–3). Then the singsong figure is repeated, not in the first violin, but in the higher of the two violas, as the lower one doubles in thirds. From this point in the second key area onward, Mozart increasingly begins to realize the potential of the opening of the second key area, by emphasizing closure. It later emerges that one of the principal achievements of the second key area is not merely an emphasis but, perhaps, an overemphasis on closure. This is part of the strategy of undermining the authority of the first key, and also of prolonging the resulting tension. Two cadences, in measures 95–96 and 97–98, are followed by a fantasylike section that culminates in a six-four chord in measure 107. The promise of this closural sign is partially avoided in measures 108–9. While the avoidance is essentially a harmonic one, it may be perceived that the melody in measures 108–9 in the second violin does reach the tonic. But since melodic closure is not accompanied by harmonic closure, and in view of the forthcoming coincidence of the two dimensions, it seems appropriate to place this "cadence" low in the hierarchy of closes. As before, it is only the third time around that full closure is attained on the downbeat of measure 115.

As we observed at the close of the first key area, it is not enough simply to supply a cadence in order to secure the tonal meaning of a period; it is also necessary to confirm it. In fact, it is necessary that the confirmation be "seen to be done," to borrow Rosen's argument about modulation in sonata form.[3] Beginning in measure 115, a closing theme is introduced whose characteristic syncopation, by disrupting a nominally regular rhythmic succession, introduces a slight element of tension before the cadence in measures 118–19. This, however, is not the end of the process of nailing down the second key. The syncopated phrase begins again in measure

[3] Rosen, *The Classical Style*, 24.

119, but instead of closing as before, it introduces a number of internal expansions that serve to heighten the effect of closure already considerable in this second period. These changes include a major-minor alternation in measures 121–22 (recalling the brutal plunge into C minor in measure 21) and an averted cadence in measure 128 despite the explicit $\hat{3}$–$\hat{2}$ melodic approach. The gesture of measures 125–27 is repeated in 128–30 before leading to the full close at the beginning of measure 131. At this point, the pedal with which the second period was launched returns, thereby creating the gestural effect of a symmetrical period. Above the pedal is another singsong figure, the proper closing theme of the exposition, which dominates measures 131–51. When, in measure 143, the pedal migrates to the first violin, we read this as a sign that a reorientation toward the next stage of the argument is about to be effected. And, as usual with Mozart, this reorientation is Janus-faced, capable, on one hand, of being joined seamlessly to the beginning of the movement (for the repeat of the exposition) and, on the other, of leading directly to the development.

The similarities as well as the differences between the strategies of the two key areas are equally significant. In terms of a tension-resolution axis, both areas exemplify that property of Classic phrase structure that concentrates its harmonic-dynamic process in its middle.[4] Both open with a period leading to a half-close. Both are rich in topical signification (as we shall see presently). But whereas the first distributes its teleological energy evenly across the span of the period as a whole, the second concentrates this energy into its closing moments, making a big point of closure. At least half a dozen clearly articulated cadences (see measures 95–96, 97–98, 100–101, and 114–15, 118–19, 130–31) assist in this signifying process.

Let us pause briefly to remind ourselves of how the foregoing action enacts the formal discourse that we call sonata form, and of the sorts of residual tensions left in its wake. We have witnessed a single dynamic trajectory in which two keys confront one another directly. C major, the home key, has chronological and referential superiority, and, as we shall see later, it also has hierarchic supremacy. G major is heard against the background of C major, thereby revealing its dependent, dissonant status. Because of this natural hierarchy stemming from the properties of the tonal system and corroborated in numerous conventional usages, the actual rhetoric of the exposition reveals an inverse relationship between the structural importance and gestural prominence of the two keys. That is, with closural signs, for example, as the main criterion, the second key area is shown to be superior to the first. By dwelling close to its tonic, G, and cadencing frequently on that tonic, its phenomenal quality is greatly enhanced. Moreover, it also lasts longer than the first key area. Key Area 1 is sixty measures long, and takes another twenty-six measures to lead to Key Area 2, which is already established by measure 69. Key Area 2, on the other hand, lasts seventy-seven measures. The point to emphasize here is one that we shall see manifest in many different ways throughout the movement: the apparent noncoincidence of dimensional processes. This is, in fact, the source of the music's essential drama. Just as the conventional disposition of dissonance and consonance is a phenomenal accent on dissonance, so the hierarchically subsidiary dominant is given greater durational representation. Mozart can, in other words, disrupt a nominally secure conventional tonal world, knowing all along that such disruption is illusory, that the security guaranteed by a closed, hierarchic tonal structure remains an immutable law. This is artistic play of a subtle and alluring kind.

---

[4] For further discussion of phrase expansion, see Sisman, "Small and Expanded Forms," and Ratner, *Classic Music,* 37–47.

The aim of the next section, the development, is to postpone the arrival of the tonic by exploring a variety of harmonic areas within the confines of the ruling dominant key. This is no wild, unbridled excursion into forbidden territorry, but, again, one of those stylized contradictions that lies at the heart of the Classic style. The music gives the impression of veering far away when, in fact, it is securely anchored. Measure 152 marks the beginning of the development section. The opening dialogue, in its diminished version, is first heard. During the repeat, the cello in measure 156 seems a bit impatient, reluctant to wait for the completion of the first violin's answer. This is already a sign that previously exposed material and ideas are being transformed, their validity questioned, and the whole elaborated upon, drawing as much attention to the process of elaboration itself as to the material content. The exchange between cello and first violin is a fourfold one this time, bringing us to a cadence in A minor (measures 170–71) and signaling, in harmonic terms, the point farthest removed. A significant textural transition takes place within measures 167–71, marking the cadence in A minor. Then, half notes and suspensions gradually oust the metronomic eighth-note motion and prepare for an exercise in species counterpoint. The "filling" of this alla breve section (beginning in measure 171) is the final singsong of the exposition (the eighth-note figure in the cello in measure 171 is inherited from the first violin in measure 132). This self-consciously learned section exploits not only the "heavy" alla breve pulses, but also a circle-of-fifths progression (measures 184–90) and a long dominant pedal. The pedal, introduced in measure 193, signifies the beginning of what is sometimes called the "retransition." Pitch class G is now heard, not as a temporary tonic, but as a structural dominant. In this context, it gathers a lot of momentum as it goes along, most obviously though the increased rhythmic articulation from whole notes to quarter notes with rests, and the minor coloration. It even changes its surface profile from the previous closing figure to a playful dancelike figure in measure 197 and subsequently in measure 201. The tremendous tension thus generated finally dissipates at the beginning of measure 205, which marks the beginning of the recapitulation.

This seems to be a rather short development section. It lasts only 53 measures, about half the length of the exposition, and shorter than the individual periods of Key Area 1 and Key Area 2. But length is less important than function in sonata form, and only by listening for the particular functions can we best understand this drama. With this orientation, we can see that despite its brevity, the development is not lacking in activity. First, it discusses several of the thematic ideas from the exposition, including the opening question-answer exchange and the dancelike figure introduced in measure 93. The closing idea of the exposition is also given some representation in the development. Moreover, the fact that these ideas do not appear here in the order in which they were introduced adds to the sense of elaboration. Second, although there is enough tonal instability to dramatize the apparent absence of a single controlling triad, the dominant chord through which we entered the development (in its capacity as tonic) and that leads us out of the development (in its capacity as dominant of the home key) regulates the overall tonal-harmonic orientation.

We have now been treated to a polarized conflict in the exposition, a conflict that has been intensified in the development. The principal function of the recapitulation is to effect a reconciliation between the utterances of the exposition's key areas. This means, first, restating the material of the first key area, and second and more importantly, allowing that key, C major, to appropriate the material of the second key. Phrased in those terms, we can understand the rhetorical basis of the gesture—namely, that the recapitulation provides an opportunity to reinterpret the exposition's harmonic dissonance (I–V) as a higher-level consonance (I–I). But this is far from implying a mechanical repeat or transposition of the exposition. In some ways, the most interesting and absorbing aspects of the recapitulation are precisely those recompositions that Mozart introduces in order to round off this tonal argument within the norms of an Enlightenment dialectic.

The recapitulation begins in measure 205. Only the first nine measures of the reprise are identical to those of the exposition. The appearance in measure 214 of a C♯ in place of a C♮ enables a compression of the events of the first period. It is as if we jumped from measure 8 to measure 29, cutting out twenty-two measures. The rationale for this may be seen in the difference between functions of the exposition and the recapitulation. Where the exposition introduced instability and internal expansion, the recapitulation, no longer needing to generate comparable tension, leaves out some of this potentially excessive rhetoric. The effect of doing so further recalls the opening of the development section, thereby undermining, for one brief moment, the security of a formal return. The first period of the recapitulation closes in measure 242 with the same perfect cadence as in the exposition, although the latter period is considerably shorter than its predecessor. In addition, where the A♭/G♯ enharmonic equivalence gave us a view of D♭ major in the exposition (measures 48–51), G♯ is now brought into the service of A minor (measures 231–36).

The cadence over, a short confirmation is given, followed by an explicit transition to the dominant (not of the dominant as before, but of the home key). Part of the rationale for Mozart's recomposition is to enhance the fantasy effects of the first violin's approach to the material in the second key area—see the diminished harmony in the lower voices in measures 269–70. From the moment in which the profile theme of the second key area appears (measure 273), a significant chunk of the recapitulation rhymes with the exposition until measure 320. Here, a diminished-seventh chord cuts through the surface of the piece, altering the course of the movement, and ushering in what might be considered a written-out cadenza (measure 322), itself preceded by another silent bar strongly reminiscent of measure 20 of the exposition. From measure 322, the sense of home-going is strongly apparent. A dominant pedal supports the closing theme of the exposition. This pedal point remains active throughout the circle-of-fifths motion in measures 332–35 and the recollection of dancelike figures beginning in measure 341. Finally, what Schenker calls "the definitive close of the composition"[5] takes place in measure 353, in which the long dominant leads to a coincidence of $\hat{1}$ and I. But, as always with these syntactical attainments, the mere appearance of a cadence, for all that it signifies one level of closure, requires further levels of resolution to bring the movement to a satisfactory close. One such necessity is a purely phenomenal one—a pause on C to enable the listener to take in the "C-ness" of the argument of the work as a whole. A number of confirmations of melodic closure take place, but there is one dissenting voice, register, which is left unresolved in the cadence of measures 352–53, for the line closes not where it was initiated, but an octave below on middle C. Measures 353 to the end are therefore concerned with register in fundamental ways, performing a spectacular balancing act that finally secures both harmonic and melodic closure on several levels of structure.

And so the movement closes, the listener having been taken through a clearly articulated dramatic course in which a basic harmonic polarity, enhanced in various ways and on several levels, is prolonged and finally resolved. To follow the outlines of this argument is to be aware

[5] Schenker, *Free Composition*, 129.

of the essential drama of this remarkable movement.

In its attempt to identify the major signposts in this movement, the preceding narrative has been conducted within the norms of what might be called a "traditional" analysis. This entailed a crossing of conceptual categories, the justification for which rested on an intuitively felt factor of significance. Although such an approach may succeed in illuminating the salient features of a work, it requires corroboration through more systematic analyses of individual dimensional processes. It is, therefore, not that there is anything wrong with what is by now an old-fashioned critical account, but rather that it is incomplete. Let us turn, then, to the attendant signifying processes by thinking through the extroversive dimension of the work.

III

Even on first hearing, the richness and variety of content in the first movement of this quintet do not escape the attentive listener. Consider, for example, the strategy of the opening period (measures 1–57). We have mentioned that this is an extraordinarily long period, and that part of its dynamic quality derives from the harmonic effect of modal interchange introduced in measure 21. But there is surely another dimension to explaining why such a long period can be sustained without the slightest feeling of redundancy: the play of topic. The dialogue between cello and first violin at the beginning of the movement involves two distinct but relevant ideas, ideas that become the subject of discussion in the first nineteen measures. Then, after a measure of rest, the same set of ideas is given to a different set of actors, and the effect is not without some parody. Then, in measure 38, we have a significantly different melodic profile. Again, beginning in measure 46, another melodic idea ensues. After the cadence in measure 57, the confirmation of tonal arrival is accomplished by means of yet another idea—and so on.

Or consider the strategy of the second key area: it was mentioned that this part of the piece is saturated with closure, and we may wonder how it is that Mozart gets away with repeating himself. The thematic surface holds the clue to this answer. The melodic idea stabilized in measure 86 (first violin) passes over to the two violas in measure 94, at which point a new idea is introduced by the two violins. When a cadence is reached in measure 115, it is followed by quite a different tune, and when a further cadence is reached in measure 131, the thematic surface is again different.

Figure 3 displays the topical content of the movement as a whole, in paradigmatic form. The topical universe invoked is the one discussed in Chapter 2. In addition, these topics are set in the context of Mozart's other quintets in order to suggest a broadly conceived musical discourse. The intertextual implications of Figure 3 will not be explored beyond the obvious observation that practically every topic exposed in this movement occurs in at least one of the other quintets, and therefore that these works share a common material fund even though their individual strategies are different.

As a supplement to the schematic presentation in Figure 3, a brief account of topical succession may help clarify the process of extroversive semiosis. The strident figure with which the cello opens the work is reminiscent of a Mannheim rocket, while its conjunction with the first violin response, a broken figure or expanded sigh, signifies sensibility. In measures 18–19, we hear a subtle anticipation of the dance gavotte, which is to emerge more emphatically in measure 57. The brutal plunge into minor is an unmistakable allusion to Sturm und Drang, an allusion that becomes even clearer with the subsequent introduction of diminished chords in measures 26–28 and 31–33. Notice, therefore, that Mannheim rocket has been transformed to yield Sturm und Drang, a transformation made possible by the fact that the former topic prescribes triadic, rhythmically incisive motion whereas the latter merely denotes instability. A brief passage of learned style (measures 34–37) is followed by an allusion to the pastoral topic. This plagal orientation also contains in embryo the next topic, the bourrée (see first violin phrasing in measures 37–42), which emerges in measure 46 but awaits a fuller and clearer exposition beginning in measure 94. Implicit in the exposition of the bourrée is the learned style, which is succeeded by a compressed fanfare in the approach to the long-awaited first cadence of the piece (measures 55–56). A gavotte confirms the closure of the period, and also forms the substance of the transition to the next key. In measure 69, Mannheim rocket and sensibility are again heard, followed by the learned style in measure 77, leading finally to the musette at the official opening of the second key. After the half cadence in measure 93, a bourrée gives profile to the repetition of the first half-period. The period continues with a mixture of chromatic elements and zigzag figures, which create a sense of fantasy (measures 99–105). The cadence in measures 114–115 is followed by the alla zoppa, or limping-style topic, which also contains (in measure 118) a hint of march. There has been present throughout a latent march, a topic also metrically compatible with gavotte and—insofar as it is metrically neutral—with fanfare, but nowhere is this topic made explicit. A faint allusion to Sturm und Drang in measure 122 is followed by the gesture of brilliant style (measure 125 onward) leading, finally, to musette again in measure 131.

In the development section, no new topics are introduced, except that they appear in a different order from that in the exposition, and are subject to different modes of articulation. The development opens with the Mannheim rocket-sensibility exchange that is now under the influence of Sturm und Drang—leading, in measure 171, to a full-fledged learned style in alla breve. Musette returns in measure 193, followed a few measures later by bourrée. The recapitulation follows the same sequence of topics as the exposition until measure 321, at which a written-out cadenza for all four instruments appears in the context of a musette. Bourrée is again prominent toward the close of the movement, appearing in measures 341 (violins), 346 (second viola and cello), and 349 (violas). The arrival at the tonic in measure 353 is also signified by a normative musette, which carries us to the end of the movement.

It is tempting, in view of the extremely rich musical surface, to speculate on a plot for this movement. The movement as a whole embodies a set of contradictions in topical signification, contradictions that serve to enrich its musical meaning. First, there is the frequent but by no means exclusive "learnedness" of the movement, which reaches a climax in the development section. This self-conscious display of contrapuntal skill constitutes a high style, and contrasts with the frequent recourse to a second topical area: the decidedly low style epitomized by the musette. Of course, if we regard every pedal point as a musette, then that would be stretching the evidence somewhat, but the fact that there are long stretches of music refusing to act harmonically is significant to the plot of the movement. Furthermore, the orbit of musette includes another low-style topic, the pastoral, which appears briefly but significantly both in the exposition and at the equivalent moment in the recapitulation. The picture that we are painting is therefore of a confrontation between high and low styles, or, phrased in operatic terms, a confrontation between high- and low-born characters. To counterbalance this conflict, there is a significant exploitation of dance elements throughout the movement. The two

Figure 3. Topics in K. 515, First Movement, compared with topics in other Mozart string quintets

K. 515	Mannheim Rocket	Fanfare	Sensibility	Gavotte	Sturm und Drang	Learned Style/Alla Breve	March
	1 – 13	55 – 56	4 – 5	18 – 19	21+	34 – 37	118+
	21 – 33	240 – 41	9 – 10	57+	152+	77+	
	69 – 75		14+	118+	215+	171+	
	152 – 66		24 – 25	242+		218 – 21	
	205 – 17		72 – 73	308+		262 – 68	
	255 – 61		155+				
			208 – 9				
			213 – 14				
			258 – 59				
			262 – 63				
	174/1/23 – 25	614/1/ 75 – 76	406/1/13 – 16	614/2/1 – 16	614/1/ 90 – 96	174/4/ 95 – 103	406/1/66 – 74
	406/1/ 1 – 5	593/1/ 21 – 23	614/1/ 8 – 15		614/1/100 – 106	406/1/115 – 22	406/4/16 – 24
	593/3/47 – 53	174/2/ 20 – 23	614/1/78 – 86		406/1/ 10 – 12		515/4/83 – 97
		174/4/280 – 91	516/1/20 – 22		516/1/ 18 – 19	614/1/ 19 – 31	593/1/21 +
		406/1/ 34 – 39	593/1/ 1 – 21		516/3/ 18 – 22	516/1/ 43 – 48	
		516/1/ 25 – 29	593/2/43 – 52		593/1/ 81 – 85	593/1/ 81 – 84	
		516/1/ 64 – 68				593/1/206 – 11	
					593/2/ 16 – 26	406/3/ 1 – 16	
						593/3/ 39 – 47	

Brilliant Style	Cadenza	Pastoral	Bourrée	Musette	Fantasy	Alla Zoppa
125+	322+	38 – 41	46 +	86 +	94+	115+
315+		222 – 25	94	131	269+	305+
322+			197 +	193 +	281+	
			230 +	273 +	315+	
			281 +	322		
			341 +	353 +		
614/1/31 – 38	516/1/78–85	174/1/70–78	593/1/21–22	614/2/16–20	614/2/ 78– 87	593/1/23–5
174/1/78 – 80	515/2/48–56		593/1/75–81	516/2/84–90	515/4/118– 36	406/1/28–34
174/1/94 –116			406/4/ 1–16	593/1/89–97	516/1/ 96–106	406/4/48–63
174/4/11 – 26			515/2/23–28		516/3/ 5– 8	
406/4/72 – 80						
516/1/72 – 76						
516/5/10 – 15						
593/1/81 – 85						
593/1/122 – 41						

Key: In the references to other quintets, the first figure is the Koechel listing, the second is the movement, and the third is the specific location by measure number. Thus, 515/2/23–24 denotes the second movement of K. 515, measures 23 and 24

principal dances, gavotte and bourrée, may be located in the center of a metrical spectrum reflecting the stratification of eighteenth-century society.[6] These dances, in fact, occupy the most space in the movement. And so Mozart can have his cake and eat it too, so to speak. He can travel easily between the extremes of his metrical spectrum, while locating the fulcrum of the work in the middle. In short, the opposition of high style to low style is balanced in the middle by dance. From a topical point of view, this movement's mode of signification embodies an essential conflict. And it is this play of styles that constitutes a plot for the movement.

Not all analysts will wish to carry the identification of topics per se to such an interpretive level, especially when the latter stages of the exercise involve speculation. Yet, it would be a poor analysis that ceased at the point at which the taxonomic enterprise came to an end. Data must be interpreted, and if that interpretation involves speculation, so be it.

Besides providing a plot for the movement, the conjunction of topics illustrates aspects of Mozart's syntactical control deriving from the grouping of similarly functioning topics. The first is the significance of topical classes. The point to be stressed here is that, although there are *Ur*-topics that abstractly embody the properties of each topical class, there is also considerable latitude in the actual compositional representation of individual topics. Consider, for example, the learned style: when it first appears in measures 34–37, it is represented by imitation between cello and first violin. In measures 77–81, the entire ensemble participates in this process of imitation resulting in a one-measure strettolike effect. Then, beginning in measure 171, we hear the learned style in its archetypal form, a self-conscious attempt at species counterpoint, complete with suspensions in half notes, enbellished with groups of running eighths. Whereas the first two passages are linked by the fact that they each involve the imitation of a single idea, the third passage reinterprets learnedness by alluding to a pedagogical tradition, a sort of double signification of the learned style. That is, while the alla breve denotes learned style, the contextual appearance of the passage gives a further signifying property to the passage as a whole. We may speak of a second-order semiotic system.[7]

The learned style is, in fact, capable of further expansion in order to account for many other passages in this movement, but we run the risk of confusing a specific, definable topic with the inevitable result of having five instruments play together. That is, since the quintet medium affords the composer an opportunity to display material in different lights, it is inevitable that a certain amount of imitation will take place. On this point, we pause to consider the words of Koch. Although they refer to the quartet rather than the quintet, they allude to what we might interpret as topical signification—which, in Koch's terms, is essentially a melodic process. The nonhierarchic organization of the ensemble that Koch implies is perhaps questionable, but his remarks about the ideal nonhierarchic ensemble requiring fugal treatment point to a residue of learned style. We may say that the "topical home" of Mozart's quintet is the learned style. Within this, however, the pull of a galant aesthetic produces other topics, ultimately forcing the learned style to reemerge as a characteristic type, and not only as an inevitable by-product of this particular textural arrangement:

> The quartet, currently the favorite piece of small musical societies, is cultivated very assiduously by the more modern composers. If it really is to consist of four obbligato voices of which none has priority over the others, then it must be treated according to fugal method. But because the modern

---

[6] On the eighteenth-century metrical spectrum, see Allanbrook, *Rhythmic Gesture in Mozart,* 15–23.

[7] For further discussion of this principle, see Barthes, "Myth Today," 114–15.

quartets are composed in the galant style, there are four main voices which alternately predominate and sometimes this one, sometimes that one forms the customary bass. While one of these parts concerns itself with the delivery of the main melody, the other two...must proceed in connected melodies which promote the expression without obscuring the main melody. From this it is evident that the quartet is one of the most difficult of all kinds of compositions, which only the composer who is completely trained and experienced through many compositions may attempt.[8]

Koch's list of "completely trained and experienced" composers includes Haydn, Pleyel, Franz Anton Hoffmeister, and Mozart.

It should not be inferred from the rich and varied musical surface that topical discourse is characterized by disjunction. Although topics display contrasting surface features, they are diachronically compatible, and also reveal noncontiguous associations. For example, the juxtaposition in the opening measures of a Mannheim rocket (cello) with a gentle sigh figure (first violin) points simultaneously to an opposition and a unity. The contrast of register and articulation is balanced by a continuity of pitch. Specifically, the first violin completes the space-opening arpeggio initiated by the cello. Similarly, the concluding C–B descent in the sigh figure (measure 5) reappears in measure 18 at the moment in which the gavotte is first hinted at. Again, Sturm und Drang, although it is marked by a very different character (evident mainly in mode, texture, and harmony), is a transformation and intensification of the Mannheim rocket–sensibility succession in the first five measures—and so on. It would be tautological to demonstrate all the possible connections between contiguous and noncontiguous topics. The point is that such a method involves switching from parameter to parameter in order to demonstrate what might be called Mozart's "art of transition," or, as Ratner describes it, his "felicity in motive connection."[9] There is, then, no necessary disjunction between topics, although this observation should not be allowed to obscure the effect of apparent gestural discontinuity. To grasp foreground discontinuity in terms of background continuity—or, rather, to grasp both simultaneously (albeit on different perceptual levels)—is to gain a sense of the richness of Mozart's music.

IV

Topical universe, topical classes, topic, and topical connection: these are layers within the musical foreground. It is time, therefore, to look beneath the surface and fill in the gaps left by the earlier discussion of topics. For theoretically minded analysts, an account that is unduly selective (although it may represent good intuitions about a piece) needs to demonstrate, rather than merely assert or assume, the evident subsidiariness of other possible accounts. And so, although the modes of topical signification point to one dimension of meaning, they also point up the need for a less selective framework for making sense of the movement. Let us think through the movement a third time, focusing now on harmony.

In Chapter 3 the beginning–middle–ending paradigm was introduced as a useful construct for processing the harmonic rhetoric of Classic music. The functions enshrined in this model are entirely compatible with, but not limited to, those of normative sonata form. Thus, the

---

[8] Koch, *Introductory Essay*, 207.
[9] Ratner, *Classic Music*, 104.

exposition may be described as "beginning," since it represents the presentation of the movement's premises. The development is equivalent to a "middle" insofar as it is premised on the absence of the tonic, and is also characterized by the foregrounding of process. And the recapitulation is equivalent to "ending," since it provides the resolution of the harmonic tension set up and prolonged during the two preceding sections. The harmonic reality of the movement may be further distributed into lower-level beginning–middle–ending paradigms, so that whole sections, periods, and phrases may be further understood hierarchically. In turning to an explanation of harmonic syntax, we shall proceed hierarchically, from the largest level to the smaller ones.

Example 4.1 summarizes the harmonic structure of the movement, and may be regarded roughly as a graphic "translation" of the verbal account given at the beginning of this chapter. The graph shows that an area in the tonic moves through the dominant of the dominant, to an area within the dominant. Then, after a prolongation of the dominant, we enter a period of tonic prolongation. In terms of normative Schenkerian voice-leading, I have read the movement as a descent from $\hat{3}$ rather than from $\hat{5}$, because $\hat{3}$ seems to offer a more cogent explanation of background coherence. Although the $\hat{3}$–$\hat{2}$–$\hat{1}$ reading is confirmed on several local levels (as we shall see presently), it is also contradicted by a number of clear descents from $\hat{5}$. The conflict of head tones is therefore a real one, one that needs to be retained on some level of the analysis rather than reduced away in the interests of theoretical economy.

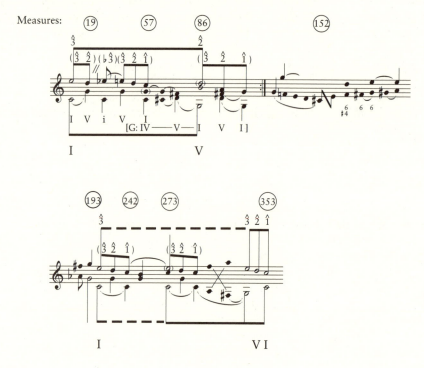

Example 4.1. Voice-leading synopsis of Mozart's String Quintet in C Major, K. 515—
First Movement

Since the essential tonal-harmonic strategy of the movement is contained in the opening period (measures 1–57), a close analysis of this period will suffice to demonstrate the nature of Mozart's harmonic rhetoric. Example 4.2 displays the structure of the opening period, which, as a large-scale beginning, preempts the course to be traveled by the movement as a whole. This beginning, in turn, has its own beginning, middle, and ending. The beginning function here encompasses the first nineteen measures, which show a progression from I to V. The details of this progression include a I–IV–V progression, the I and IV separated by an arpeggiation of I and, in the top voice, an *Anstieg* to $\hat{3}$ followed by a preliminary descent to $\hat{2}$ in the next-lower register (see alternative reading of measures 1–14 given below Example 4.2). The placement of $\hat{3}$ and $\hat{2}$ in different registers is an event of considerable structural implication, as we shall see when we examine registral play at the end of the movement. Various neighbor-note patterns, passing notes, and unfoldings serve to prolong this I–V progression.

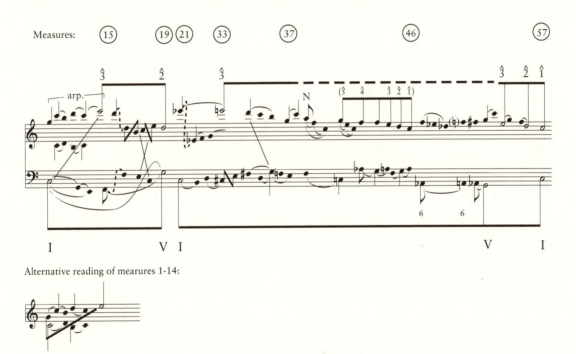

Example 4.2. Voice-leading synopsis of Mozart's String Quintet in C Major, K. 515—
First Movement, measures 1–57

Measures 21–46 may be considered middle. Although this section opens on the tonic, it is tonic minor rather than tonic major—serving, therefore, to weaken the parallelism with the opening. Measure 21 is heard in the shadow of the preceding half-cadence. Nor does the two-fold occurrence of the tonic chord in measures 39 and 41 undermine the overall transitional sense of measures 21 onward since these are plagal cadences lacking the directionality of a structural dominant. More significant still is the circle-of-fifths progression that supports the learned style in measures 34–37. This is the archetypically middle progression, which provides a means of traversing a given harmonic territory without committing itself to either a confirmatory or a stabilizing function. There is even a preliminary attempt at closure toward the end of this section (measures 39–46), the top voice outlining a $\hat{3}$–$\hat{4}$–$\hat{3}$–$\hat{2}$–$\hat{1}$ progression but having been denied the cooperation of the bass, which cadences deceptively on VI instead of on I.

The elements of the ending consist principally of a V–I bass progression, the V approached via the flatted sixth, which, in its dying stages, supports a strongly implicative augmented sixth chord (measure 54). The intense directional sense of this chord is unchallenged, providing a heightened feeling for the tonic. It is at this point that the explicit $\hat{3}$–$\hat{2}$–$\hat{1}$ descent, the archetypal melodic-closural sign, serves to close off the opening period.

As indicated earlier, the teleological energy released in this fifty-seven measure period is much too great to be contained by a single cadence, so Mozart provides a confirmatory cadence (measures 57–60) to emphasize the sense of an ending. Example 4.3 displays the structure of this confirmation, which may be heard as a recomposition of the opening period. This is, in

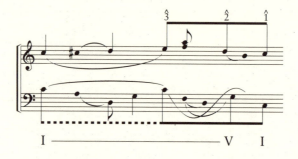

Example 4.3. Voice-leading synopsis of Mozart's String Quintet in C Major, K. 515—
First Movement, measures 57–60

other words, a three-measure compression of the fifty-seven-measure period. Like the larger period, it composes out a $\hat{3}$–$\hat{2}$–$\hat{1}$ descent, the $\hat{3}$ approached by the same stepwise ascent that led to the $\hat{3}$ of the opening period (Example 4.2, alternative reading). The bass cooperates in its essential I–V–I obligation. Measures 57–60 are therefore confirmatory in a very real sense: they do not merely provide another cadence in the tonic, but replicate the actual voice-leading pattern of the larger period.

The parallels noted among the three structures just discussed—the movement as a whole, the opening period, and the cadential phrase in measures 57–60—illustrate a technique of "motivic parallelism," whereby copies of a motive appear on several different hierarchic levels of structure.[10] These three instances do not, however, exhaust the instances of motivic parallelisms in the movement. The second key area, for example, also begins with structural $\hat{3}$, so that its first period may be profitably compared with Examples 4.1, 4.2, and 4.3. Similarly, one could take various passages throughout the movement in which an overall $\hat{3}$–$\hat{2}$–$\hat{1}$ descent is functional and compare their individual strategies. This would point up the consistency of voice-leading

[10] Charles Burkhart, "Schenker's 'Motivic Parallelisms'."

and show how Mozart varies an archetypal progression using temporal, registral, and rhythmic means. Since such an exercise would only add further substantiation to the point already made about the consistency of syntax, there is no need to pursue it any further in the present context. Instead, we might return to the beginning–middle–ending paradigm in order to consider in a bit more detail the function of two of its parts—middle and ending. Implicit in this shift of focus is one principal claim—that the middle-ending portion of the paradigm plays a more significant *rhetorical* role in this movement than beginning.

Evidence for the significance of middle lies in the extensive use of the circle of fifths. The principal property of this circle, which makes it the archetypically middle progression, is its ability to generate a succession of dominants by turning every one of its members into the dominant of its immediate successor (this property is available only if the fifths are perfect rather than diatonic; as we shall see, Mozart uses both schemes either separately or together). The property thus implies process, making it suitable for moments in the musical discourse at which process is foregrounded. Example 4.4a, 4.4b, and 4.4c show three prominent uses of the circle of fifths. Example 4.4a displays the structure of measures 34–38, where a circle-of-fifths progression provides a preliminary lead to an understated, nonstructural tonic in measure 39. The degrees traversed as shown in reduction are E–A–D–G–[C]–F (C is only implied). Having given a preliminary hint at the use of this device, Mozart proceeds to expand its domain

Example 4.4a. Circle-of-fifths progression in Mozart's String Quintet in C Major, K. 515—
First Movement, measures 34–39

significantly between measures 60 and 67 (Example 4.4b). It will be recalled that these are the explicitly directional measures in which the music heads for the alternative tonal premise. A total of seventeen fifth-related progressions are used here, the whole amounting to two and a half times the (diatonic) circle. The circle of fifths also serves a prolongational purpose in the course of the development, where four contiguous fifths from B♭ to G (measures 184–90) lead to the retransition to the home key in measure 205 (Example 4.4c). Notice that this third use of the circle is also the most expressive because of the added 9–8 suspensions distributed between various voices. Again their explicit goal-directedness is not underplayed, functioning in this case as preparation for the recapitulation.

Example 4.4b. Circle-of-fifths progression in Mozart's String Quintet in C Major, K. 515—
First Movement, measures 60–67

The emphasis on middles is rivaled only by an emphasis on ending signs. For example, the principal source of dynamic tension in the second key area is a play with closural signs. Cadences are promised and withheld, some articulated weakly, others strongly. In measures 86–115, for example, the first half-period, eight measures long, displays a $\hat{3}$–$\hat{2}$ and accompanying I–V progression, a miniature "interrupted" structure in Schenkerian terms. And, as always with periods that are divided at the halfway point, the resumption of the process (measure 94), although it represents in gestural terms a new beginning, is not in fact disjunct, in terms of voice-leading, with the preceding ending. It is possible to hear a $\hat{2}$–$\hat{1}$ progression in the two violin parts (by octave transference) and also in the cello. But the sense of closure is weak, since this is only the halfway point in the unfolding of the period.

Example 4.4c. Circle-of-fifths progression in Mozart's String Quintet in C Major, K. 515—
First Movement, measures 184–90

Between measures 94 and 115, the structural progression is a closed $\hat{3}$–$\hat{2}$–$\hat{1}$, the $\hat{3}$ of measure 94 being equivalent to that of measure 86, despite the change in register and instrumentation. But by far the most explicit denial of closure is the series of cadential approaches in measures 108–9 and 110–11, which are finally superseded in 114–15. Here too, it is possible to find linear $\hat{3}$–$\hat{2}$–$\hat{1}$ progressions (see the second violin lines), but any closural sense that these lines carry is greatly weakened by the refusal of the bass to cooperate, terminating each progression on a six-four chord. This makes the arrival of the cadence in 115 all the more exciting, since the preparation for it has been played out so obviously.

A little farther along in the exposition, the arrival of another postponed cadence becomes the occasion for introducing a surplus of closural signs. The close onto $\hat{1}$ in measure 131 leads, via a technique of underlapping, to a sequence of closural gestures—a $\hat{3}$–$\hat{2}$–$\hat{1}$ and two statements of its truncated version, $\hat{2}$–$\hat{1}$.

The most dramatic play with closural signs occurs at the very end of the movement, and primarily involves the parameter of register. Example 4.5 provides a summary of measures 349 to the end. Between measures 349 and 352, the first violin articulates a $\hat{3}$–$\hat{2}$ progression whose goal is clearly $\hat{1}$. Had Mozart maintained a mechanical continuation of the descent, the attainment of $\hat{1}$ (C^2) would have occurred on the downbeat of measure 353 (C represents Middle C, C^1 represents the octave above, and so on). Note, however, that the first violin drops

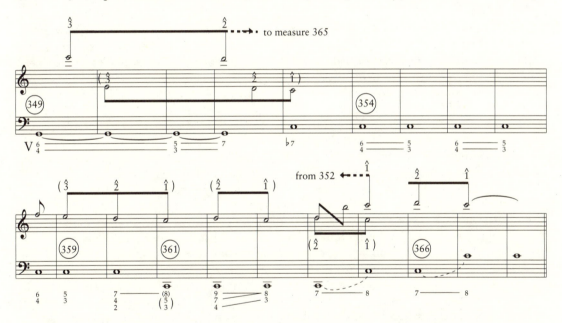

Example 4.5. Registral/structural connections in Mozart's String Quintet in C Major, K. 515—First Movement, measures 349–68

down two octaves to resolve the line onto Middle C. This registral disjunction is a clear indication that although measure 353 represents a point of harmonic arrival—indeed, the rest of the movement sits happily on the tonic pedal—the piece cannot close there, for there are still registral issues to be resolved. Of course, the upper viola moves up to C^1 to provide a perceptually weak resolution in that register, but C^2 is left hanging. Then, beginning in measure 358, the melody again descends from $\hat{4}$ to $\hat{1}$, this time in the middle register (i.e, toward C^1). After confirming this arrival of $\hat{1}$, the first violin again moves back up to the register of the unresolved D^2, reaching it on the downbeat of measure 366 and resolving it finally to $\hat{1}$ in the next measure. Note, meanwhile, how the bass note C moves upward through three octaves (measures 361–68), thus playing out another dimension of the registral story.

What is striking about this passage is the care that Mozart has taken to resolve the registers left in various states of incompletion from the beginning of the work. All the movement's three active (melodic) registers (i.e., Middle C, the octave above it, and the octave above that) are brought to appropriate points of convergence. This necessitates a splitting off of harmonic function from melodic function. That is, once structural I is attained in measure 353, there is no further harmonic obligation; registral (including melodic) processes are then foregrounded.

V

By way of summary and conclusion, let us once more think through the three perspectives from which we have examined Mozart's movement. (There is no need to proceed in the order in which these perspectives were introduced.)

1. As a work that embodies a specific historical moment, the first movement of Mozart's C Major Quintet is best understood as partaking of a universe of stylistic signs current in the eighteenth century—signs that formed the listening environment of its composers and listeners, and were used consistently in work after work by Mozart and his contemporaries. This exercise has unearthed a number of references to various dances such as gavotte and bourrée, to styles such as musette and the pastoral, to historical styles such as sensibility and Sturm und Drang, to gestures such as fanfare, and to procedures such as the learned style. By their mere presence, these topical signs embody that historical reality.

Identification is easy enough, but in order to interpret topical content, we need a mediating construct. For example, by invoking a metrical spectrum ranging from high to low styles, from ecclesiastical to galant, from the exalted passions to the terrestial passions,[11] we are able to postulate a fulcrum for an idealized social signification in this movement, and to liken the overall strategy to a tussle between high- and low-born characters. This strategy mainly refers to content rather than order, for the specific temporal succession of topics, although significant on local levels of structure as indicators of certain dimensional behaviors, is not as invariable as that of other dimensions.

Topics may be seen to embody one aspect of the movement's intertextual resonance. To distinguish between texts is easy enough. To spot the occurrences of topics in other works is equally easy. In order to reach a level of analytical significance, however, we need to be able to show, for example, that some works or sections thereof are recompositions of others. For example, the first movement of the D Major Quintet, K. 593, part of which was dicussed at the end of the previous chapter, forms a valuable comparison with the C major movement. Both movements are centrally concerned with the learned style, the D major much more thoroughly than the C major. Both partake of similar topics—fanfare, bourrée, pastoral, and so on. Yet the

---

[11] Allanbrook, *Rhythmic Gesture in Mozart*, 66–70.

aesthetic effects of the two movements are significantly different, perhaps even opposed—for whereas the C major movement essays its course carefully and with exemplary dimensional balance, that in D major offers a decidedly jerky utterance, whose appeals to the realm of the learned represent more of a struggle in their self-consciousness than an effortless and natural trafficking in the style.

Turning the analytical procedure inward, we may say that topics give profile to the harmonic argument of the movement; they are markers of harmony. But although the dependency relationship implied in this view of topical function is supported by certain parts of the Mozart movement, it is also challenged by others. For example, it would be too limiting to describe the bourrée figures introduced in measure 94 as simply giving profile to the underlying harmony. Could it in fact be that the opposite is true—that, because the harmonic motion is severely restricted to dominant-tonic confirmation, topics step into center stage to carry the dynamic sense of the passage? Here the argument is based not on a fixed notion of what constitutes musical structure, but rather on a pragmatic perceptual interpretation that takes its point of departure from the uncontroversial assumption that at different points in the course of the movement, different things are highlighted. If this turns out to be a chicken-egg question, then it will serve as a gentle reminder that surface and subsurface elements are locked in a genuine dialectic. An analytical plot which excludes or downplays the significance of the surface can have no preordained priority over one that takes the surface seriously.

2. Hearing Mozart's movement through a sonata-form grid comes with mixed blessings. The form's basic dynamic resides in a rhetorical dialectic in which a polarized tonal-harmonic relationship is composed out in frankly dramatic terms. The broad outlines of this formal process are assumed to be within the competence of listeners, but they are very much in the background, coming to the fore only when other dimensional processes subside momentarily. The perspective of sonata form is best conceived as the composer's working mechanism and, by transfer, as a comparable background working mechanism for the listener. We do not listen for sonata form; we simply hear it.

3. The beginning–middle–ending paradigm attempts to capture the rhetoric of harmony. Moreover, the paradigm imputes characteristic use to its members. Thus within the broad dimension of the movement, a number of small temporal worlds are nested in larger ones. For the listener, this may well be the most important perspective from which to view harmonic connections.

If we now ask how the first movement of Mozart's C Major Quintet, K. 515 means, it will immediately be obvious that a summary meaning cannot be reduced to a single propositional statement or set of statements, but must draw on each of the perspectives outlined here (and perhaps others also), respecting continuities and discontinuities, and consonances as well as dissonances. It will also have emerged that the three accounts overlap considerably. An umbrella notion of play serves to mediate between these accounts, so that a play in the articulation of the fictional construct that we call sonata form is, at the same time, both a play in referential structuring and a play in the rhetoric of harmony. The fragmentary nature of each account, the potential as well as the actual conflicts between accounts, and the nonduplicitous nature of aspects of each account: these factors suggest that the movement's semiotic resides in a large number of inter- and intradimensional connections. Our task has been to suggest ways in which we might begin to unravel some of this complexity.

FIVE

A SEMIOTIC INTERPRETATION OF THE FIRST MOVEMENT OF

HAYDN'S STRING QUARTET IN D MINOR, OP. 76, NO. 2

I

IN DEVELOPING a semiotic analysis of the first movement of Mozart's C Major String Quintet, we relied on the dual framework of extroversive and introversive semiosis. The underlying assumption of that discussion was that there are, on one hand, events that can be characterized in terms of a value-laden surface saturated with stylistic signifiers, and, on the other hand, events that, while not nonreferential, disclose their secrets in specific reference to conventions of grammar and syntax. To what extent does this distinction apply to the first movement of Haydn's Op. 76, No. 2, and what is the nature of the disposition of the introversive-extroversive dichotomy?

To the extent that there was a stable conclusion at the end of the Mozart analysis in the previous chapter, it was that extroversive and introversive modes of signification are comparably significant in the music. This is not to say that they are weighted equally in perceptual terms, but rather that if we subtract the givens of the tonal system, then they may each be said to retain an irreducible and nonredundant primitive in the articulation of the music. By contrast, Haydn's movement seems not to yield particularly compelling results when heard simply as a chain of topical signs. Why? Part of the answer is hinted at by the popular subtitle "Quinten," which points to the saturation of the musical foreground with a single interval, the fifth.[1] By dominating the surface of the entire movement, providing in fact a line of discourse and argument by which we may interpret the piece, the fifth, a pure sign, promises to act as the most reliable guide to the movement's meaning. When a composer makes extensive use of a single musical element, the result, from the listener's point of view, is a heightened awareness not only of that element but also of the transformational processes that it undergoes. Thus, we are right to suspect that the fifth's local contexts will reveal one aspect of Haydn's craft: his contrapuntal skill. And by drawing attention to such skill, the movement acquires, almost by default, a conventional topical or referential quality: it emerges as a rigorous study in the learned style.[2]

Haydn, however, follows normative generic constraints in shaping this first movement as a sonata-form piece. How are we to understand this interpenetration of learned style and sonata form? In semiotic terms, we need to redistribute the reality of the movement onto an axis that can accommodate the two frameworks, because both learned style and sonata form are describable as topics—albeit from different perceptual viewpoints. The topicality of sonata form is a point that will emerge more fully in the analysis that follows, but I might remind the reader

---

[1] The nickname "Quinten" by which this quartet is generally known is apparently not Haydn's, although this in no way lessens its descriptive appropriateness.

[2] A fuller discussion of this movement, which came to my attention only after I had written my own analysis, may be found in László Somfai, "'Learned Style' in Two Late String Quartet Movements of Haydn." Somfai argues that "in 1797 Haydn could have been stimulated under the direct influence of reading the fugue section of Albrechtsberger's book [*Gründliche Anweisung der Komposition*], to try out a bold compositional idea [i.e.,] the adaptation of principles of the fugue to the thematic-motivic elaboration of the sonata-form opening movement of a string quartet" (338).

of a point made in Chapter 4: saying that a piece is in sonata form is also claiming that sonata form not only acts as a formal constraint, but is itself the subject of discussion—the two attributes are inseparable. This condition arises from the fact that, in practice, sonata form is both output and input; it is a post facto abstraction from the works of composers for whom it provided an effective communicative channel. Every time that composers wrote pieces in sonata form, they also made a statement about sonata form by concretizing, if only temporarily, their understanding of the form. This understanding could remain merely implicit in the works' processes, or it could be made rhetorically explicit.

Although the broad outlines of sonata form provide a reliable framework for tracing and evaluating a possibly self-referential discourse, there is a more neutral semiotic frame, the beginning–middle–ending paradigm, for understanding the internal gestures of this Haydn movement. As we have seen, the paradigm is, of course, compatible with sonata form, not only on the level of a simple equation of exposition with beginning, development with middle, and recapitulation/coda with ending, but also on several lower levels within and between these sections. Even more than in the Mozart quintet, the rhetorical functions of beginning, middle, and ending are so boldly articulated in Haydn's movement that they weaken considerably the listener's perception of the sonata-form process.

The chief purpose of a semiotic interpretation of this movement, then, is to mediate between these perspectives by coming to terms not only with the interplay of introversive and extroversive semiosis but also, and more importantly, with what will emerge as a transformation of one into the other, a merging of semiotic identities. This is another manifestation of the phenomenon of play in Classic music.[3]

II

The first twelve measures of the movement, which form a closed period in the tonic, offer in microcosm the essence of the movement's semiotic play, and may be analyzed in detail to prepare for the less detailed discussion of the rest of the work. (From this point onward the reader will need to refer to a copy of the score of the work in order to follow my argument.) The beginning–middle–ending paradigm is distributed as follows:

Beginning 1	measures 1–4
Beginning 2	measures 5–7
Middle	measures 7^4–10^3
Ending	measures 10^4–12

Example 5.1. Beginning, middle, and ending functions in measures 1–12 of the First Movement of Haydn's String Quartet in D Minor, Op. 76, No. 2

This shows a twofold beginning, a middle, and an ending. It goes without saying, however, that such a division, which relies principally on surface harmonic articulation, must not be allowed to obscure the more dynamic process that cuts across the phrase's obvious divisions and lends it continuity and unity.

[3] By focusing on the nonreferential aspects of this movement, I am merely following an initial intuition about the imbalance between extroversive and introversive semiosis. This is not to deny the presence of topics in the movement: in addition to the learned style given in alla breve, fantasy, cadenza, sensibility and Sturm und Drang may be heard.

The work may be heard to announce its intramusical intentions in the pair of descending fifths heard at the beginning of the movement. This twofold descent characterizes both beginning 1 and beginning 2, gaining rhetorical strength with the latter. Two features of this event are worth noting: first, the interval of a fifth or its equivalent interval class of a fourth, and second, the specific scale degrees and pitch classes by which it is articulated. Separating out these identities enables us to perceive the diverse contexts in which each property (or subproperty) is played with. For example, the fifth may be heard to expand or contract, while retaining its essential "fifth" identity, so that the apparent illogicality of equating another interval (such as a descending semitone) with the descending fifth will be shown to be no fallacy at all. And with this fluid intervallic process comes an expanded pitch framework for various kinds of harmonic/contrapuntal exploration.[4]

In proposing to trace the intramusical process of the movement through the interval of the fifth, we have not overlooked its arguably unavoidable place in the tonal system. To refuse to accord the fifth-inspired process any sort of priority, however, is to fail to appreciate a crucial aspect of the movement's semiotic: the use of a commonplace in ways that expand its universe, thus exposing different, sometimes startling, connections with others, while retaining its essentially fixed signification within the tonal system. We will therefore distinguish between various fifths in the thematic process, invoking the general principle that significance is measured either by the coincidence of more than one signifying factor, or the retention of a salient previous identity, one that arises either by force of contiguity—in which case it may be immediately perceptible—or by association—in which case it may be less perceptible, but no less significant.

Manifestations of the fifth in measures 1–12 may now be elucidated. In measures 1 and 2, the fifth is given in its pure form, although the $\hat{3}$–$\hat{1}$ presentation, because it connects with fundamental melodic and tonal functions, will be accorded priority over the $\hat{2}$–$\hat{5}$ form. The significance of scale degree $\hat{3}$ is further evident from the fact that it frames the opening two measures melodically, and, in so doing, confirms its compatibility with both the tonic and the dominant triads. We must resist the temptation to construct a hierarchy or weighting of the various kinds of fifth signification in these opening two measures, however, because this embryonic presentation offers a complex from which various latent elements and procedures may be extracted for later use. For example, the $\hat{3}$–$\hat{1}$ progression of measure 1 returns as $\hat{3}$–$\hat{8}$ in measures 3–4, marking the melodic high point of beginning 1. Similarly, motivic $\hat{3}$–$\hat{1}$ may be heard mapped onto the harmonic structure of beginning 1 such that the overall I–V progression provides a harmonic interpretation of the motivic unit—note here the identity of pitch, in spite of the reversal of order.

In beginning 2, the internal relations established within beginning 1 are not affected by the change of register—but it is in the progression from beginning 2 to middle that we sense yet another interpretation of the fifth. Measures 7–8 can be heard as embodying two main fifth partitions—an immediate and a less immediate (i.e., durationally expanded) one, both involving the succession of pitches F–A–C. The immediate form occurs on the third, fourth, and fifth eighth notes of measure 8, while the less immediate form takes in the F at the end of measure 7, the A on the downbeat of measure 8, and the C on the third main beat of that measure. This simple arpeggiation of the F major triad hints at a future event—the control of the second key area by this triad—while revealing already a different aspect of the basic interval: its embodiment

---

[4] An exhaustive inventory of "fifths" in the movement may be found in Raimund Bard, *Untersuchungen zur motivischen Arbeit in Haydns sinfonischem Spätwerk.*

in a decorative texture. And finally in ending, not only the melodic approach to the cadence but the actual cadential measure contains a prominent reference to the point of departure. The $\hat{3}$–$\hat{1}$ progression of measure 1 is now entrusted to the bass as V–I and, with an interpolated $\hat{7}$, to the melody ($\hat{3}$–$\hat{7}$–$\hat{1}$). Measure 12 may therefore be interpreted both as the symmetrical equivalent of measure 1, and also as a concentrated summation of the broad harmonic sweep of the phrase, I–V–I.[5]

The play of this opening period, then, derives from the necessarily symbiotic nature of the relationship between two subgroups of the domain of introversive semiosis. On one hand, the pure sign, the fifth, infuses Haydn's texture in various ways (harmonic, motivic, thematic, and registral), although one could not make a claim for a self-sufficient and coherent explanation along these lines only. On the other hand, the functional domain of the beginning–middle–ending paradigm, itself a product of essentially harmonic processes, overlaps significantly with that of the fifth. It is my claim that the apprehension of these mutually reinforcing dramas provides the richest experience of the opening period.

If we ask how this opening period means, the answer is that meaning is inherent in the play of conventional and formal signs. The world of topical signs is no longer a strong presence here, because the period makes only implicit reference to alla breve and the learned style. By contrast, the concerns of internal manipulation are uppermost, hence my earlier reference to a self referential discourse. We might risk a tautology, and assert that the music refers to one of its own elements: the fifth, an acoustical phenomenon, the material stuff of the music. It lacks not referential associations, but meaningful ones that might provide an extroversive line of discourse for the listener.

In contrast to the first twelve-measure period, the next formal segment, measures 13–19, is tonally open. It progresses from F in measure 13 to its dominant in measure 19. The formal obligation here is the setting up of an alternative tonal premise, the principal source of tension in sonata form. To the extent that this alternative premise emerges as F major, Haydn may be said to adhere to a regular stylistic norm. Having said that, however, one should qualify the statement and note the extent to which Haydn has played with what would normatively be a bridge passage, whose signifiers are tonal instability and the foregrounding of process—a middle, in our terms. There is no question that this seven-measure passage can be described as a middle, but the fact that its entire harmonic orientation is squarely within F major partly undermines the essential instability of a middle. Measure 13 not only represents the beginning of a middle, but also points to the beginning of a mini beginning. It is in this sense that beginning, middle, and ending functions are level-specific.

By projecting the beginning–middle–ending paradigm onto the sonata-form model, we can continue to underscore the point that not only the internal functions of each model but also the functions that authorize their interaction overlap significantly. These functions are also treated recursively, so that a development can begin as a beginning, while an exposition necessarily includes development. In recognizing the fluidity of these sign functions, we gain a further appreciation of the nature of the constraints posed by a model such as sonata form; these constraints, in fact, begin to seem gradually less relevant beyond their broad, perhaps inevitable, functional roles.

---

[5] In arguing that a relationship of equivalence may be heard between the global I–V–I progression of measures 1–12 and the local cadential progression involving the six-four chord in measure 12 itself, I have not overlooked the dependent status of the six-four chord. It is the identity of intervallic content between the two progressions that I wish to stress, although they share a functional dissimilarity.

The role of fifths in signifying the dual nature of measures 13–19—as both middle (in terms of the larger formal strategy) and also as a beginning–middle (in terms of a local projection of the paradigm)—may now be described. The phrase divides into three subphrases, measures 13–14, 15–16 and 17–19. The identity of these subphrases is shaped by the falling fifth that is presented here in different harmonic contexts. We may display these within the framework of paradigmatic harmonic functions as follows:

Subphrase	Measure		Harmonic structure	
1	13–14	I	–IV–V	–I
2	15–16		V/ii–ii–V	–I
3	17–19		V/V–V^7–vi–ii–V	

Example 5.2. Harmonic functions in measures 13–19 of the First Movement of Haydn's String Quartet in D Minor, Op. 76, No. 2

We thus have an initial subphrase that is closed at both ends, a second that is open at one end (it is both a simple, expanded cadence and a motivic variation of the previous subphrase), and a third that is open at both ends (a dominant prolongation). The first subphrase constitutes a total structure complete with its own beginning, middle, and ending, the second is an ending, and the third is a middle. The odd temporal succession (ending followed by middle) suggests that the beginning–middle–ending paradigm is not fixed with respect to a temporal spectrum, but may be subject to play on lower levels of structure. This exercise of redistributing beginning–middle–ending functions enables us to compare the first twelve-measure period with this one, and to observe two types of continuity between the segments. First, in measures 13–19, the fifths appear as bass (13–14), then as an inner voice (15–16), and again as bass (17–19); the overall F–C progression also frames a fifth. We may speak, therefore, of movement between foreground and middleground. Second, despite the apparent gestural discontinuity between measures 12 and 13, measures 13–19 clearly continue from where the previous music left off. We saw in measures 7–8 a parenthetical reference to the F major triad, which could not, however, be called the key of F, since the elements of that triad, typically in minor-mode keys, are in one respect diatonic to D minor. Measures 13–19 therefore intensify a previous parenthesis.

We are on the verge of assigning to this exposition a monothematic or even a monointervallic structure, thereby placing it in the company of several other Haydn first movements. Without the benefit of the "second subject," such a designation must be provisional, however directly the singlemindedness of the thematic process and the interpenetration of theme and harmony point to its plausibility. But, as always with the assignment of traditional categories, the label both hides and illuminates aspects of the music. It is, for example, silent regarding the factor of process, which is crucial to both monothematic and bithematic expositions, in which an initial Gestalt may appear transformed in order to yield apparently "contrasting" material. The gap between monothematic and bithematic expositions may therefore be a conceptually small one. What the semiotic interpretation makes evident are those intramusical processes that confirm the monothematic structure.

The principal function of the next section, measures 20–32, is to intensify the sense of the alternative key by making explicit gestures toward closure. In fact, measure 32, which I have designated the provisional end of this section, initiates what will emerge later as a digression, therefore heightening the expectation of a formal close. Heard against the abstract norms of Classic music—as distinct from contextually-sensitive Haydnesque norms—this phrase may be perceived as a request for the music to "settle down" into its new key and offer a formal utterance. The facts that it does not, and that it makes strong pleas for closure are both signs that the structural process of this exposition, while, so to speak, paying lip service to the constraints of sonata form, are internally directed, leading to where the material wills it, rather than to where the form wills it.

Measures 20–32 both maintain and transform aspects of the fifth-practice. Three types of transformation are evident: transformation of contour and therefore of intervallic identity, linearization, and harmonic reinterpretation. The first type may be heard in measures 20 and 21 (first violin), which retain the basic descending motion, although the first of the fifths is now a diminished interval within a V^7 harmony. Similarly in measure 22, durational diminution is applied to the referential half-note succession of fifths. Then follows an explicit preparation for closure beginning in measure 25. This falls into two main phases, measures 25–27 and 28–(32). The melody of measures 25–26 shows one way in which we might hear the fifth D–G (measure 26) as preceded by another "version" of itself, the semitone B♭–A (measure 25), the point being that, perceptually, the association of the two descents belongs to the same Gestalt. A second type of transformation, linearization, begins on the upbeat to measure 27. Here the explicit $\hat{3}$–$\hat{4}$–$\hat{3}$–$\hat{2}$ preparation for a cadence is thwarted, the $\hat{2}$ failing to arrive on $\hat{1}$. I have described this as another manifestation of the fifth because it constitutes the linear framework whose realization we anticipate. The fact that the melody actually only spans a fourth does not undermine the fifth's latent presence.[6] The third transformation is heard in measures 29–31, in which the fifth-descent in the bass, now in the familiar circle-of-fifths configuration, underpins the final preparation for a close; this last reinterpretation is a harmonic one.

The discourse of measures 20–32 may therefore be heard in terms of both the transformation of the fifth into other intervals and the emergence of its closural function. Were we to approach the analysis of this work by means of a first-hearing strategy, we would, at this point in the movement, be seeking to resolve an essential conflict: the juxtaposition of two keys, D minor and F major (implying discontinuity), and the presence of an organic thematic process (implying continuity). We may speak of being "in" the alternative key without receiving a formal reassurance that such an event has taken place.

Measure 32 is a moment of double significance. Locally, it provides the resolution of the dominant prepared in the previous period, thus fulfilling one of the expectations generated by the overt representations toward closure. But the resolution is the 'wrong' one for, although the key is F, the mode is minor, not major. The point signified here is that further activity is about to take place, and we are not yet ready to make a formal utterance about closure. As we come to understand in retrospect, measure 32 in fact initiates a digression or parenthesis, which is not closed until measure 49. Syntactically, a progression from measure 31 to measure 50 is conceivable. But what is syntactically conceivable does not necessarily make the most effective rhetorical explanation. The digression has a life of its own, and calls for separate comment.

Measures 32–50 develop in two phases, 32–44 and 45–50. In terms of the beginning–middle–

---

[6] For a different interpretation, see Somfai, "Learned Style," in which the sequence D–G–C–F in the first violin of measures 26–32 is described as an instance of the contrapuntal device *interruptio*. Thus, the D–G–C of measure 26 finds completion only in measure 30, after which the C–F is repeated in measures 31–32.

ending paradigm, the overall orientation of this passage is toward a middle, despite the beginning in "tonic minor" and the progression to the dominant—qualities that normatively define a beginning. The latter reading is weak because it makes sense only in a purely local context, one that assumes that measure 32 represents some sort of beginning. But if this measure is heard in the context of the previous material, then its modal challenge, which later emerges as temporary, serves to orient it toward process—that is, toward a middle. More implicative is the goal of the passage, the dominant, which is reached in measure 41 and prolonged through measure 44. Then, taking up previously heard material from earlier on (measures 45–49 are identical to measures 15–19), the music leads to the "correct" tonic resolution in measure 50.

The principal function of measures 32–50, therefore, is to postpone the resolution to F major, the alternative tonal premise from a D minor tonic. This function is made palpable by the essential recomposition of previous material, so that while postponing a formal resolution to F major, Haydn can offer, almost in prismatic fashion, different angles from which to view previous material. Thus, the music beginning at measure 36 is a recomposition of what began in measure 13, while that in measure 45 is taken over from measure 15. Even the melodic approach to V in measure 41 recalls the cadential gesture of measure 11. Harmonically, the fifth may be heard composed out in a larger dimension, by means of an arpeggiation, F, (measure 32)–A♭ (measure 36)–C (measure 40)—the latter assuming hierarchic significance as V of F and thus absorbing the sense of both F and A♭. The fifth may also be heard on more local levels of structure, notably in the accompaniment of measures 36–41, where its transformation into other intervals is also observable. To describe measures 32–50 as parenthetical may be adequate from the point of view of harmonic syntax, but such a designation must not blind us to the intervallic processes within the parenthesis and their participation in the larger semiotic process.

Measures 50–56 complete the process of the exposition. It is not merely this terminal position that confers on them the status of an ending, but an additional gestural quality, the alternation of short V-I progressions. Both the syntax and the reiterations combine in Classic music to signify closure. In terms of the beginning–middle–ending grid, the distinctly nonexpository function of these measures—obvious from the figuration—rules out a possible beginning quality. And the relative stability of a V–I progression, emphasized through repetition, rules out a middle.

Perhaps the most important conclusion to be drawn from this interpretation concerns the realization of a sonata-form model in this movement. There is no question that harmonic obligations continue to exert an important structuring influence here. But, however important the harmonic progressions are, they tell an incomplete story, for Haydn has not signified the normal sequence by which the first key area is followed by a bridge, then by a second key area, and then by a closing theme sequence. For one thing, as remarked earlier, there is, strictly speaking, no bridge. The music moves directly from D minor to F major, without apology and without ceremony. Moreover, it never really settles down to give the listener a contrasting thematic idea or second subject. The movement is, as we have seen, monothematic, so that there is an interpenetration of ideas in both key areas, placing the thematic process on a different, but not separate, level from the harmonic one. A semiotic interpretation, in isolating a cellular organization based on the fifth and a set of conventional gestures regarding a particular segment's membership of the syntagmatic chain, throws the entire process into relief. These factors continue to enhance the observation that, for Haydn, sonata form itself could be taken as a semiotic object, complete with a normative set of relations between signifier and signified— which, in turn, serve the analyst as points of reference.

In turning to the development section (beginning in measure 57), we must stress both its continuities and discontinuities with the exposition as regards a "developmental" function. Although a process of elaboration or development characterizes this section, it is not restricted to it. There is essentially no difference between the types of elaborative process heard in the exposition and those heard in the development; the latter's *extent* is what constitutes the difference. The principal sign of development is the absence of stability in several, but by no means all, dimensions. Harmonically, this is achieved most readily by setting up a strong expectation of the tonic. To enhance this basic gesture, Haydn continues to elaborate on the movement's basic sign, the fifth, changing its contexts and its identity throughout this section. The continuity between the exposition and the development will be seen to lie not just in the identity of thematic content but, more significantly, in the identity of process. What separates them is a more global intention: the exposition is concerned with the undermining of an initial tonal premise, while the development is given over to the prolongation of the resulting conflict.

The developmental process may be heard in three phases, measures 57–63 , 63–71, and 72–98. Although the section as a whole carries the normative quality of a middle (globally speaking), it displays both beginning and ending qualities on more immediate levels of structure. The first phase, measures 57–63, serves a transitory function from the F at the end of the exposition, through G minor, to B♭ major (measure 63). Measures 57–58 present an inverted and transposed form of the opening two-measure motif (cello), measures 59–60 a transposed form (first violin), and measures 61–62 an inverted and transposed form once again (first violin). This accretion of learned devices within an unstable harmonic environment is the first sign of formal development.[7]

In the second phase of the development, measures 63–71, the material from measure 13 returns in measure 63, now in B♭ major, and its second measure becomes the basis of a sequence that leads to the dominant of D minor (measures 67–72), a dominant that is subsequently prolonged until measure 72. Of particular interest in this second phase is the rhythmic compression of the fifth in measures 68–69 to create a stretto effect. Again, it is this more conscious kind of transformation that signifies "development," for its *raison d'être* is internally directed, gaining perceptual prominence in the absence of any other process. We have spoken in Chapter 3 of the foregrounding of process, a technique that may be invoked in this context, too.

The third phase of development begins in measure 72, and offers the farthest-reaching harmonic explorations before the return to the tonic. Measures 72–76 present a concentrated passage of descending fifths, a canon in fact, symbolizing one high point of the learned style. From then on, the fifth appears in various guises—as a diminished fifth in measures 76 and 77, as a diminished fourth in measures 79 (first violin) and 80 (second violin), as a diminished fifth again in measures 81, 83, and 84, and so on. The point farthest removed harmonically, the dominant of the mediant minor, A, is reached in measure 82. This dominant never finds resolution to its tonic, but is prolonged by neighbor-note motion until measure 92. The succession of measures 92–93 is harmonically abrupt, involving a drop of a third from an E major chord to a C major chord, but the motivic process cuts across this apparent disjunction, lending it continuity (B–E in measure 92, G–C in measure 91, and D–G in measure 92). C then leads by descending chromatic bass motion to the dominant of D minor in measure 98. The final stage of the developmental process, saturated as it is with the basic sign of the movement on a surface or motivic level, may also be heard in a downward arpeggiation, E (measure 92)–C (measure 93)–A

---

[7] The joint presence of fifths and unstable harmony is what distinguishes the beginning of the development from earlier passages such as measures 13–19, in which fifths are active within a relatively stable harmonic environment.

(measure 98)—yet another middleground manifestation of the fifth, and one that complements the overall harmonic gesture of measures 32–49.

The strategy of the development therefore takes three essential paths. First, as is to be expected of a characteristic middle, process is foregrounded, the imitative back-and-forth reaching a climax in measures 72–76. Second, harmonic instability, notably the quick succession of tonal centers, highlights the absence of the tonic—in spite of a perilously close moment in measure 72 that, however, turns out to be illusory. Third, the beginning–middle–ending paradigm "normalizes" the orientation of each passage in the development as follows:

Phase 1	measures 57–63	Middle–Ending
Phase 2	measures 63–64	Beginning–Middle–Ending
	measure 65	Ending
	measure 66	Ending
	measure 67	Ending
	measures 68–72	Middle
Phase 3	measures 72–98	Middle

Example 5.3. Beginning, middle, and ending functions in measures 57–98 of the First Movement of Haydn's String Quartet in D Minor, Op. 76, No. 2.

This digest shows not only how the section is framed by middle, thus confirming its global function, but also how ending functions in an important gestural capacity. The overlap in function between the succession of endings in measures 65–67 is also noteworthy. Least significant in this section is beginning, whose association with D minor makes it something of a potential intruder—although, in a different guise, it may be heard to service measures 63–64. Thus, the weighting of the components of the beginning–middle–ending paradigm underscores the continuities as the well as the discontinuities between exposition and development.

In the recapitulation, the essential conflict of the exposition is resolved, the home key effecting a reconciliation of the two previous keys. And as invariably happens in sonata form-pieces, this reconciliation calls for a certain amount of recomposition. Haydn's tonal adjustments follow sonata-form norms, but the recompositions, ranging from trivial filler-material (as in measure 102, the equivalent of measure 4) to extentions through repetition and sequence (measure 110, the equivalent of measure 11) are not to be underplayed. No new strategies are displayed in this section.

It remains to comment on the coda (measures 139 to the end). The normative closural function of these bars is met in two ways: first, by a dominant prolongation (measures 139–149) in whose texture is embedded a set of fifths distributed among various instruments (violins and cello play D and G respectively in measure 139, then C and F in measure 140, and so on), and second, by various conventional signals of closure. The first signal occurs in measures 150–52, in which the resolution of the previous dominant prolongation takes place and   supports a full beginning–middle–ending paradigm over a tonic pedal; the effect is one of recollection, as well as of a compressed summary. Then, the ending portion of the paradigm is given special emphasis through a fourfold statement (measures 152–54). Just as the end of the exposition served to give rhetorical emphasis to the temporary closure attained, so the end of the piece emphasizes the attainment of the tonic by foregrounding the procedure of an ending.

The movement's pure sign, the fifth, occurs in the bass here as a final "fling" with the dominant sign of the movement.[8]

III

The process of this movement represents a triumph of pure signs over referential signs, a triumph of introversive semiosis over extroversive semiosis. Such a description must, however, not obscure the fact that in all Classic music, the ultimate determinants of structure are intramusical elements, so that in a fundamental sense introversive semiosis always triumphs over extroversive semiosis. But what is available as a property is not always what is made perceptually apparent; nor is it what communicates the drama of the piece. I have sought, therefore, to explicate the nature of Haydn's drama without negating the background inevitabilities. To focus on the latter at the expense of the former is to risk ending up with a tautological analysis—an analysis that merely affirms the obvious. Although focusing on the former does not eschew altogether the tautology of the latter, it manages to show how that tautology may be positively interpreted.

The fact that the interpretive approach adopted in this chapter overlaps significantly with what some might call a "traditional analysis" of the motivic variety continues to underscore the point made at the beginning of this study: that no semiotic analysis can meaningfully claim to sever its bonds with so-called traditional analysis—or, put in a different way, that our traditional modes of analysis include (at least implicitly) a semiotic perspective. Thus, the invocation of an intramusical or pure sign, the fifth, enabled an exploration of the various ways in which this particular sign mapped out the drama of the movement. We saw several levels of use, including a purely motivic one that included not just the fifth itself but its numerous derivatives, a harmonic level including V–I progressions and arpeggiations, and a linear-melodic level such as $\hat{5}$–$\hat{4}$–$\hat{3}$–$\hat{2}$–$\hat{1}$ descents.

Perhaps the most important (and paradoxical) consequence of this emphasis on pure signs is the substitution of an evident self-referentiality for referentiality. By this, I mean that although the movement continues to be nominally referential—its cadences, its intervals, its phrase structure all "refer to" other Classic pieces, not to mention topical allusions that have been excluded from this account—its discourse forces the listener to confront the work on its own terms. It dwarfs the sense of referentiality that emerges from topical structuring, substituting in its place one that is internally directed. This does not mean that the movement cannot continue to offer a basis for comparison; indeed the overall "pointing towards the learned style" may be taken as a condition for comparison. Finally, the implications of a semiotic analysis for genre were shown to involve another element of self-referentiality, this time a treatment of sonata form itself as a compound sign. Its evident signifiers are engaged in a remarkable play of pure signs, a play that, while pointing to various lower-level generic signs, includes a most significant "circular pointer" to a quartet movement in sonata form.

[8] There may well be symbolic value in the concluding pattern of fifths, D-A-B♭-C♯ (measures 150–51), which interverts the elements of a common eighteenth-century pathetic figure, A-D-B♭-C♯.

SIX

A SEMIOTIC INTERPRETATION OF THE FIRST MOVEMENT OF
BEETHOVEN'S STRING QUARTET IN A MINOR, OP. 132

I

THE INTERPRETATIONS offered in the two preceding chapters were directed more toward method and individual illumination than toward a broader stylistic synthesis. In turning to Beethoven, our aim will be to use the same technical apparatus to forge an interpretation in which traditional questions of style occupy a central place. This more explicit engagement with style is motivated by the fact that the String Quartet Op. 132, composed in 1825, although it lies within the chronological limits set at the beginning of this book (1770–1830), belongs to that much-discussed—and supposedly enigmatic—late period of Beethoven. A necessary part of my argument will therefore be that an interpretation authorized by a normative, synchronic definition of the Classic style is sufficient for late Beethoven. I shall proceed as follows: As background to later discussion of musical meaning in late Beethoven, I first summarize the main generalizations concerning the historical-stylistic allegiances of late Beethoven, the aim being in part to demonstrate the limited applicability of generalization to the subject. Then, I shall formulate a semiotic analysis in three stages. Stage 1 takes the condition of contrast in the musical surface as the point of entry, redefining contrast in terms of the play of semiotic signs. Stage 2 takes a look at the movement "from within," demonstrating the logic of harmony, and contrasting the nature of this logic with that implicit in the play of surface signs. Stage 3 then offers a synthesis of these two approaches, arguing that a normative coincidence between surface and deep articulations is under siege here, and attributing the uneasy character of this movement to this radical transformation of a premise of the Classic style. A brief final section contrasts the conclusions of a semiotic interpretation with those reached in other studies of late Beethoven.

II

The works of Beethoven's late period, the years from 1813 to 1827 broadly defined, occupy a central place in the history of Western music. They are thought to contain some of the most profound utterances of their composer—or, for that matter, any composer. Until recently, however, the kind of commentary they have elicited has been concerned less with technical explication of compositional logic than with an assembly of superlatives to register what is in effect a confession that these works are beyond analysis. Thus J.W.N. Sullivan, tracing what he termed the composer's "spiritual development," heard in the late works "the greatest of Beethoven's music" and the exploration of "new regions of consciousness," while leaving the necessary *explication de texte* to his readers' imagination.[1] Only with the publication of studies by, among others, Tovey, Schenker, Deryck Cooke, Joseph Kerman, Erwin Ratz, Charles Rosen,

---

[1] J.W.N. Sullivan, *Beethoven*, 148–49.

and Edward T. Cone have technical commentaries been offered as corollaries to critical judgment.[2]

Although the absence or presence of technical commentary per se does not guarantee an illuminating analysis, the nature of technical analysis forces an engagement with nuts and bolts; it conflates both assertion and demonstration in one critical image, leaving the reader or listener to accept or reject some or all facets of the analysis. Among the factors that seem implicative for the analysis of the late quartets, the most important is something of a paradox, mirroring a conflict between what is "free" and what is "strict": on one hand, the apparent introspective and experimental character of these works, including a certain otherworldly and improvisatory character, and on the other, the preponderance of what may be termed "technique-dominated" genres such as fugue and theme and variation. One implication of this condition is that an analytical model that is based on an aesthetic of conflict or irreconcilability may well provide the most valuable key to understanding late Beethoven.[3]

Two schools of thought may be discerned among assessors of late Beethoven. The first comprises the writers who wish to sever completely any bonds that might exist between Beethoven's late style and mainstream Classic music. "It is impossible to describe [Beethoven's late works] as Classical," writes Gerald Abraham.[4] But if these works are not classical, what are they? Romantic? Postclassical? Neobaroque? Neoclassical? Another writer rules out the possibility of a classical background to the methods of formal organization found in late Beethoven: "The old academic attempts to analyze the final works in terms of 'expanded' or 'modified,' 'sonata form,' 'variation form,' and all the other quaint old formulae of nineteenth century pedagogy will some day have to be abandoned. Beethoven no longer thinks in these terms, superficially as his procedures may resemble them here and there."[5] Ernest Newman's desire to free Beethoven analysis from the grip of unsuitable prescriptive models, and to view each work within the framework of its internal constraints, is a healthy critical premise; but, like Abraham, Newman only tells us what Beethoven's late style is *not*, rather than what it *is*.

The second and more influential school of thought emphasizes the influence of tradition on late Beethoven—not merely that of the recent past (by which I mean the style of Haydn and Mozart), but also that of a more distant past, the styles of Bach and Handel, and even of Palestrina. Maynard Solomon contends that Beethoven "never relinqished his reliance upon Classic structures," while Kerman hears a "persistent retrospective current" in late Beethoven.[6] Warren Kirkendale, writing specifically about a work whose historical allegiances seem almost self-conscious, the *Grosse Fuge*, asserts that "only before the background of tradition can its uniqueness and the personal accomplishment of the composer be determined."[7] What Kirkendale fails to do is return his meticulous documentation of historical sources to the context of the piece as a single, self-regulating structure—that is, to demonstrate the principles of continuity (or discontinuity) and coherence (or noncoherence) at work in the *Grosse Fugue*.

---

[2] Among Schenker's and Tovey's numerous Beethoven publications are *Beethovens Neunte Sinfonie* and *A Companion to Beethoven's Pianoforte Sonatas'* respectively. See also Deryck Cooke, "The Unity of Beethoven's Late Quartets," Joseph Kerman, *The Beethoven Quartets*, Erwin Ratz, *Einführung in die musikalische Formenlehre*, Charles Rosen, *The Classical Style*, and Edward T. Cone, "Beethoven's Experiments in Composition."

[3] An example of such an aesthetic is Adorno's model for late Beethoven discussed in Subotnik, "Adorno's Diagnosis of Beethoven's Late Style."

[4] Gerald Abraham, ed., *The Age of Beethoven*. Vol. 7, *The New Oxford History of Music*, vi.

[5] Ernest Newman, "Beethoven: The Last Phase," 250.

[6] Maynard Solomon, *Beethoven*, 294–95, Kerman and Tyson, *The New Grove Beethoven*, 125.

[7] Warren Kirkendale, "The 'Great Fugue' Op. 133."

It will be obvious that neither school of thought fully represents Beethoven's practice, for whereas one can argue that without some sense of origin and tradition tonal music is of very limited comprehensibility, there is the danger of letting the shadow of influence mask the uniqueness and individuality of particular works. The dialectic is therefore a rich one, one that is only marginally threatened by a third, relatively less important school of thought, which, failing to appreciate the vitality of the aforementioned critical dichotomy, offers a middle-of-the-road view of Beethoven as part Classic and part Romantic. In the absence of a *bona fide* synthesis, this "double perspective" serves only to drown a healthy debate in the deadly seas of compromise.[8]

III

Perhaps the most striking characteristic of this movement is the extreme contrast that dominates the musical surface. Many of the late quartets share this characteristic, whether it is between movements (as in, Opp. 130, 132, and 135) or within a single movement (the first movements of Opp. 127, 130, and 132). I quote Walter Riezler's description of this condition:

> Beethoven's contrasts, significant and expressive as they were from the very beginning, have now acquired an altogether unparalleled profundity. Movements are juxtaposed in seeming incompatibility—in sharper contrast than ever before; and there are "surprises" of astounding magnitude, such as the sudden unison in the Trio of op. 132, which comes in the midst of the unconstrained ease of the dance-like measures, or—and this is far more important from the point of view of the construction of the movement as a whole—the major phrase that twice appears (bars 56 and 216) in tempestuous minor of the Finale of op. 131, only to fade away each time in gentle sighs. Not only this, but there are even whole movements in which contrasts prevail without interruption, such as the first of op. 132, in the first forty bars of which, and later also in long passages, there are continual changes of mood—contrasts even occurring simultaneously—without the homogeneity of construction, which in spite of all is very strict, being [not] in the least impaired.[9]

The dual implication of Riezler's insight is, on one hand, that contrast be taken as the basic premise for analysis, so that norms are formulated with the premise of discontinuity rather than continuity (note the subtly formulated phrase "contrasts prevail without interruption"), and on the other, that the threat to coherence implicit in this condition is ameliorated by the pull of a background structure in which these contrasts are regularized. While seeking to demonstrate this high degree of contrast, therefore, the analyst is obliged to retain an awareness of the forces of integration. With the first of these aims in mind, let us consider two passages in which this maximization of contrast is evident measures 1–23 and measures 74–110.

The slow and regular half-note figuration that dominates the first seven and a half bars is followed, or rather, interrupted, by a rapid sixteenth-note figure in the first violin (measures 9–10). Then, with the emergence of what appears to be a coherent musical idea or motif (the dotted figure in measure 11, cello), the music seems to be on its way—but only for eight measures, for midway through measure 18 another erratic change occurs, arresting the motion in the manner of measures 9–10, and leading not to a relatively stable passage as before, but to a full Adagio measure on six-

---

[8] See Amanda Glauert, "The Double Perspective in Beethoven's Opus 131." A concise summary of nineteenth-century critical responses to late Beethoven may be found in Robin Wallace, *Beethoven's Critics.*

[9] Walter Riezler, *Beethoven,* 235.

four harmony (measure 21), a partial recollection of the effect of the opening measures. This, in turn, gives way in measure 22 to the sixteenth-note idea from measure 9, and then to the dotted figure again in measure 23. On this immediate level of structure, then, there is much change, contrast, and, summarily, instability. Riezler's characterization of this musical surface in terms of "contrasts...without interruption" is shown to be particularly apt.

Consider, too, measures 74–110. Over an augmented and transposed version of the opening four-note idea emerges the dotted figure, which is developed for a while and then followed by one of the most violent contrasts in the entire movement: measures 91–92. Here, a seemingly new thematic idea—superficial rhythmic affinities with the dotted figure notwithstanding—initiates a brief dialogue between lower and upper strings. This passage is however cut off in midstream at measure 103, not, as in measures 91–92, by being followed by silence, but rather by delaying gesturally the resolution to tonic (E minor). The delay is caused by the return of the opening four-note idea, now in yet another transposition. The principle at work here—which we shall discuss more fully later on—is the noncoincidence of domains, specifically the harmonic-gestural and the thematic. From a harmonic-gestural point of view, measure 103 is unnecessary (registral discontinuities notwithstanding); but from the thematic point of view, this measure is indispensable. There is clearly an overlap in function, with discontinuities in one domain approaching the status of continuities in others.

Many more passages could be cited from this movement to illustrate the nature of contrast, but I think we can consider these two examples representative and sufficient to establish the phenomenological validity of contrast. To point out these contrasts, to point out the stuff of which they are made, however, is only the beginning of an analysis. We require an explanation. In what terms can we best formulate the nature of this musical surface? Faced with such an unstable musical surface, contemporary music analysis (especially that of the neo-Schenkerian variety) invokes the neutral notion of *design* to account for the changes of texture and figuration. In an article entitled "Design as a Key to Structure in Tonal Music," John Rothgeb undertakes to demonstrate the significance of "the design of the surface...for the study of voiceleading."[10] He puts forward a "general principle" whose generality is questionable: "Changes in surface design usually coincide with crucial structural points." Doubtless there are tonal works in which this principle applies, but there are perhaps just as many works in which the principle does not apply. In a Bach prelude or a Chopin étude, where the surface figuration remains constant throughout, there is no question that harmonic processes are foregrounded, making the explication of these processes the highest goal of an analysis. Such changes in design as there may be will inevitably accompany "structural points," especially when "structural" is defined so flexibly. It may be argued, however, that the basis of any expressive structure must be premised on the noncoincidence of domains. In general, structuralists invoke aspects of surface patterning on a somewhat ad hoc basis: if the surface confirms a structural point, then the coincidence is considered significant; at the same time, structural significance is not compromised by the absence of a striking foreground feature.[11]

A more serious objection to Rothgeb's conception of design is the implication that the variables that generate a musical surface —such as the ones we described earlier—are in any sense neutral or value-free, and therefore that the notion of design is differential only of the musical

[10] John Rothgeb, "Design as a Key to Structure in Tonal Music," 73. For another approach to the same problem, see Joel Lester, "Articulation of Tonal Structures as a Criterion for Analytic Choices."

[11] I do not mean to deny the value (perhaps even necessity) of ad hoc reasoning in music analysis, only to note the difficulties that arise from not making one's premises explicit.

surface. To hold this view is to remove oneself completely from the implications of an intertextual musical discourse in which referentiality plays a major role. It does not seem to matter, for example, that the biting acciaccaturas in the first movement of Mozart's A Minor Sonata, K. 310, which Rothgeb analyzes, are hallmarks of a Turkish topic, or, more broadly in the eighteenth century, an "exotic" topic, and that its alternate presentation in minor and major is an important pointer to expressive meaning.

Rothgeb's notion of an ahistorical, value-free design, while valuable at later stages of the analysis, must, in the initial stages, be replaced by a semiotic approach sensitive to the historical and stylistic specificity of this particular musical surface. Two things emerge from adopting the latter perspective. First, it enables us to specify the intertextual world of this movement of Beethoven's, and to establish a framework for comparing works with similar "utterances." Second, by pursuing the morphology of topics, we arrive at a unique structural rhythm for this work.

In Figure 4, I have, as in previous analyses, distributed the reality of the entire first movement among various topical classes. Although the objects isolated are self-evident, I wish to comment briefly on the chart and to stress the intertextual implications of this categorization. Measures 1–8 suggest learned style by virtue of the strict, almost fugal-expository imitation. Kerman, in fact, hears this as a "miniature fugal exposition."[12] The temporal unit is alla breve, and the slow tempo, soft dynamics, and generic thwarting of expectations—what sort of piece is this?—conspire to create a sense of fantasy. The conjunction of learned style and fantasy already encapsulates a conflict, for fantasy implies a lack of order and discipline, whereas learned style implies the strictest possible discipline. Measures 9–10 suggest, in their improvisatory, virtuosic, and unmeasured manner, a cadenza, while the dotted-note idea initiated by the cello in measure 11 is clearly a reference to a march (whose narrow range and sighing effect hint simultaneously at singing style). There is something odd about this march, however, for it is missing a crucial downbeat. This is, in fact, a "defective" march, whose "ideal" form does not occur until the very end of the movement.

We hear hints of the learned style in measures 15–17, while the celebratory triadic outline in measures 18–19 describes a fanfare; in addition, given its disposition within a musical context in which contrast is a premise and such aural flights emerge almost unannounced, we can hear hints of the midcentury sensibility style in measures 19–21. The first violin cadenza returns in measures 21–22, followed by march in measures 23, from which point it begins to establish itself as the main topic of the movement. A striking, if parenthetical reference to gavotte may be heard in measure 40, and the brief imitation of the head of this dance suggests learned style. We will refer to a gavotte in learned style underpinned by march, a complex from which the listener selects one or two components depending on which line of discourse he or she wishes to follow. Finally, with the arrival of the second key, an Italian aria emerges, complete with an introductory vamp and a near-heterophonic presentation. From this point onward, no generically new topics are introduced (with the exception of the brilliant style, which serves to provide an appropriate flourish for the end of the movement). The rest of Figure 4 tells the topical history.

Before drawing specific conclusions from this succession of topics, we might digress briefly and note that if we consider the last five string quartets of Beethoven to be a closed world, then there are no unique topics in this movement—indeed, the notion of a unique topic is a contradiction in terms, given that a fundamental property of topic is its commonality. Some basis for further analysis of this aspect of intertextuality may be gained by pointing to topics in other late quartets. Consider for example the march topic, which dominates this movement. It may be heard in the second

---

[12] Kerman, *The Beethoven Quartets*, 249.

Learned Style	Alla Breve	Fantasy	Cadenza	March	Sensibility	Gavotte	Aria	Brilliant Style
1–8	1–8	1–8	9–10	11+	18–20			
			21–22	23+				
25–28					28–29			
				30+				
40–44						40+		
							48+	
		60+						60+
					67–74			
75–91				75–91				
				92–102				
	103–106							
107+				107+				
			119+					
				121+				
125+								
					129+			
			131–32	134+				
151–54						151+	159+	
		176+						176+
					182+			
	193+			195				212
214–17						214+		
							223+	
				232				236
	247			247+				
				254–64				251+

Figure 4. Topics in Beethoven's String Quartet in A Minor, Op. 132—First Movement

variation of the second movement of Op. 127, in the seventh movement of Op. 131, perhaps in the opening movement of Op. 135, and in the fourth movement (Alla marcia) of Op. 132. This last occurrence, which plays Haydnesque tricks with articulation, displays one kind of subversive treatment of topic in late Beethoven. There is both a challenge to a vital and defining component (meter) and, at the same time, a summary affirmation of its essential structure. This strategy of questioning certain basic assumptions—departing from the full-fledged and normally direct presentation of topics in Mozart, especially—is a hallmark of late Beethoven, providing further support for Edward Cone's thesis that Beethoven, in the late Bagatelles, calls into question the basics of tonal articulation such as cadence, antecedent-consequent construction, and so on.[13]

Other topics similarly provide material for a comparison of content and disposition between Op.132 and other late quartets. The aria of the second key area in Op. 132, striking in its regularity in context, may be compared with other arias: the fourth variation of the second movement of Op. 127, the development section of the first movement of Op. 130 with its allegiances to da capo aria and the theme of the fourth movement of Op. 131. These more formal presentations may be contrasted with arioso-type references, as in the Cavatina of Op. 130 or the sixth movement of Op. 131. The learned style is another useful intertextual pointer. It is epitomized in the *Grosse Fuge* (which, however, includes topics other than the learned style), but may be heard in the range of imitative procedures in both the variation movement and the cantus firmus writing in the finale of Op.131, in the first movement of Op. 135, and in both the development section of the first movement (measure 97) and the "Viennese counterpoint" in the third movement of Op. 127.

So much for topical references between Op. 132 and other late quartets. A list such as the foregoing, however, can only provide a framework for further study. It offers no explanation for the nature of Op. 132's internal conjunctions, beyond the observation that the movement is marked by contrast and a plurality of topical references. But let us not underplay the significance of the main point demonstrated by the first stage of the analysis. We can confidently assert that the piece is nominally referential in the manner of earlier Classic music. On this level alone, therefore, Beethoven's classical heritage is given some support. We are also able to mention the differences—in terms of topical play—between Beethoven and such contemporaries as Hummel, Weber, and to a lesser extent, Schubert. The point is not that eighteenth-century topics may not be found in the music of these other composers, but rather that they do not normally form an essential component of the musical texture. We might even go farther and draw a distinction between late Beethoven and middle-period Beethoven, between the severe and self-conscious classicism of the late style and the freer, exploratory style of the middle quartets, to name just one example.

In placing this movement in the context of other Classic pieces, I have not overlooked one crucial aspect of topical signification: the presentation of topics by understatement. In the majority of cases cited in previous chapters, we have seen both clear and forthright presentations on one hand, and allusions on the other hand. The former usually outweigh the latter. By contrast, allusion seems to be more central in late Beethoven than explicit statement, as is certainly the case with gavotte, cadenza, learned style, and march—although aria is subject to a very formal presentation. To understate topics is to endow them with a greater structural power. We might adapt Donald Grout's

[13] Cone, "The Late Bagatelles." See also the provocative analysis of the first movement of Op. 135 by Jonathan Kramer, "Multiple and Non-Linear Time in Beethoven's opus 135," *Perspectives of New Music* 11 (1973), 122, which seeks to demonstrate a fascinating play in the temporal dimensions of the piece.

naturalizing metaphor for formal procedures in late Beethoven to topical signification, and say that topics "remain as the former features of a landscape after a geological upheaval—recognizable here and there under new contours, lying at strange angles underneath the new surface."[14]

The exercise of distributing the reality of this movement into various topical categories does not represent the end of referential-semiotic analysis, but can be pursued further in two ways. First we might examine the variables themselves to see how their succession is regularized by a higher-level structural rhythm; second, we might speculate on a plot for the movement. A metaphor for structural rhythm in this piece is movement to and from points of metric stability—which could be conversely formulated. We arrive at this metaphor by isolating the various dimensions that define each topic and finding out what is occurrent as opposed to nonoccurrent. Rhythm and meter are the obvious choices, and the succession of topics reveals a gradual shift from metric instability to metric stability. Thus, the learned style at the beginning of the piece defines a pulse, not a rhythm. The cadenza then erases this pulse. The march, though inherently rhythmic, is presented without its crucial downbeat. The arrival of the gavotte reinforces the shift toward metric regularity, a condition that is fully established with the arrival of aria. A process of destabilization begins soon after the aria, and from this point on we experience various dynamic transitions to and from points of metric regularity. The "background" of this movement as defined by topical signification consists, therefore, not of a pitch-defined, arhythmic *Ursatz,* but rather of a rhythmically defined functional stability that moves in and out of subsidiary levels of instability. One therefore does not impose a dimensional hierarchy on the piece, but approaches the idea of background metaphorically.

A possible compositional plot for this movement derives from the erratic surface, the understatement of most topics, and the overall quality of instability—this is so even at the end of the movement, as we shall see later. The oppositions between high and low styles, between sacred and profane, and between the spontaneity of aria and the self-consciousness of learned style: these constitute an attractive framework for a plot. This helps to explain why a solemn motet for strings in a decidedly high style and infused with fantasy elements is suddenly interrupted by virtuoso display, then by a middle-style march, and then by a high-style dance (gavotte), and finally by the emergence of an operatic character.

So much for topical signification and issues arising out of the play of referential elements in this movement. For certain analysts, the foregoing commentary has been concerned only with the foreground or surface, so that, at best, it provides a characterization of a very small part of the piece. But leaving aside for now the point that some music may be genuine foreground music— and challenging the value system that goes with the familiar foreground-middleground-background hierarchy—we need to acknowledge the inadequacy of topics as ontological signs, and replace that formulation with structuralist notions of arbitrary signs, for it seems clear that even those listeners for whom the referential elements are real and substantive would agree that the individual gestures derive their importance less from their paradigmatic or associative properties than from their syntagmatic or temporal ones. For if the relationships between phenomena determine their nature rather than any intrinsic aspect of the phenomena themselves, then it is to the domain of absolute diachrony that we must turn.

---

[14] Donald Grout, *A History of Western Music,* 3d ed., 540.

IV

As a rhetorical process, the argument of this movement, like that in the Haydn and Mozart works studied in the two preceding chapters, is conducted within the framework of sonata form. But in turning to the nature of tonal signification in this movement, we should be immediately aware that both sonata form and the beginning–middle–ending paradigm, like the disposition of topics, achieve their explanatory power more negatively than positively. That is, it is the departures from a normative enactment of sonata form, or from the use of material conventionally symbolizing beginning, middle or ending that constitute the key characteristic of the movement.

Despite the formal unorthodoxy of this movement, commentators have persisted in identifying an underlying sonata form. Here are three possible schematizations of the movement:

Version 1	Exposition	Development	Recapitulation 1	Recapitulation 2
Measures:	1-74	75-102	103-92	193-end

Version 2	Exposition 1	Exposition 2	Recapitulation
Measures:	1-102	103-92	193-end

Version 3	Exposition	Development	Recapitulation	Coda
Measures:	1-74	75-102	103-92	193-end

Figure 5. Three possible schematizations of the form of the First Movement of Beethoven's String Quartet in A Minor, Op. 132

These divergences in the reading of the formal layout arise out of certain representations that Beethoven makes toward sonata form—representations that are, however, never normatively enacted. By virtue of the aria in F major alone, one can rightly speak of a second subject or, more properly, of a second key area, just as one can speak confidently of a recapitulation, since material presented earlier in A minor and F major is reconciled in the reappearance of A minor (with a touch of A major) later on. On the other hand, the appearance of the thematic substance of the A minor and F major areas in the middle of the movement in E minor and C major respectively disrupts the normative gesture of sonata form, and embarrasses both the analyst who sees it as a thematic but not a harmonic recapitulation, and the one who sees it as a mere development—the former because the harmonic environment makes nonsense of any notion of a recapitulation, and the latter because such a wholesale restatement is uncharacteristic of a genuine development section (Schubert's essentially anticlassical procedures notwithstanding).

The questions of two expositions versus one development, two developments versus one exposition, or one exposition versus two recapitulations need not detain us further, because the issue will never be settled. Indeed a search for the "truth" may not lie with those analysts anxious to distribute the reality of this movement into a sonata-form model, especially if conflict and lack of resolution are essential to late Beethoven. If we think of sonata form as a signifying model against the backdrop of a normative, harmonically-defined process, then the logic of Beethoven's formal strategy is at once evident. There is, first, a statement of contrasting premises (A minor and F major), then a prolongation of the resulting conflict (E minor, C major, and others), and finally a resolution (A minor/A major/A minor). It may therefore be argued that it is unimportant how one chooses to label the individual sections of the movement, so long as one grasps the logic of

Example 6.1. Structural elements of Beethoven's String Quartet in A Minor, Op. 132—
First Movement

Example 6.1. (*cont.*)

tonal relations. Formulated in terms of harmonic function, we might say that a i–VI relationship on the triads of A minor and F is repeated on the triads of E minor and C and resolved on the triads of A minor, A major, and A minor once more. It is the high degree of invariance between members of controlling triads that is striking here: A minor and F, like E minor and C, may be said to display maximum intersection with respect to pitch class within the diatonic triadic universe.

The statement–conflict–resolution scheme may also be seen to represent a beginning–middle–ending paradigm on a global scale, but the paradigm loses its explanatory power in application to more local levels. For example, the absence of tonic in the first nine measures suggests middle rather than beginning, while the nominal V–I progression of the first ten measures suggests ending. In the second key area, on the other hand, the regular phrase structure of the tune makes a beginning–middle–ending distribution possible, and shows Beethoven to be playing tricks with the ending (see measures 55 onward). The rhetorical emphasis on ending in the last seven measures of the movement is perhaps the strongest representation of any one of the elements of the paradigm—although even here there are further challenges to the sense of an ending.

Without listing all the details in the workings of the beginning–middle–ending paradigm, we may observe that while its elements are subject to play, there is a more fundamental logic operative on lower levels of structure. Example 6.1 attempts to convey some sense of this logic by distributing the reality of the piece over two levels labeled Middleground 1 and Middleground 2. The *modus operandi* is the familiar complex of neighbor-note motions in both diatonic and chromatic forms, unfoldings, arpeggiations, and tonicizations of various scale steps. Rather than embarking on a further explication of technical procedures enshrined in this graph, I suggest that the reader play through the graph at the piano in order to experience not only the logic, but also the conjunction in the harmonic unfolding. The smoothness and evenness of that reduction are striking, presenting a remarkable contrast to the near-disjunction that characterizes the musical surface.

There is one final stage of this discussion of harmonic syntax, whose relevance derives from the fact that the conventional formal grid does not provide the most effective reading of the harmonic process. Rather, a familiar construct, which we have referred to in Chapter 4 as the archetypal middle progression—the circle of fifths—may be shown to underlie the harmonic process of the entire movement, cutting across the obvious points of formal articulation and lending the whole process a subsurface continuity. In the third line of Example 6.1 I show that, beginning with A, the movement travels through five cycles of the circle. All seven possible points are occurrent, although not in any one cycle. Each cycle is, in other words, defective—there is no enactment of the ideal. Specifically, three, then one, then four, then two, and then, again, two steps are omitted from the respective cycles. Although Beethoven, here as elsewhere, does not deploy the cycle mechanistically, he provides us with a statistically significant unfolding of its elements to guarantee both the local and large-scale tonal progressions.

With each point of entry into the world of harmonic syntax in the first movement of Beethoven's Op. 132, we have encountered either an obstacle or a signficant absence. The disposition of the beginning–middle–ending paradigm, with its largely absent beginning, its covert emphasis on middle throughout, and its rhetorical stress on ending, is a case in point. The use of the circle of fifths is another. The business of defective cycles continues to underscore the significance of instability, lack of completion, and perhaps even lack of unity. For although—to take the circle of fifths as an example—there is never a complete journey through its span, familiarity with the construct serves to guarantee its perceptual significance, making the notions of ideal and defective purely theoretical phenomena.

V

The results of the first two stages of the analysis show that the varied, highly contrasted, even apparently disjunct topical discourse that characterizes the surface of the movement contrasts sharply with the high level of continuity in harmonic process. There are no "bumps" in the latter, and where there are shortcuts, their articulation counters any feeling that something is inconsequential. The point of this third stage is to examine certain aspects of the relationship between domains. I shall suggest that that relationship is one of disjunction, a disjunction whose rhetorical force transcends the normative disjunction between domains that lies at the heart of every expressive structure. More specifically, by comparing topical articulation with harmonic articulation, I wish to show that the signifying function of topics is seriously questioned in this movement. Five separate examples, given in voice-leading reduction as Examples 6.2a, 6.2b, 6.2c, 6.2d, and 6.2e will serve to illustrate this feature of the movement.

Example 6.2a (measures 9–11). This example shows that the major point of topical articulation

Example 6.2a. Interaction between topic and harmony in Beethoven's String Quartet in A Minor, Op. 132—First Movement, measures 9–11

fails to coincide with the major point of harmonic articulation, thereby making for dissonance as premise. The homorhythmic writing in the first eight measures, coupled with the relative neutrality of the alla breve topic, serve to bring the resultant vertical sonorities into greater prominence. The harmonic orientation of these opening measures is toward the dominant, a function that is intensified in measure 9 in the form of a diminished-seventh chord presented simultaneously on the downbeat, and successively in the first-violin cadenza. It is not until the fourth beat of measure 10 that this prolonged dominant resolves to the tonic—but what a resolution! The tonic appears in first inversion, on the weakest beat of the measure, and is marked piano. Surely the weight of the extensive dominant prolongation is much too great to be absorbed, let alone neutralized, by this most understated of resolutions. To speak merely of a V–I progression in measures 1 –9 is to fail to appreciate the provisional status of measure 9, or the fact that, while meeting a syntactical obligation, this measure is not given comparable rhetorical or gestural force. More important is the subsequent appearance of march, the principal topic of the movement. No ceremony accompanies its articulation; it does not even appear in the moment of resolution, but only subsequently. Topic is therefore exposed at a subsidiary point in the structural-harmonic process.

It is not that one cannot find examples of such displacement in earlier Classic music; it is rather that displacement as premise is not the norm. When this becomes the order of the day in late Beethoven, we are able to sense the ways in which it sounds different from earlier Classic music and, through the particular mechanism used analytically, to appreciate what it preserves of this earlier style. Consider one other example of this misalignment in another late quartet, that in Eb major, Op. 127. The principal topic of the first movement, probably waltz, appears in measure 7 over subdominant harmony, in what seems harmonically to be the middle of a passage. Beethoven avoids the kind of gesture that would ensure that the topic was introduced at the beginning of a phrase and with a harmonic gesture associated with beginning.

Example 6.2b (measures 19–22). This example shows that, by the terms of a fixed background hierarchy of tonal function, the articulation of topic and harmony remain noncoincident. In this passage, the outbursts of sensibility function as space-filling material in the approach to the structural dominant in measures 21–22. The essential harmony of the passage, Neapolitan–dominant–(implied) tonic, reveals an increase in the functional status of each chord. Note, however, that fanfare occurs on the first of these chords, the Neapolitan. And although it is not unusual in Classic music to hint at the later use of material in this way—the Neapolitan obviously prepares

Example 6.2b. Interaction between topic and harmony in Beethoven's String Quartet in A Minor, Op. 132—First Movement, measures 19–22

the approaching modulation to F major— the topical event acquires special significance in this context, first, because of its durational prominence, and second, because of the special affinities between fanfare and the more prominent march. Here, too, the individual hierarchies of topic and harmony do not necessarily function complementarily.

One argument against comparing topical and harmonic processes may be that, unlike topic, the domain of harmony is virtual, always present. To place the two domains on the same level is therefore to compare unequal forces. But note that, while acknowledging the dependent status of topical signs, I have also been concerned about pointing out the matter of articulation, without which our analysis will remain on a normative, perhaps even mechanical background level.

Example 6.2c (measures 39–48). In this example, an important topic—structurally important

Example 6.2c. Interaction between topic and harmony in Beethoven's String Quartet in A Minor, Op. 132—First Movement, measures 39–48

insofar as it reinforces the broad shift from metric instability to metric stability—is introduced over parenthetical harmony. By measure 39 the preparation for the second key is well under way. We are effectively in the new key; it only remains for this key to acquire a profile theme. Then beginning in measure 39, the cello initiates a dominant prolongation that includes a circle-of-fifths progression. The gavotte is thus introduced within the unfolding of a harmonic process, rather than at its beginning or end (the more traditional points of topical articulation). Like the march and fanfare, the gavotte appears at a structurally subsidiary point.

Example 6.2d (measures 91–94). We have already mentioned this passage as displaying one of the most striking contrasts in the movement, and that point can now be reformulated in terms

Example 6.2d. Interaction between topic and harmony in Beethoven's String Quartet in A Minor, Op. 132—First Movement, measures 91–94

of the interaction between harmony and topic. The passage involves a progression from G to C, but the articulation of this V–I progression is handled in a remarkable way. Gesturally, the topical unfolding takes precedence over the harmonic process, demoting the latter. This is so because the listener accepts as a matter of course an implicit V–I progression (note especially how the high D in the first violin is resolved four octaves lower!), while being treated to the marchlike idea. Topic is not displaced from harmony as such; rather, the relationship between the two domains is inverted from earlier Classic practice.

In interpreting these features of Op. 132 as inversions of Classic practice, I do not wish to imply that their apprehension carries a normative disposition. That is, I am not claiming that one hears the harmony less than the topic. On the contrary, I mean to describe the way in which the two domains are articulated, to show how one is given prominence over the other. For the listener, however, hearing this passage in context will be strongly informed by the premises given at the beginning of the movement, so that by this point he or she is more likely to expect such displacements rather than coincidences.

Example 6.2e (measures 258–60). The structural tension between the two domains is perhaps most violent at the end of the movement, specifically in the last eleven measures of the piece. Prior to this, closure has been signaled by means of a number of representations toward the tonic. Then in measures 254–57 we hear a passage that functions, on one hand, as a harmonic parenthesis—we could easily dispense with these four measures so far as syntactic necessity is concerned, and go directly from 253 to 258—but, on the other hand, as a gestural intensification of the sense of an ending. Already, it is clear that to ignore the gestural significance of these measures is to ignore something vital. This leads to an extraordinary moment, the downbeat of measure 258—where, for the first time, the march acquires its crucial downbeat, thereby supplying the essential (and defining) component of the most prominent sign in the movement. This, in fact, is the "ideal" march whose "defective" form was given near the beginning of the movement. But that is not the whole story, for while thus resolving a tension with a long history, Beethoven undercuts this resolution

Example 6.2e. Interaction between topic and harmony in Beethoven's String Quartet in A Minor, Op. 132—First Movement, measures 258–60

by means of a rhythmic figure that shifts the accents of the dotted figure in the march (see Example 6.2e, in which I have contrasted a normative articulation of measures 259 and 261 with Beethoven's). The effect of this is to challenge the very sense of closure achieved by the arrival of the ideal march. Kerman's remark that there is "no very determined conclusion" to this movement,[15] although contradicted by the outward closural gestures of these last eleven measures, is offered some support by the present reading, which considers the sign functions to be in conflict, not in synchrony.

There are several more examples of this feature in the first movement of Op. 132, but further discussion will add nothing substantial from a theoretical point of view to this discussion. We may summarize the analysis as follows: The surface of the first movement of Op. 132 may be heard with reference to the code of stylistic signifiers or topics found in earlier Classic music. The resulting gestural syntax could itself provide a framework for understanding not just the surface paradigmatic associations, but also the syntagmatic properties that stem from reading topics as ontological signs (hence notions of "plot" and "structural rhythm"). Stripped of this surface, the formal and tonal-harmonic processes reveal a persuasive, remarkably continuous operational logic whose coordinates are locatable within the normative Classic style. Not only this higher-level contrast of articulation, but several lower-level comparisons reveal an absence of synchronicity between topic and harmony, and it is this dissonance between the domains that gives the work its unique character.

VI

One ought to guard against undue generalization stemming from an analysis of a single movement, especially when the subject is as delicate and multifaceted as Beethoven's late style. But, at the same time, it would be a pity not to place the results of this analysis within the context of recent attempts to come to terms with the principles behind Beethoven's late style. In confronting the following four points of view, my aim is not to challenge the applicability of their authors' conclusions to the works they analyze—although such an indirect critique is, in one or two cases, inevitable—but rather to challenge the relevance of those conclusions to the first movement of Op. 132. An inevitable implication of the present exercise, however, is that an aesthetic rooted in conflict holds the greatest potential for unraveling the secrets of late Beethoven. The demonstration of that implication will, however, have to await a further study.

First it is clearly an exaggeration—if not an error—to sever completely the bonds between late Beethoven and mainstream Classical style. In fact, the opposite is true. It is not that the previously cited remarks of Abraham and Newman, conceived in a more general appraisal of late Beethoven, are without merit. One can, in fact, sympathize with the need to be cautious about pushing the works of late Beethoven into the molds of earlier Classic music, but that is not the same thing as denying the presence of a palpable connection. It is difficult to imagine how one can understand late Beethoven without the classical style. Surely a neutral apparatus is patently ahistorical.

Second, the extent of the analysis should not be the detailing of sources, either procedural or material, from earlier music. Both Warren Kirkendale's impressive assembly of "sources" for the *Grosse Fuge* and Sieghard Brandenburg's elucidation of the background to the "Heiliger

---

[15] Kerman, *The Beethoven Quartets*, 249.

[16] See Kirkendale, "The 'Great Fugue'," and Sieghard Brandenburg, "The Historical Background to the 'Heiliger Dankgesang' in Beethoven's A Minor Quartet," in *Beethoven Studies* 3, ed. Alan Tyson (Cambridge, 1982), 161–91.

Dankgesang" movement from this quartet seem to me to stop too soon.[16] As the earlier description of topical process has shown, material sources, once identified, need to be returned to their proper context so that we can understand the logic or lack of logic that governs their actual compositional disposition. To fail to advance an explanation for coherence is tantamount to listing ingredients without indicating how they are to be mixed, or providing a vocabulary without a syntax.

Third, there is no evidence here of a "double perspective." Amanda Glauert's contention, based on a study of the Op. 131 quartet, that "the revolutionary aspect of the late works was their insistence on the right to forge their own relationship to established procedures, from a position no longer within, but outside the sphere of classical norms"[17] runs counter to the conclusion reached here. "Forge their own relationship to established procedures" they certainly did, but the position is squarely within the sphere of Classic norms, not outside of it. I have emphasized that there are precedents for this dissonance between domains, thus showing a continuity between earlier Classic music and Beethoven. Even where I have referred to an "inversion" of earlier Classic practice, I have not implied that the procedures are traceable to a different tradition. It seems necessary to insist on this classicist view of late Beethoven in order to distinguish between him and the early nineteenth-century line of Schumann and Chopin, whose structural premises differ significantly from Beethoven's.

Fourth, and finally, there is no "reconciliation of contrasts" as Brodbeck and Platoff have argued in connection with Op. 130.[18] My own desire to uphold a fundamental dissonance between domains, to retain contrasts as premises, may be no more than an ideological difference from Brodbeck and Platoff. But this difference points to a bigger difficulty in the practice of music analysis. Few analysts have taken it upon themselves to prove that a piece of tonal music is unified; fewer still have attempted to demonstrate the absence of unity in a tonal piece. What one often finds, however, is the *assumption,* inherited from nineteenth-century organicist aesthetics, that masterworks of music are unified. Analysis adopts this as premise, and, with a curiously circular logic, proceeds to demonstrate that unity. Not only have contemporary analysts largely avoided the difficult questions of value, but they have also rarely attempted a systematic demonstration of disunity in tonal music.[19] The occasional comments from critics about the decidedly inferior status of, say, Pleyel to Mozart, or Vanhal to Haydn—comments that hinge on the unity–disunity issue—are, for the most part, assertions rather than demonstrations (which is not to say that they are not motivated by good intuitive response).

In the absence of a framework for proving unity or disunity, I can only point to the specific analytical demonstration of dissonance between dimensions in order to support my contention that Beethoven here intends for us to live by this very conflict between the domains. We might modify a formulation of Adorno's, and say that the late style is concerned with the irreconcilability of dialectical opposites (in contrast to their reconcilability in the second-style period). But we could also conclude that the analytically perceived dissonance is, in fact, a conceptual consonance. This last formulation would satisfy a certain aesthetic bias for unity and higher-level consonances. At that level of the discussion, however, the subject would no longer be music, but words.

[17] Glauert, "The Double Perspective," 116.

[18] David L. Brodbeck and John Platoff, "Dissociation and Integration: The First Movement of Beethoven's Opus 130," *19th-Century Music* 7 (1983): 149–62.

[19] A notable exception is Hugh MacDonald's "Fantasy and the Order in Beethoven's Phantasie Op. 77."

SEVEN

TOWARD A SEMIOTIC THEORY FOR THE INTERPRETATION OF
CLASSIC MUSIC

I

THE AIM of this chapter is to summarize the theory that underlies the interpretations developed inductively in preceding chapters. Interpretive theories of music generally resist formalization, so that in an important (i.e., nontrivial) sense, the concerns of this chapter must be seen to renounce any claim to comprehensiveness or ultimate truth. Some aspects of music analysis are easier to formalize than others, but the degree to which a particular theory can be formalized may have no bearing on the value that it holds for musicians. Various ad hoc invocations, for example, may appeal on the basis of their rhetorical power or interpersonal resonance. The aim here, however, is not to reduce the entire music-analytical enterprise to mere rhetoric, but to facilitate a better understanding of how we understand Classic music.

The goal of the theory is to provide an analytical framework for the interpretation of Classic music. The theory seeks an answer to the question "How can Classic music mean?"—and, in so doing, recognizes not only the significance of "how" over "what" but also the inevitable intersection of the explanatory domains of the two interrogatives. Pointers to meaning, or rather, pointers to the senses in which a piece means are deemed adequate for the formulation of an interpretive theory.

A. The Domain

1. The historical-empirical domain of the theory is the period 1770–1830. There is, of course, nothing sacred about these dates, the only claim being that the theory's most effective results are obtained when it is applied to music written during this period. A synchronic view is taken toward Classic music. This means that it is assumed that there is such a thing as a self-sufficient and self-regulating body of Classic works whose broad dimensions can be isolated and defined in terms of normative features, and that these features can and should form the basis for any interpretive exercise. It is also assumed that, however closely it approaches the nature of these norms, no single Classic work embodies *only* these norms. Each work plays with or violates the expectations prescribed by norms. The postulation of a summary Classic style is therefore a necessary oversimplification, one that must yield in actual execution to the prospect of a dialectical interplay between norm and realization.

2. Although the theory adopts a synchronic view of Classic music, it includes a potential for illuminating diachronic aspects. First, the particular play of signifiers that emerges from each analysis can provide the basis for evaluating historical-stylistic changes. Nothing is built into the theory to enable a mechanical deduction of historical consequence, however. Such application must be made on the basis of a sensitive invocation of the relevant dimensions of this interpretive mechanism. Second, in the actual process of interpretation, the problem of reconciling an "in-time" awarenesss in music analysis with a "final-state" awareness is met by adopting a diachronic (verbal) account on one hand, and a synchronic graphic account (after Schenker) on the other. In

the former, the metalanguage and object-language are different, whereas in the latter they bear an iconic relationship to each other. Neither account is inherently superior, and both accounts must be seen as complementary. In any case, the domains of both accounts overlap significantly.

3. The generic-empirical domain of the theory is instrumental music—string quartets, string quintets, symphonies, piano sonatas, concertos, and so on. This limitation should be seen as pragmatic rather than binding, for an application of a semiotic approach to vocal genres such as opera, oratorio, and lieder is not only conceivable, but potentially equally illuminating. At the same time, the added complexities of other systems—language, drama—should discourage a premature application of semiotic principles. Since instrumental music forms the common denominator in all these genres, the approach developed toward it may serve as a model for the development of other analyses.

B. The Analytical Method

1. Defining the Fields of Investigation

The theory recognizes the extraordinary complexity of the musical object and the potentially infinite number of dimensions whose interaction defines that object. A necessary imperative, therefore, is a narrowing of focus. For reasons considered in the beginning of Section III, the theory postulates two fundamental properties of Classic music: "expression" and "structure" (and in a variety of rough synonyms, including foreground-background, semantics-syntax, rhetoric-structure, and extramusical-intramusical). Although useful as a mechanism for distributing the reality of a piece into various dimensions, the dichotomy is later shown to embody intersecting perspectives. The dichotomy may therefore be used in service of a preliminary taxonomy. Beyond this, it must undergo some redefinition before being subsumed into a higher-level semiotic order.

2. The Concept of Topic as Key to Expression

a. The expressive aspects of any piece of Classic music, M, may be described with respect to a set of topics, T's, which are subjects of musical discourse. The Universe of Topic, UT, is the sum total of all topics isolated so far. Theoretically, UT is open, since it continues to expand as more and more topics are uncovered; UT can only attain closure on the last day of research. The grouping of T's within UT is subject to a number of considerations. For example, T's consist of both types of music and styles of music. That is, they may point to standard dance types (minuet, sarabande, gavotte) by replicating an identifying feature or features of a particular dance, or to historically situated musical styles (sensibility, Sturm und Drang), or to musical procedures (learned style, fanfare). As pointers to expressive meaning, T's are subject to other constraints, and their ultimate significance is neither fixed nor determinable in isolation from the particular musical context in which they occur. T's may function as lower-level generic pointers—as, for example, the presence of a "concerto style" within a string quartet, or of "aria style" in the slow movement of a piano concerto. These pointers, references, and allusions are simply collected as inputs, their ultimate significance to be determined in conjunction with other properties.

b. A topic, T, may be defined as a musical sign. Each T embodies the union of a signifier and a verbally mediated signified. Signifiers are purely musical dimensions such as texture, timbre, rhythm, melody, and harmony *in a particular disposition;* the latter caveat means that references to "static" T's (such as Sturm und Drang) or to "dynamic" procedures (such as imitation) are admitted without discrimination into the domain of signfiers (albeit on different hierarchic levels). Although no explicit attempt is made to define the elementary signifying units for music, it is proposed that, within the domain of expression, signifiers be regarded as the most meaningful small-scale elements that define a particular relationship. The signified or concept is represented by an arbitrary label drawn from UT. Signifieds normally point to dimensions of historical or sociocultural specificity, including the elements of a contemporary compositional code. T's provide a useful mechanism for the pursuit of intertextual discourses both within a given M and between various M's.

c. The identity of a given T is subject to a wide variety of contextual factors. T's may be organized hierarchically, so that a sequence such as T1–T2–T3, which in the first instance describes a simple succession of T's, may, in this particular disposition, yield a secondary topic (T4) or topics (T5, T6, T7), where T4, T5, T6, and T7 arise solely from the conjunction of T1, T2, and T3. T's are therefore subject to replication as (at least) second-order semiotic systems. This possibility further implies that the identity of any T is subject to change, depending on the hierarchic level on which that identity is being measured. This instability in the status of T's suggests a theoretical switch from similarities to differences—the point being that it is the differences between T1 and T2 that matter ultimately, not the discrete identity of each. Moreover, as regards the presentation of T's, the arrangement T1–T2–T3... TN describes a normative disposition of topics within a compound musical texture as a succession. It is also possible to combine T's so that T1 and T2 may form "melodic" elements while T3 forms the substance of the "accompaniment." That is, in the context of a given M, T's may be functional both "vertically" (that is, as elements of a paradigmatic axis) and "horizontally" (as elements of a syntagmatic axis).

d. There are no virtual temporal limits to the identity of a given T as there are for M. Although the succession T1–T2–T3 may represent a succession of three different topics, it is often the case that there is a transfer of identity between contiguous topics, which places their points of origin and termination in strategic fluidity. T2, for example, may be activated in the dying stages of T1, even if it does not become clear until T1 ceases to be active. And there is always the possibility that elements of T2 may be foreshadowed in T1, those of T3 in T2, those of T3 in T1, and so on. Moreover, an associational relationship is possible between T's such that, in the succession T1–T2–T3–T4, the local contacts between T1 and T2 or between T2 and T3 may be balanced or counterbalanced by references between the noncontiguous T1 and T3, T1 and T4, and so on.

e. Although it is theoretically possible to partition M exhaustively into a T1,T2,T3... TN series, the current state of our research does not enable such a generalization. That is, while topical signification may be apprehended in several, if not most parts of M, there are often "remainders" or grey areas that seem to be topically neutral. Neutrality, in our terms, may simply be provisional, awaiting the discovery of more topics. Those areas that appear to be neutral would then be given the appropriate label, once the discovery is made. The fact, however, that such exhaustive partioning rarely takes place in practice is a significant pointer to a fundamental limitation of topic, discussed presently in Subsection 3, "Beyond Expression."

C. From Taxonomy to Interpretation

After the preliminary task of distributing the reality of M into various categories of T, a number of conclusions and methodological consequences need to be addressed. A preliminary conclusion is that, as an unordered sequence of gestures, M embodies a certain historical or sociocultural specificity. This finding merely confirms an initial intuition, but it may present an argument against reading M as a literal exemplar of the Classic style. The apparent circularity of demonstrating what one perceives by intuition may be defended, here as elsewhere in the criticism of art, as an unavoidable by-product of aesthetically motivated criticism. Beyond this confirmatory function, the disposition of T's within M may be analyzed with two further aims in mind. The first is to attempt to derive a plausible "plot" (P) for M. The second is to investigate its "structural rhythm" (SR).

1. THE PLOT

Plot denotes something like a secret agenda, a coherent verbal narrative that is stimulated by both the types of T and the nature of their disposition in M. A confrontation between high and low styles, an episode from a *commedia dell'arte*, a critique of an Enlightenment world view: these are sample plots developed for various Classic pieces. References are to so-called "extra-musical" events, and are justified by the appropriateness of the analogy. This is unquestionably a speculative step, albeit potentially profitable speculation that is motivated by the belief that some such scenario lies at the basis of most Classic works. To legislate speculation, however, may seem unnecessarily binding, if not simply embarrassing, to the structuralist, who is of course welcome to move on to the beginning of Section II of the analysis. But to the humanist for whom music is the product of human volition, such a step represents, at worst, an indulgence of his or her fantasy, and, at best, an opportunity to dip into other semiotic systems, societal structures, and specific historical events for traces of musical patterning. Plots, then, are fluid propositions arising mainly, but not exclusively, out of a reading of referential signifiers.

2. STRUCTURAL RHYTHM

If the leap from the T1–T2–T3...TN succession to a verbally mediated plot seems somewhat abrupt (especially since the leap involves crossing the boundaries of different semiotic systems), we may turn the procedure "inward" toward a purely musical "plot," describable as a structural rhythm (SR). The SR for any M is a fluidly conceived, intramusical process that represents the end result of stripping T's of referentiality and pursuing their purely musical attributes or essences. SR is neutral so far as dimensional specificity is concerned, but it often assumes the form of a rhythmic succession or flow, which is in turn describable by means of a metaphor such as the shift from instability to stability and back again. The pursuit of a deeper-level, nonreferential process may be conceptualized as a search for an answer to the question "what is the essence (E) of each individual T?" Methodologically, we investigate each T, invoking Jauss's notion of a "generic dominant" to determine its invariable elements. E's include a rhythm, a procedure, a melodic progression, a cadence, and so on. From this list of elements we find a guiding idea, which often turns out to be a lowest common denominator. Thus, the succession of E's may be subject to the same constraints as the succession of T's, only on a lower, or micro-level. The point of this exercise is to switch from a consideration of the associational nature of expressivity and reference to the morphology of expression. For just as P provides a way into the limits of expression, so SR attempts to concretize the musical substance enshrined in topics. What emerges is a fluidly defined sense of movement, often most accessible through rhythm (hence the term "structural rhythm").

3. BEYOND EXPRESSION

With the attainment of a (verbal) P and a (musical) SR, the essential analytical enterprise deriving from T's ends. P and SR can, of course, be compared for significant coincidence, but by now the level of abstraction is so great that the results are not particularly meaningful to the listener, although they may be of interest to the theorist. The most severe limitation of an analysis following T's is that expression has no syntax. The gaps that were left after the identification of topics point to the need to engage with a dimension of M in which the temporal element, undoubtedly music's most fundamental attribute, occupies center stage.

II

A. The Universe of Structure (US)

1. We accept as suggestive, but not as binding, the generic identity of M. To recognize, for example, that M is the first movement of a string quartet is to accept the (conventional) potential for signification inherent in an ensemble of four stringed instruments playing together. To recognize further that Classic first movements are usually in sonata form, or to make the specific observation that M is in sonata form, is to establish more specific constraints for interpreting M. Thus, the broad harmonic plan, I–V X–I, establishes the principal constraint for sonata form—the assumption being that the form is defined primarily by harmony. More important for a semiotic interpretation are the rhetorical gestures normatively enshrined in the sonata-form model. For whereas the harmonic obligations of the form provide a lens through which we can view the music of the Classic period—and, as with all norms, the model only establishes a very general class of expectations—the attendant rhetorical procedures, although less formalized, provide a better view of the meaning of M. Thus, the staging in frankly dramatic terms of an exposition (complete with the undermining of an initial tonal premise), the prolongation of that conflict in the development, and the stylized resolution of the conflict in the recapitulation (complete with the appropriation by the first key of the second key's thematic material, thereby rounding off perfectly a rhetorical argument), demand an investigation of the rhetoric of M— not merely a labeling of key areas. To accept generic identity as suggestive but not binding further encourages a more flexible and dynamic view of genre, admitting, for example, the interplay of "lower-level" genres within a larger one. The potential for intersection between aria and concerto, for example, or between piano sonata and symphony is made explicit by this formulation.

2. Passing M though a generic grid, indeed through several lower-level generic grids, throws into relief certain internal procedures that define the structure of a Classic piece. For the interpretation of that structure, we propose a closed beginning–middle–ending paradigm. Without doubt, tonal music's supremely hierarchical quality is most usefully captured by an analytical method that provides both a representational and a conceptual means for conveying its various levels of hierarchic organization. In Schenkerian theory, for example, the prescriptions are essentially organicist, thus enabling, on one hand, an elucidation of the local levels of structure, while discouraging, on the other hand, a mechanical application to the larger levels of structure. Classic music thrives on contrast, juxtaposition, and conflict; to reduce away these essential ingredients of the drama of M is to remove something essential. The beginning–middle–ending paradigm, on the other hand, enshrines both an aspect of convention—the notion that there are

stylized approaches to beginning, continuing, and ending—and an aspect of function. It can therefore be shown to be compatible with the Schenkerian model, although it underplays—but does not (indeed, cannot)—ultimately reject the organicism of that model.

3. Beginning defines the tonality through a I–V progression that itself contains a closed period, middle is premised on the absence of I, and ending symmetrically resolves the conflict initiated and prolonged by closing off the structure in the form of a V–I progression. The beginning–middle–ending model works on both local and larger levels of structure. The model may subsume the functions of an entire movement, for example, or of a single period, phrase, or subphrase. The beginning–middle–ending model does not operate within a strict hierarchy, however; that is, its hierarchic levels are not strictly recursive. Although we are at present unable to provide a strict formulation of the segmental levels on which beginning–middle–ending is operative, the model's conflation of order and function allows it to be flexibly invoked on several hierarchic levels. Although the paradigm does not reach a detailed level of harmonic syntax or voice-leading, it indirectly subsumes their functions. For example, ending, defined by V–I, may be given a $\hat{2}$–$\hat{1}$ melodic profile, but the latter is an idiomatic progression belonging to a paradigm that includes $\hat{7}$–$\hat{8}$, $\hat{4}$–$\hat{3}$, $\hat{2}$–$\hat{3}$, $\hat{3}$–$\hat{3}$, and so on. Of greater consequence for the development of a semiotic interpretation of M is the possibility of detaching the elements of the beginning–middle–ending model. This means that the composer can play with their functions. To stress ending at the beginning of a piece, for example, is to invert expectations—or rather, to establish a different set of expectations from normative ones. A corollary of this adoption of the beginning-middle-ending paradigm, rather than, say, a Schenkerian *Ursatz,* is the elevation of local discontinuities and miniature wholes into prominence. This does not deny the significance of long-term connections, however. The shift in emphasis is motivated by a desire to get at the palpable surface drama of Classic music—drama that tends to be lost when the connective constraints prescribed by the *Ursatz* are indiscriminately applied. One final consequence of the use of the beginning–middle–ending model is the possibility of reading its elements as topics—not referential topics or T's, but functional topics providing clues to specific locations within the work's temporal structure.

III

A. The Interaction between Structure and Expression

1. INTEROVERSIVE VERSUS EXTROVERSIVE SEMIOSIS

In order to integrate the analytical results obtained from expression and structure, we may reformulate the dichotomies of "Defining the Fields of Investigation"(Section I) in terms of introversive and extroversive semiosis (after Jakobson). Introversive semiosis denotes internal, intramusical reference, both backward and forward, retrospective and prospective, while extroversive semiosis denotes external, extramusical, referential connection. Analysis of harmonic relations, for example, or of aspects of rhythm and phrase structure, point to the domain of introversive semiosis. This is the stuff of music, enabling an explication of structure and syntax. By contrast, anything that takes us outside the domain of the piece is extroversive. A reference to sensibility is a reference to an abstracted form of a previous historical style, the style itself describable as "external" to the piece. UT may therefore be provisionally described as pointing to the dimension of extroversive semiosis, with the important qualification that this set is, in itself, extremely heterogenous. But insofar as T's take their authority from a shared commonality—the fact that there is nothing like a "unique topic"—the label may be defended. Thus, to mention topic in these terms is necessarily to go beyond the bounds of a single piece. This particular interpretation of Jakobson's terms obscures the "external" aspects of US and the "internal" aspects of UT—both of which are considered presently.

2. INTROVERSIVE-EXTROVERSIVE SEMIOSIS: A FALSE DICHOTOMY

Jakobson's claim that in music introversive semiosis predominates over extroversive semiosis is perhaps most meaningful in the context of a comparison of various semiotic systems (such as when music is set against literature, for example, where it emerges that the referential aspects of language do not find a ready equivalent in music). However, in adapting the dichotomy for the present use, we cannot propagate such a generalization. M is analyzable with respect to the two processes of semiosis. Their interaction may prove that one predominates over the other, but such a condition is piece-specific. Sometimes there may be a precarious balance between these two modes of signification. More practically, one may compare the articulation of T's with the articulation of the beginning –middle–ending paradigm. It could be shown that, in general, T's give profile to the elements of syntax and structure. On the other hand, the situation may be reversed—or at least challenged. These are specific stylistic findings that emerge from the semiotic analysis.

   As useful as it is for conceptualizing various aspects of meaning in Classic music, the introversive-extroversive interplay represents something of a false dichotomy. Just as the defining elements of UT involve aspects of introversive semiosis, so elements of US involve aspects of extroversive semiosis. To elaborate: T's assume their primal identity within a relational structure in which they are perceived as music-semiotic objects. The reference to historical styles or dances, for example, identifies only the origin of these gestures. Their adaptation to a musical context thus entails a transformation into music of what is not explicitly musical. T's therefore embody aspects of both introversive and extroversive semiosis. Similarly, aspects of structure are not completely devoid of expressive capability. In harmonic terms, an implicit recognition is often made of the elements of tension and resolution, thereby hinting at a potential expressive dimension. In Schenker's interrupted structure $\hat{3}–\hat{2}$, $\hat{3}–\hat{2}–\hat{1}$, for example, the failure of the first $\hat{2}$ immediately to reach $\hat{1}$ may be read normatively as a tension-creating event. Moreover, the descriptive medium of the principal elements of introversive semiosis is, like that of T, a relational one. A semiotic theory therefore aims to integrate the two processes, not necessarily to effect a reconciliation between them.

B. The Notion of Play

Play denotes the interaction among constituent processes both within a single domain and between different domains. By restricting the notion to only two dimensions, topic and harmony, we may investigate the essences of each dimension by adopting a reductive and generative approach to topic (extroversive semiosis) and harmony (introversive semiosis), respectively. The reductive process ultimately assumes an intramusical form in passing from concept to realization, while the generative form, conceptualized as motion from a relational deep structure to a manifestly expressive, historically unique, stylistic surface fails to generate an explicit musical surface. But it is precisely where the two processes overlap, a region described as the "region of play," that a semiotic interpretation reaps its richest harvest. The notion of play describes not the broad and inevitable interaction between topic and harmony but, more specifically, the activity at the moment of break or rupture in each mode's process of self-definition. Introversive semiosis strives for uniqueness by attempting to reconstitute itself into a specific musical surface, while extroversive semiosis systematically deprives itself of that very uniqueness.

IV

A. The Medium of Analytical Discourse

1. As with all semiotic analyses of nonlinguistic systems, we fall back on the individuation of language for expressing this element of play. The musical processes unearthed in Section II point to, but do not fully express, the meaning of the piece. That meaning must be given partly in verbal language. Typically, it leads to the adoption of a metaphor for the piece. More substantively, that metaphor is grounded on what must now be treated as the inescapable condition of any expressive structure: the noncoincidence between dimensional processes. Thus, topics may originate and terminate at moments different from the major points of articulation of the beginning–middle–ending paradigm. Within the latter, melodic and harmonic processes are under no obligation to travel *pari passu*.

2. By accepting the metaphorical or symbolic status of the outcome of a semiotic analysis, we are able to assess further the role of words in music analysis. So long as concepts are attached to language, any thinking about music necessarily involves language. The communication of analytical insights is therefore primarily a linguistic activity—but it is more than that. Where analysis has recourse to music notation—as in Schenkerian graphs—the metalinguistic status of the analysis must be understood not as the expression of an idea "in" music, but as the expression of a (necessarily) verbal idea in a notation that bears an iconic relation to the object-language. To depict a neighbor-note is not to proceed from music to music, but to proceed from an observed phenomenon, through a process of contemplation, to the representation of what is observed or apprehended. The Schenkerian graphs that are used to convey a synchronic view of M must be understood as repositories of primarily linguistic information about musical structure.

EIGHT

EPILOGUE: A SEMIOTIC INTERPRETATION OF ROMANTIC MUSIC

I

THE VIEW of a synchronic Classic style, which has been treated as an axiom in the foregoing pages, is of course a simplification of historical reality. As more than one commentator has pointed out, our arbitrarily imposed chronological limits, 1770–1830, are exactly that: arbitrary. The Classic style did not die in 1830; nor was there an inaugural ceremony for Romanticism in the same year. And yet the opposition between Classic and Romantic persists among music historians. The implied separateness from Classicism, however fragile a concept, appears to be a necessary aid to historical understanding.[1]

What exactly is the nature of the continuities and discontinuities between Classic and Romantic music? It is the aim of this brief concluding chapter to speculate on the answer to this question within the theoretical confines established in Chapters 2 and 3. We shall test the relevance of concepts of introversive/extroversive semiosis and their analogical equivalents. Are there topics in Romantic music—and, if so, do they differ from those in Classic music? What sorts of compositional attitudes underlie the disposition of the beginning–middle–ending paradigm in a Romantic work?

II

An attractive opposition between Classicism and Romanticism develops from the relative sameness or uniformity of the surface of Classic music, as distinct from the evident diversity and pluralism of Romantic music. Furthermore, the architectonic security of works in sonata form appears contradictory, both in spirit and intent, to the formal insecurities of, for example, the nineteenth-century tone poem. The claim of a universal eighteenth-century language, itself a product of an Enlightenment rationalism, is then conveniently opposed to the multiple voices of Romanticism; the latter apparently speak as individuals, rather than as representatives of particular schools, societies, or ideological groups. And so the opposition between Classicism and Romanticism can be conveniently summarized in a number of dualistic metaphors whose semantic fields intersect in significant ways, but that ultimately remain distinct: an emphasis on structure in Classic music is opposed to an emphasis on expression in Romantic music, purely musical meanings in Classic music are contrasted with extramusical meanings in Romantic music, autonomy in the Classic style is opposed to nonautonomy in Romantic music, abstract tendencies in Classic music are opposed to concrete ones in Romantic music, and Classicism's public language is opposed to Romanticism's private discourses.[2]

The first step toward developing a semiotic interpretation of Romantic music is to begin to

---

[1] Three recent titles are Carl Dahlhaus, *Between Romanticism and Modernism: Four Studies in the Later Nineteenth Century*, Leon Plantinga, *Romantic Music: A History of Musical Style in Nineteenth-Century Europe*, and Arnold Whittall, *Romantic Music: A Concise History from Schubert to Sibelius*.

[2] For further discussion of similar or analogous oppositions between Classicism and Romanticism, see Meyer, "Exploiting Limits" and Subotnik, "The Cultural Message of Musical Semiology."

undermine these oppositions. Consider, for example, the public-private opposition. The following statement by Subotnik captures a familiar claim for ready intelligibility in Classic music, without the props of the extramusical, as opposed to the mediated intelligibility of the Romantic work: "Classicism aimed at a high ideal of human universality, in which all rational structures would be self-evident without recourse to a supplementary knowledge of particular individuals, circumstances, or cultures."[3]

Yet the technical procedures of Classic composers are replete with private, divisive meaning. The opposition between connoisseurs and amateurs that is frequently invoked in discussions of the reception of Classic music threatens any claims for universality. The notion of topic, which calls for degrees of intertextual competence, works paradoxically: to enhance, on one hand, a global, self-evident musical intention while, on the other hand, undermining that intention by making certain meanings accessible only to those "in the know." One thinks, for example, of the private "jokes" in Haydn's string quartets—jokes whose appreciation demands "recourse to... supplementary knowledge of particular individuals, circumstances, or cultures." Again, Haydn took advantage of the élite private circumstances of Esterhazy in order to project a public voice, a cosmopolitan musical language understood elsewhere in eighteenth-century Europe.

A parallel dialectic is evident in Romantic music. The private codes of Schumann, Liszt, and Wagner seem to close off the outer world and forge an internal, self-sustaining discourse. But the grandiose utterances of these composers, which seem to acknowledge a self-evident meaning based on powerful analogies between musical expressivity and the expressive structures of the human mind, are decidedly outgoing or universal in intent. The paradox of Mahler is another case in point. His unabashedly public angle plays on the listener's familiarity with various topics including marches, ländler, bugle-calls, chorales, and so on; yet that same compositional voice contrasts with, or sometimes merges into, an extremely personal and—some might claim—autobiographical one.

Yet another instructive contradiction is the case of Beethoven. Vincent d'Indy's still-useful model for the composer's stylistic development, Imitation–Externalization–Reflection, carries a normative opposition between private and public. To imitate is to accept an external, usually public code by using it. But to use it is necessarily to alter it, to stamp the code with one's personal identity. Externalization implies, on one hand, a more direct public voice, and on the other, the suspension or transcendence of previous constraints. And Reflection implies introspection, a retreat into a private world. And yet the results of this introspection remain inescapably public because of the musical content that provides the medium for reflection.

Again, consider the demonstrations of syntactical coherence in the music of eighteenth- and ninteenth-century composers by Schenker and his disciples. Here, the synchronic view of the tonal language requires the analyst to suspend surface dissimilarities and concentrate on underlying continuities. Thus, in a collection such as the *Five Graphic Music Analyses*, important strategic parallels are shown among works by Bach, Haydn, and Chopin, composers belonging ostensibly to three different historical eras.[4] While it is possible to spot differences and perhaps to develop a theory of opposition, it is equally possible—even desirable—to suspend those temporal changes and support a theory of sameness.

It would not be an exaggeration to claim, even on the basis of these few examples, that for every trend within and between Classic and Romantic musics there is an opposite trend. One way of

[3] Subotnik, "On Grounding Chopin," 116.
[4] Schenker, *Five Graphic Musical Analyses*.

concretizing these continuities and discontinuities is to invoke notions of introversive and extroversive semiosis. While a superficial assessment might lead one to posit introversive and extroversive tendencies for Classic and Romantic music respectively (the claim being one of autonomy for Classic music and the absence thereof for Romantic music), such an assessment will not withstand careful scrutiny. The decisive differences between Romantic and Classic musics stem from the pattern of *weighting* within the individual sets of signs. But there can be no simple formula for determining the nature of this weighting.

III

Topics abound in the music of Romantic composers. The category "march," for example, is to be found in the instrumental music of practically every great composer—several movements from Beethoven's late string quartets, Berlioz's *Symphonie Fantastique*, numerous works from Schumann's piano cycles, Liszt's *Les Preludes*, various passages from Wagner's operas and music dramas, and many movements from Bruckner's Symphonies. Mahler, the march composer *par excellence*, offers a wide choice among both instrumental and vocal works, including the funeral marches of the Second and Fifth Symphonies, the great march songs like "Revelge" and "Der Tambourgesell," and the interplay between different high- and low-style marches in the first movement of the Third. Consider another topic, such as "singing style," whose affinities with aria make it eminently suitable for analyzing the music of an age that celebrated melodic distinctiveness. The singing quality of many of Chopin's Nocturnes, itself indebted to Italian opera, of Mendelssohn's *Lieder öhne Wörte*, and of Bruckner's glorious Adagios: all these are usefully approached via the concept of singing style. Similarly, the nominally disruptive topic "Sturm und Drang" resonates readily with the essential instability of Romantic harmony, while the broken rhetoric and interrupted continuity epitomized in the sensibility style find ready parallels in numerous instrumental recitatives in Romantic music. The list is endless.

Endless, but valuable? The major problem with a straightforward transfer of eighteenth-century topics to Romantic music is what may be described as a dislocation of the signifier from the signifed. The various arbitrary labels that are applied to topics and drawn from eighteenthth-century historiography seem increasingly less relevant when applied to the socio-historical context of Romantic music. It appears, therefore, that while the *morphology* of various topics is retained by Romantic composers, their conventional association is displaced. Thus, one way of describing the Classic-Romantic relationship is in terms of a morphological continuity and a referential discontinuity. Of course, this displacement is already implicit within the bounds of the Classic style; Romanticism merely exaggerates that tendency.

We may also speak of a transformation of sign into symbol. Despite our earlier comments about the comparable oppositions within Classic and Romantic musics, there is an important strand in Romantic music that, while not new, nonetheless assumes increasing importance in characterizing the musical surface. Musical symbols, such as Schumann's league of composers, Wagner's leitmotifs, and Mahler's programs all challenge the universality of the sign by questioning the self-evident nature of the signified. One needs to consult a different kind of lexicon, itself a product of various biographical sources, or simply legendary titles or subtitles, in order to get at the meaning of the sign. The sign thus assumes symbolic status. Facile generalizations about Romanticism's interrelatedness with "life," its attack on autonomy, and its widening of the bounds of the work of art need to be carefully considered in light of this semiotic transformation. Whereas eighteenth-century music defamiliarizes "ordinary" materials such as fanfares, hunt-calls, brilliant-style effects, and so on, therefore making them properly and self-consciously artistic, Romantic music, without abandoning this gesture, often prefers a break with the outside world by entering into private, biographical realms in which the cryptic sign holds the key to meaning in the musical work.

The second group of signs, embodying aspects of introversive semiosis, points to a similar set of continuities and discontinuities between Classicism and Romanticism. We have already seen examples of play in the disposition of the beginning–middle–ending paradigm in Classic music. Romantic music retains and exaggerates this play in respect to both the elements themselves and their actual disposition. First, the integrity of the beginning–middle–ending model is brought under attack, with the result that its three component parts are no longer held to be in a necessary syntactical relationship. For example, the model could be conceptually truncated to beginning–middle or middle–ending without any loss of meaning. Extensive permutation is also possible, so that beginning–middle-ending could become ending–beginning–middle, middle–ending–beginning, and so on. The usefulness of the paradigm, however, seems strained when it is subject to so much play, and yet an appreciation of deviation is not possible in the absence of some such postulated norm. For example, it is often remarked that many Romantic works, such as Schumann's Piano Fantasy Op. 17, begin *in medias res*—in our terms, with the component middle. Which "res," one might ask immediately, and why "medias"? It soon emerges that the metaphor is typically grounded on the assumption that a piece must begin on or in the tonic, and therefore that beginning on the dominant implies beginning in the middle of a process that has already begun. But this is a highly strained norm. If the apparently normative tonic beginning of Classic music is being consulted, then the metaphor may be defended; but it is equally likely that the Classic protocol is irrelevant to the Romantic composer.

A second way in which the beginning–middle–ending model is utilized by Romantic composers is by the weighting of individual components. The agents of this weighting are rhetorical, and include duration, proportion, rhythm, and dynamics. On this point, too, we carry over an unstable norm from Classic music, and read Romantic music against it like a grid. It is quite likely that the weighting within the paradigm will itself produce new paradigms.

By weighting and reordering its components, Romantic music reduces the explanatory power of the beginning–middle–ending model to the identification of position within a temporal whole (or fragment), rather than an indication of the function of those temporal segments. Beginnings are those things that come first, middles follow beginnings, and endings complete the succession. Onto this natural order is grafted the true functions of the musical segments themselves, so that a natural-order beginning may, in fact, appear as a functional ending, a natural-order middle as a functional beginning, and so on. These rich oppositions are not, of course absent from Classic music; they are merely highlighted in Romantic music.

Two brief examples of the sense that the beginning–middle–ending paradigm projects may be mentioned. First, the theme of Brahms's "Variations on a Theme of Schumann" Op. 9 begins with an expanded cadence, a normative ending. This casts a shadow over the rest of the work, giving it a quality of closing. It is against the considerable weight of this sense of an ending that the piece unfolds its own beginning, middle, and end. It is almost as if one were swimming upstream rather than downstream. Second, in many of Schubert's late piano sonatas, there appears to be a problem of closure, of just when to say farewell. The oft-used phrase "heavenly lengths" implies that generic signs of closure are often indicated, and that the realization of their implications are often postponed, but not ultimately denied. The problematic of closure, which may well have sociohistorical resonances in the nineteenth century, challenges the integrity of the beginning–middle–ending model.

One final pointer to the compositional dynamic of Romantic music is the opposition between periodicity, with its implication of recurrence or regularity, and the claims of a narrative or dynamic curve—an ascent to a tensional high point and a descent therefrom.[5] Although this contour is implicit in the three-phase beginning–middle–ending model of Classic music, it receives greater foreground emphasis in Romantic music. The formal imperative of Romantic music is the product of the competing and mutually contradictory claims of a periodicity that seeks a normative regularity in its grouping structure and a climactic process that eschews any such process.

Example 8.1 quotes the opening phrase from the middle movement of Beethoven's Piano Sonata in C Major, Op. 7 to show how its compositional dynamic derives from the competing claims of grouping and narrative structure. Although this sonata dates from 1796–1797 and is therefore only nominally a "Classic" piece, it is cited here not as an example of "Romantic music"

Example 8.1. Beethoven, Piano Sonata in E♭ Major, Op. 7—
Second Movement, measures 1–8

but simply as a musical phrase that embodies an aspect of Romantic utterance. A crude distribution of Classic and Romantic allegiances might assign the grouping structure to the former and the high-point structure to the latter. According to the grouping structure, the phrase is, first of all, an eight-measure period. Although there is an implicit 4 + 4 segmentation, the continuity between measures 4 and 5 greatly undermines the sense of this segmentation. Yet it would not be hard to construct a foil for the progression in these measures and argue that Beethoven exploits the listener's expectation of a half cadence in measure 4. The 4 + 4 segmentation is therefore both present and absent, manifest and latent. On the next level of grouping, it is no longer possible to divide measures 5–8, whereas measures 1–4 may be grouped as 2 + 2 (with the caveats given above in mind), and further as 1 + 1 + 2. But the ambivalent status of measure 4 promotes other plausible segmentations: 3 + 5, 1 + 1 + 1 + 5, 2 + 1 + 5, and so on.

These multiple meanings are mirrored in the disposition of the beginning–middle–ending paradigm on at least four levels (see Example 8.2). The largest of these, encompassing the eight-measure level, includes a beginning, a middle, and an ending. On the next level, there is an interrupted structure in which beginning does not go straight on to an ending, but instead returns to a second beginning before concluding. Level 2 describes one complete paradigm—two successive beginnings and an ending. Finally, the most local level, Level 1, includes a beginning, two endings, a complete beginning–middle–ending, and a middle. While retaining something of the external periodic structure of Classic music, this period also includes many small universes, whose potential independence points to one of the central traits of Romantic music.

Working against this tendency toward small wholes is the global gesture of an ascent to a high

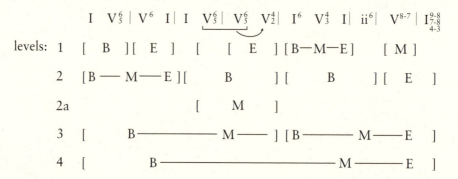

Example 8.2. Beginnings, middles, and endings in Beethoven's Piano Sonata in E♭ Major, Op. 7—Second Movement, measures 1–8

point or turning point on the downbeat of measure 6, and a descent therefrom. This moment is the most dissonant in the phrase, it bears (by implication) the highest dynamic level, it occurs about two-thirds of the way through the phrase, and it offers a rhetorically memorable recomposition of the head tone, E. It constitutes the most decisive turning point in the phrase.

It is the competing claims of these diverse tendencies that endow this phrase with its unique sense. So, even within the realm of introversive semiosis (putting aside the possible implications of this movement's reference to a sarabande), we note an irreducible conflict between competing tendencies in the music. This is one of Romanticism's essences.

IV

We leave the last word to the musical poet *par excellence* of early Romanticism, Robert Schumann. Example 8.3 quotes the concluding piece from the collection *Kinderszenen*—a work that may serve as a model of Romantic expression and structure. In isolating it from context, we do violence to the collection's additive sense; we also underplay the feeling of repose that the piece brings after the cumulative effect of the twelve preceding character pieces. But we can still capture something of the style and spirit of Romanticism in this excerpt.

The fact that this, like preceding pieces in the cycle, bears a title ("Der Dichter spricht") points to one of the central concerns of Romanticism: devising a bridge between the world of words and the world of sound. The poet speaks with dignity, with some hesitation, but without external obligation. Both listener and performer accept the suggestiveness of the title. But the code is decidedly private. There are as many poets as there are composers, and each speaks a different language. Even Schumann speaks differently depending on the occasion. To stress this "one-offness" of the title is to stress its resistance to generalization without underplaying its communicative potential. The particular and the general are thus locked in a genuine dialectic.

It is in the realization of the poetic idea that Schumann makes the most explicit use of a public code. The piece begins as a chorale, which carries implications of archaicness, age, authority, and

Example 8.3. Schumann, "Der Dichter spricht," from *Kinderszenen*

a certain purity. In measures 9–10, the first three melodic notes of the chorale are transformed into an arabesque—a hesitant arabesque, on the verge of renouncing its own capability for forward movement. Next comes recitative (measure 12), the poet's natural language. Our soliloquizing poet speaks deliberately, but with restrained passion, rising in measure 12 to the highest point of the piece (G^2). Then the line of discourse is abandoned, without warning and without apology, as the chorale returns in measure 13. This leads to a cadence on the tonic, G major—the first such cadence in the entire piece. Only with its completion do we gain some sense of a structure whose highly fragmentary character forces the listener to engage directly with various levels and kinds of temporality, a "polyphony of periodic forms," to borrow Lawrence Kramer's phrase.[6]

[5] See my "Structural 'Highpoints' in Schumann's Dichterliebe" for further discussion of this organizing shape.
[6] Kramer, *Music and Poetry*, 7.

The sequence of topics, chorale–arabesque–recitative–chorale, does not command a single temporal spectrum; it has no syntax. What it succeeds in doing is loading the associative dimension in such a way that listener and performer are invited—indeed, compelled—to construct a metaphorical scenario or plot for the piece.   Unlike the neat plots of Classicism, however, those of Romanticism could be fragmentary and internally contradictory, without the slightest loss of expressive power. There is thus something decidedly improvisatory about the poet's utterance, evident most clearly in measures 9–12. The meditation on the head of the chorale theme (measures 9–10), repeated in an inexact sequence (measures 11–12), and then abandoned: this is stylized indecision of the sort that lies at the heart of Schumann's Romanticism. It calls to mind the reflective and retrospective quality of some of Schumann's final moments (such as the close of the *Dichterliebe* cycle), and highlights not the intertextual premises of the work, but rather the extraordinary weight of an unavoidable past. But this is no routine summary of a forgotten past; the poet now proclaims an enticing liberty by overturning many aspects of Classical syntax. In measures 7–8, for example, a normative close on the tonic, which might have provided an "answer" to the first four measures, is replaced by a cadence on the supertonic. The essence of the phrase therefore resides in the contradiction between a gestural or morphological exterior (the Classical eight-measure phrase) and an apparently noncausal relationship between its two four-measure segments.

In measure 12, resolution of the diminished-seventh harmony is initially postponed, and eventually forgotten. The otherworldly recitative—the height of the poet's fantasy—simply evaporates upon reaching a high point (Schumann has even added a double bar here to emphasize the separateness of thought and idea). And finally, in measures 21–25 the music simply leads were it wills, challenging but never completely eroding the listener's capacity for synoptic comprehension.

There is considerable play with the elements of the beginning–middle–ending paradigm as well. On the broadest level, the piece enacts an ending, for it is open until the end. Its beginning suggests a middle, and this floating sense persists throughout, challenged only occasionally by local cadences that suggest ending (measures 8 and 20). In this sense, the piece is open until the very last chord, possibly even beyond, and it is this ultimate deferral that enhances its function in the *Kinderszenen* collection as a whole.

The idea that the piece leads not necessarily to an implied goal, but rather to a point of arrival whose appropriateness is only retrospectively perceived, is suggestive for considerations of narrative. Just as the discussion in Chapter 2 drew attention to the dramatic and possibly narrative aspects of topical unfolding, so may we speak of drama here too, albeit on a small scale. But the crucial difference is that whereas Mozart's topics do not command the essence of the narrative, Schumann's appear almost to acquire that function by default. So, in spite of token gestures to the contrary—such as the four-measure phrase that begins the piece—the foundations of periodicity and harmony fail to assume the same constructive function in Schumann that they do in Mozart and Haydn. We accept a periodic structure that appears to concretize the present at the expense of the past. At the same time, its ontology is apprehended more in retrospect than in prospect. But this should not lead us to the conclusion that only the present matters in Romanticism, for the strategy of this lived present is erected upon a felt past of Classical syntax— felt, whether or not actually present.

And thereby hangs a long tale. Romanticism dissolves the props of a semiotic interpretation without ever renouncing their function. It blurs their visibility, questions their validity, and extends their functional domain, but remains inextricably linked to the fundaments of Classicism. It is in this sense that Romanticism remains inescapably paradoxical and profoundly parasitic. By merely rearranging the weights attached to the various components of Classicism, Romanticism retains its inevitable dialectic with what is only an apparent uniformity.

REFERENCES

Abbate, Carolyn. "What the Sorcerer Said." *19th-Century Music* 12 (1989): 221–30.

Abraham, Gerald, ed. *The Age of Beethoven* Vol. 7, *The New Oxford History of Music*. London: Oxford University Press, 1982.

Abrams, M. H. *A Glossary of Literary Terms*. 4th ed. New York: Holt, Rinehart and Winston, 1981.

Actes du 1er Congrès Internationale de Semiotique. Pesaro, Italy: Centro di Iniziativa Cuturale, 1975.

Adler, Guido. *Der Stil in der Musik*. Leipzig: Breitkopf and Härtel, 1911. 2d ed. 1929.

Agawu, V. Kofi. "Structural 'Highpoints' in Schumann's *Dichterliebe*." *Music Analysis* 3 (1984): 159–80.

———. "Concepts of Closure and Chopin's Opus 28." *Music Theory Spectrum* 9 (1987): 1–17.

———. "Schenkerian Notation in Concept and Practice." *Music Analysis* 8 (1989): 275–301

Allanbrook, Wye Jamison. *Rhythmic Gesture in Mozart: Le Nozze di Figaro and Don Giovanni*. Chicago: University of Chicago Press, 1983.

Anderson, Emily, ed. *The Letters of Mozart and His Family*. 3d ed. London: Macmillan, 1985.

Baker, Nancy, and Roger Scruton. "Expression." In *The New Grove Dictionary of Music and Musicians*, edited by Stanley Sadie, Vol. 6, 324–32. London: Macmillan, 1980.

Bard, Raimund. *Untersuchungen zur motivischen Arbeit in Haydns sinfonischem Spätwerk*. Kassel: Bärenreiter, 1982.

Baroni, Mario. "The Concept of Musical Grammar." *Music Analysis* 2 (1983): 175–208.

Barthes, Roland. "Myth Today." In *Mythologies*. Selected and translated from the French by Annette Lavers. New York: Hill and Wang, 1972.

Benjamin, William. "Schenker's Theory and the Future of Music." *Journal of Music Theory* 25 (1981): 155–73.

Bent, Ian. *Analysis*. London: Macmillan, 1987.

———. "The 'Compositional Process' in Music Theory 1713–1850." *Music Analysis* 3 (1984): 29–55.

Benveniste, Émile. "The Semiology of Language." *Semiotica*. Special Supplement (1981): 5–23. Reprinted in *Semiotics: An Introductory Reader,* edited by Robert E. Innis, 228–46. Bloomington: Indiana University Press, 1985.

Bernard, Jonathan. "On Densité 21.5: A Response to Nattiez." *Music Analysis* 5 (1986): 207–31.

Berry, Wallace. *Structural Functions in Music*. Englewood Cliffs, N.J.: Prentice-Hall, 1976. Reprint. New York: Dover, 1987.

Blume, Friedrich. *Classic and Romantic Music*. London: Faber, 1970.

Boilès, Charles. "Processes of Musical Semiosis." *Yearbook for Traditional Music* 14 (1982): 24–44.

Brandenburg, Sieghard. "The Historical Background to the 'Heiliger Dankgesang' in Beethoven's A Minor Quartet." In *Beethoven Studies* 3, edited by Alan Tyson, 161–91. Cambridge: Cambridge University Press, 1982.

Brodbeck, David, and John Platoff. "Dissociation and Integration: The First Movement of Beethoven's Opus 130." *19th-Century Music* 7 (1983): 149–62.

Buelow, George. "The Concept of 'Melodielehre': A Key to Classic Style." *Mozart-Jahrbuch* (1978–1979): 182–95.

———. "Rhetoric and Music." In *The New Grove Dictionary of Music and Musicians*, Vol. 15, 793–803.

Burkhart, Charles. "Schenker's 'Motivic Parallelisms'." *Journal of Music Theory* 22 (1978): 145–75.

Burmeister, Joachim. *Musica Poetica*. Rostock, 1601.

Burney, Charles. *The Present Music in France and Italy*. London, 1773.

Castil-Blaze, François Hénri Joseph. *Dictionnaire de musique moderne*. Paris: Au magasin de musique de la Lyre moderne, 1821.

Charlton, David. "Orchestra and Image in the Late 18th Century." *Proceedings of the Royal Musical Association* 102 (1975–1976): 1–12.

Chatman, Seymour. "How Do We Establish New Codes of Verisimilitude?" In *The Sign in Music and Literature*, edited by Wendy Steiner, 26–38. Austin: University of Texas Press, 1978.

Churgin, Bathia. "Francesco Galeazzi's Description (1796) of Sonata Form." *Journal of the American Musicological Society* 21 (1968): 181–99.

Clarke, Eric. "Structure and Expression in Rhythmic Performance." In *Musical Structure and Cognition,* edited by Peter Howell, Ian Cross, and Robert West, 209–36. London: Academic Press, 1985.

Coker, Wilson. *Music and Meaning: A Theoretical Approach to Musical Aesthetics*. New York: Free Press, 1972.

Cone, Edward T. *Musical Form and Musical Performance*. New York: Norton, 1968.

———. "Beethoven's Experiments in Composition: The Late Bagatelles." In *Beethoven Studies* 2, edited by Alan Tyson, 84–105. London: Oxford University Press, 1977.

Cook, Nicholas. *A Guide to Musical Analysis*. London: Dent, 1987.

Cooke, Deryck. "The Unity of Beethoven's Late Quartets." *The Music Review* 24 (1963): 30–49.

Crotch, William. *Substance of Several Courses of Lectures on Music Read in the University of Oxford and in the Metropolis*. London: Longmann, Rees, Orma, Brown, and Green, 1831.

Curtius, Ernst Robert. *European Literature and the Latin Middle Ages*. Translated from the German by Willard R. Trask. New York: Harper Torchbooks, 1953.

Dahlhaus, Carl. "Harmony." In *The New Grove Dictionary of Music and Musicians* Vol. 8, 175–88.

———. *Between Romanticism and Modernism: Four Studies in the Later Nineteenth Century*. Translated from the German by Mary Whittall. Berkeley: University of California Press, 1980.

———. *Foundations of Music History*. Translated from the German by J. B. Robinson. Cambridge: Cambridge University Press, 1983.

Daube, Johann Friedrich. *Anleitung zur Erfindung der Melodie und ihrer Fortsetzung*. 2 vols. Vol. 1, Vienna: Schaumberg, 1979. Vol. 2, Vienna: Taubelz, 1798.

Dreyfus, Laurence. "J. S. Bach's Concerto Ritornellos and the Question of Invention." *The Musical Quarterly* (1986): 327–58.

———. "J. S. Bach and the Status of Genre: Problems of Style in the G Minor Sonata, BWV 1029." *Journal of Musicology* 5 (1987): 55–78.

Dunsby, Jonathan. Review of Nattiez, *Fondements d'une Sémiologie de la Musique, Perspectives of New Music* 15 (1977): 226–33.

———. "Editorial: A Hitch-Hiker's Guide to Semiotic Music Analysis." *Music Analysis* 1 (1982): 235–42.

———. "A Bagatelle on Beethoven's WoO 60." *Music Analysis* 3 (1984): 57–68.

Easthope, Antony. *Poetry as Discourse*. London: Methuen, 1983.

Eco, Umberto. *A Theory of Semiotics*. Bloomington: Indiana University Press, 1976.

Einstein, Alfred. *Mozart: His Character and Work*. Translated from the German by Arthur Mendel and Nathan Broder. New York: Oxford University Press, 1945.

Epstein, David. *Beyond Orpheus: Studies in Musical Structure*. Cambridge, Mass.: MIT Press, 1979.

Faltin, Peter. "Musikalische Syntax: Ein Beitrag zum Problem des musikalischen Sinngehaltes," *Archiv fur Musikwissenschaft* 34 (1977): 1–19.

———. "Musikalische Bedeutung: Grenzen und Möglichkeiten einer semiotischen Aesthetik." *International Review of the Aesthetics and Sociology of Music* 9 (1978): 5–33.

Finscher, Ludwig. *Studien zur Geschichte des Streichquartetts, 1: Die Entstehung des klassichen Streichquartetts: von den Vorformen zur Grundlegung durch Joseph Haydn.* Kassel: Bärenreiter, 1974.

Fischer, Wilhelm. "Zur Entwicklungsgeschichte des Wiener klassichen Stils," *Studien zur Musik Musikwissenschaft* 3 (1915): 24–84.

Forte, Allen, and Steven Gilbert. *Introduction to Schenkerian Analysis*. New York: Norton, 1982.

Galeazzi, Francesco. *Elementi teorico-pratici di musica*. Vol. 1, Rome: Cracas, 1791. Vol. 2, Rome:

Puccinelli, 1796.

Glauert, Amanda. "The Double Perspective in Beethoven's Opus 131." *19th-Century Music* 4 (1980–1981): 149–62.

Grout, Donald. *A History of Western Music*. 3d ed. with Claude V. Palisca. New York: Norton, 1980.

Hatten, Robert S. Review of Nattiez, *Fondements d'une Sémiologie de la Musique, Semiotica* 31 (1980): 139–55.

———. Review of Tarasti, *Myth and Music, Semiotica* 30 (1980): 345–58.

Hawkes, Terence. *Structuralism and Semiotics*. London: Methuen, 1977.

Heartz, Daniel. "Classical." In *The New Grove Dictionary of Music and Musicians*, Vol. 4, 449–54.

Ingarden, Roman. *The Work of Music and the Problem of Its Identity*. London: Macmillan, 1985.

Innis, Robert E. *Semiotics: An Introductory Anthology*. Bloomington: Indiana University Press, 1985.

Jakobson, Roman. "Language in Relation to Other Communication Systems." In *Selected Writings*, Vol. 2. The Hague: Mouton, 1971.

Jauss, Hans Robert. *Toward an Aesthetic of Reception*, trans. by Timothy Bahti. Minneapolis: University of Minnesota Press, 1982.

Keiler, Allan. "Bernstein's 'The Unanswered Question' and the Problem of Musical Competence." *Musical Quarterly* 64 (1978): 195–222.

———. "Two Views of Musical Semiotics." In *The Sign in Music and Literature*, 138–68.

———. "On Some Properties of Schenker's Pitch Derivations." *Music Perception* 1 (1983–1984): 200–228.

Kerman, Joseph. *The Beethoven Quartets*. New York: Alfred A. Knopf, 1967.

———. *Listen*. 3d edition. New York: Worth Publishers, 1972.

Kerman, Joseph, and Alan Tyson. *The New Grove Beethoven*. London: Macmillan, 1983.

Kirkendale, Warren. "The 'Great Fugue' Op. 133: Beethoven's 'Art of the Fugue.'" *Acta Musicologica* 35 (1963): 14–24.

Kivy, Peter. *The Corded Shell: Reflections on Musical Expression*. Princeton: Princeton University Press, 1980.

Koch, Heinrich Christoph. *Musikalisches Lexikon*. Frankfurt am Main: A. Hermann, 1802.

———. *Introductory Essay on Composition: The Mechanical Rules of Melody, Sections 3 and 4*, trans. and edited by Nancy Kovaleff Baker. New Haven: Yale University Press, 1983.

Kramer, Jonathan D. "Multiple and Non-Linear Time in Beethoven's opus 135." *Perspectives of New Music* 11 (1973): 122–45.

———. "Beginnings and Endings in Western Art Music." *Canadian Music Review* 3 (1982): 1–14.

Kramer, Lawrence. *Music and Poetry: The Nineteenth Century and After*. Berkeley: University of California Press, 1984.

Krebs, Harald. "Alternatives to Monotonality in Early Nineteenth-Century Music." *Journal of Music Theory* 25 (1981): 1–16.

La Rue, Jan. *Guidelines for Style Analysis*. New York: Norton, 1970.

Le Huray, Peter, and James Day. *Music and Aesthetics in the Eighteenth and Early-Nineteenth Centuries*. Cambridge: Cambridge University Press, 1981.

Lenneberg, Hans. "Johann Mattheson on Rhetoric and Affect." *Journal of Music Theory* 2 (1958): 47–84, 193–236.

Lerdahl, Fred, and Ray Jackendoff. *A Generative Theory of Tonal Music*. Cambridge, Mass.: MIT Press, 1983.

Lester, Joel. "Articulation of Tonal Structures as a Criterion for Analytic Choices." *Music Theory Spectrum* 1 (1979): 67–79.

Levy, Janet. "Gesture, Form and Syntax in Haydn's Music." In *Haydn Studies*, edited by J. Peter Larsen, H. Serwer, and J. Webster, 355–62. New York: Norton, 1981.

———. "Texture as a Sign in Classic and Early Romantic Music." *Journal of the American Musicological Society* 35 (1982): 482–531.

Lidov, David. "Nattiez's Semiotics of Music." *The Canadian Journal of Research in Semiotics* 5 (1978): 13–54.

———. "Musical and Verbal Semantics." *Semiotica* 31 (1980): 369–91

———. "The Allegretto of Beethoven's Seventh." *American Journal of Semiotics* 1 (1981): 141–66.

MacDonald, Hugh. "Fantasy and the Order in Beethoven's Phantasie op. 77." In *Modern Musical Scholarship*, edited by Edward Olleson. Stockfield, Northumberland: Oriel Press, 1978.

Marmontel, Jean François. "Mouvement du style." In *Élémens de littérature*. 6 vols. Paris: Née de la Rochelle, 1787.

Mason, Wilton. "Melodic Unity in Mozart's Piano Sonata K. 332." *Music Review* 22 (1961): 28–33.

Mattheson, Johann. *Der vollkommene Capellmeister*. Hamburg: Herold, 1739. Reprinted 1954. Translated from the German by Ernest C. Harriss. Ann Arbor, Mich.: UMI Research Press, 1981.

Maus, Fred. "Music as Drama." *Music Theory Spectrum* 10 (1988): 56–73.

McGrath, William. *Dionysian Art and Populist Politics in Austria*. New Haven: Yale University Press, 1974.

Meyer, Leonard. *Explaining Music*. Berkeley: University of California Press, 1973.

———. "Exploiting Limits: Creation, Archetypes, and Style Change," *Daedalus* 1980: 177–205.

Micznik, Vera. "Gesture as Sign: A Semiotic Interpretation of Berg's Opus 6, No. 1." *In Theory Only* 9 (1987): 19–35

Monelle, Raymond. "Symbolic Models in Music Aesthetics." *British Journal of Aesthetics* 19 (1979): 24–37.

Nägeli, Hans-Georg. *Vorlesungen über Musik mit Berücksichtigung der Dilettanten*. Stuttgart and Tubingen, 1826.

Nattiez, Jean-Jacques. *Fondements d'une Sémiologie de la Musique.* Paris: Union Générale, 1975.

———. "The Contribution of Musical Semiotics to the Semiotic Discussion in General." In *A Perfusion of Signs*, ed. Thomas A. Sebeok, 121–42. Bloomington: Indiana University Press, 1977.

———. "Varèse's 'Density 21.5': A Study in Semiological Analysis," *Music Analysis* 1 (1982): 243–340.

———. *Musicologie Générale et Sémiologie*. Paris: Bourgois, 1987.

Newcomb, Anthony. "Sound and Feeling." *Critical Inquiry* 10 (1984): 614–43.

———. "Schumann and Late Eighteenth-Century Narrative Strategies." *19th-Century Music* 11 (1987): 164–74.

Newman, Ernest. "Beethoven: The Last Phase." In *Testament of Music*. London: Alfred A. Knopf, 1977.

Newman, William S. *The Sonata in the Classic Era*. Chapel Hill, N.C.: University of North Carolina Press, 1963.

Noske, Frits. *The Signifier and the Signified: Studies in the Operas of Mozart and Verdi*. The Hague: Nijhoff, 1977.

———. Review of Nattiez, *Fondements d'une Sémiologie de la Musique*. *Ethnomusicology* 24 (1979): 144–48.

Osmond-Smith, David. "Music as Communication: Semiology or Morphology?" *International Review of Aesthetics and Musical Sociology* 2 (1971): 108–11.

Pauly, Reinhard G. *Music in the Classic Period*. 3d ed. Englewood Cliffs, N.J.: Prentice-Hall, 1973.

Pestelli, Giorgio. *The Age of Mozart and Beethoven*. Cambridge: Cambridge University Press, 1984.

Plantinga, Leon. *Romantic Music: A History of Musical Style in Nineteenth-Century Europe*. New York: Norton, 1984.

Powers, Harold. "Language Models and Music Analysis." *Ethnomusicology* 25 (1980): 1–60.

Quantz, Joachim Johann. *On Playing the Flute*, trans. from the German by Edward R. Reilly. 2d ed. New York: Schirmer Books, 1985.

Ratner, Leonard G. *Classic Music: Expression, Form, and Style*. New York: Schirmer Books, 1980.

Ratz, Erwin. *Einführung in die musikalische Formenlehre*. 2d ed. Vienna: Universal Edition, 1968.

Riezler, Walter. *Beethoven*, trans. from the German by G.D.H. Pidcock. New York: Vienna House, 1938.

Ringer, Alexander L. "The Chasse as a Musical Topic of the 18th Century." *Journal of the American Musicological Society* 6 (1953): 148–59.

Rosen, Charles. *The Classical Style*. London: Faber, 1971.

———. *Sonata Forms*. New York: Norton, 1980.

Rothgeb, John. "Design as a Key to Structure in Tonal Music." In *Readings in Schenker Analysis and Other Approaches*, edited by Maury Yeston, 72–93. New Haven: Yale University Press, 1977.

Rowell, Lewis. "The Creation of Audible Time." In *The Study of Time*, Vol. 4, edited by J. T. Fraser, N. Lawrence, and D. Park, 198–210. New York: Springer-Verlag, 1981.

Said, Edward. *Beginning: Intention and Method*. New York: Morningside, 1975.

Schenker, Heinrich. *Free Composition*, trans. and edited by Ernst Oster. New York: Longmann's, 1979.

———. *Five Graphic Musical Analyses*, edited by Felix Salzer. New York: Norton, 1969.

Schneider, Reinhard. *Semiotik der Musik: Darstellung und Kritik* Munich: Fink, 1980.

Scholes, Robert. *Semiotics and Interpretation*. New Haven: Yale Univeristy Press, 1982.

Schwartz, Judith. "Opening Themes in Opera Overtures of Johann Adolf Hasse: Some Aspects of Thematic Structural Evolution in the Eighteenth Century." In *A Musical Offering: Essays in Honor of Martin Bernstein*, edited by Edward H. Clinkscale and Claire Brook, 243–59. New York: Pendragon Press, 1977.

Scruton, Roger. Review of Nattiez, *Fondements d'une Sémiologie de la Musique*. *The Cambridge Review* 2 (June 1978). Reprinted as "The Semiology of Music" in *The Politics of Culture and Other Essays*, 75–79. Manchester: Carcanet Press, 1981.

———. *The Aesthetic Understanding*. London: Methuen, 1983.

Sisman, Elaine. "Small and Expanded Forms: Koch's Model and Haydn's Music." *The Musical Quarterly* 68 (1982): 444–75.

Solomon, Maynard. *Beethoven*. New York: Schirmer Books, 1977.

Somfai, László. "The London Revision of Haydn's Instrumental Style." *Proceedings of the Royal Musical Association* (1973–1974): 159–74.

———. "'Learned Style' in Two Late String Quartet Movements of Haydn." *Studia Musicologica* 28 (1986): 325–49.

Stopford, John. "Structuralism, Semiotics and Musicology." *British Journal of Aesthetics* 24 (1984): 129–37.

Subotnik, Rose Rosengard. "Adorno's Diagnosis of Beethoven's Late Style: Early Symptom of a Fatal Condition." *Journal of the American Musicological Society* 29 (1976): 249–75.

———. "The Cultural Message of Musical Semiology: Some Thoughts on Music, Language, and Criticism Since the Enlightenment." *Critical Inquiry* 4 (1978): 747–68.

———. Review of Nattiez, *Fondements d'une Sémiologie de la Musique*. *Journal of Aesthetics and Art Criticism* 35 (1976): 239–42.

———. "On Grounding Chopin." In *Music and Society: The Politics of Composition, Performance, and Reception*, edited by Susan McClary and Peter Leffert, 105–31. Cambridge: Cambridge University Press, 1987.

Sullivan, J.W.N. *Beethoven: His Spiritual Development*. New York: Alfred A. Knopf, 1927.

Sulzer, Johann Georg. *Allgemeine Theorie der schönen Künste*. 4 vols. 2d ed. Leipzig: M. G. Weidmann, 1792–1794.

Tarasti, Eero. *Myth and Music: A Semiotic Approach to the Aesthetics of Myth in Music, Especially That of Wagner, Sibelius and Stravinsky*. The Hague: Mouton, 1979.

Tovey, Donald Francis. *A Companion to Beethoven's Pianoforte Sonatas*. London: Associated Board, 1931.

———. "Some Aspects of Beethoven's Art Forms." In *Essays and Lectures on Music*. London: Oxford University Press, 1949.

Tunstall, Patricia. "Structuralism and Musicology: An Overview," *Current Musicology* (1979): 51–64

Türk, Daniel Gottlob. *School of Clavier Playing*, trans. from the German by Raymond H. Haggh. Lincoln: University of Nebraska Press, 1982.

Unger, Hans Heinrich. *Die Beziehungen zwischen Musik und Rhetorik im 16–18 Jahrhundert*. Würzburg,

1941. Reprint. Hildesheim: G. Olms, 1969.

Vogler, Georg Joseph. *Betrachtungen der Mannheimer Tonschule*. Mannheim, 1778, 2 vols. Reprint. New York: G. Olms, 1974.

Walker, Alan. *An Anatomy of Music Criticism*. London: Rockliff, 1966.

Wallace, Robin. *Beethoven's Critics: Aesthetic Dilemmas and Resolutions During the Composer's Lifetime*. Cambridge: Cambridge University Press, 1986.

Webster, James. "Sonata Form." in *The New Grove Dictionary of Music and Musicians*, Vol. 17, 497–508.

Whittall, Arnold. "Analysis as Performance." Paper read at the International Musicological Society Meeting, Bologna, 1987.

———. *Romantic Music: A Concise History from Schubert to Sibelius*. London: Thames and Hudson, 1987.

Wolf, Eugene K. *The Symphonies of Johann Stamitz: A Study in the Formation of the Classic Style*. Utrecht: Bohn, Scheltema, and Holkema, 1981.

INDEX

Abbate, Carolyn, 36n

Abraham, Gerald, 111, 125

Abrams, M. H., 35n

Adler, Guido, 5n

Adorno, Theodor, 126

Alberti bass, 31, 45

alla breve, 30, 31, 84, 87, 90, 101n, 114

alla zoppa, 87, 89

Allanbrook, Wye Jamison, 13, 30n, 33, 38n, 45n, 48, 56, 90n, 98n

amoroso, 30, 48

analysis: ad hoc reasoning in, 113, 127; descriptive and/or intuitive adequacy of, 19, 22–23; limitations of, ix, 79; relations to theory and criticism, 4. *See also* interpretation; theory

arabesque, 141

aria, 28, 30, 32, 44, 45, 114, 115, 137

ars combinatoria, 78

autonomy: in Classic music, 33n; in Romantic music, 135–36

Bach, C.P.E., 44, 47

Bach, J.S., 111, 136

background, 117. *See also* Ursatz

Baker, Nancy, 26n

Bard, Raimund, 102n

Baroni, Mario, 7

Barthes, Roland, 90n

Beethoven, Ludwig van: 4; Bagatelle WoO. 60, 16n; Piano Sonata in E♭ Major, Op. 7, 139–40; Piano Sonata in D Major, Op. 10, No. 3, 61–62; Piano Sonata in C Minor, Op. 13 ("Pathetique"), 42–44, 46; Piano Sonata in C Major, Op. 53 ("Waldstein"), 56; Piano Sonata in E♭ Major, Op. 81a ("Les Adieux"), 41n; String Quartet in F Major, Op. 59, No. 1, 6; String Quartet in E♭ Major, Op. 74, 32; String Quartet in E♭ Major, Op. 127, 32, 116; String Quartet in B♭ Major, Op. 130, 116, 126; String Quartet in C♯Minor, Op. 131, 116, 126; String Quartet in A Minor, Op. 132, 32, 110–26; String Quartet in B♭ Major, Op. 133 ("Grosse Fuge"), 111; String Quartet in F Major, Op. 135, 116; Symphony No. 3 in E♭Major ("Eroica"), 31–32; Violin Sonata in D Major, Op. 12, No. 1, 57–58

beginning–middle–ending model, 20, 51–79, 91–92, 99, 131–32, 138–40

beginnings, 56–62. *See also* beginning–middle–ending model

Benjamin, William, 23n

Bent, Ian, 7n, 52n

Benveniste, Émile, 10, 14–15

Berio, Luciano, 47

Berlioz, Hector, *Symphonie Fantastique*, 33, 137

Berry, Wallace, 45n

binary oppositions, 15

Blume, Friedrich, 5n, 7, 9

Boilès, Charles, 13n, 15n

bourée, 30, 87, 89

Brahms, Johannes, "Variations on a Theme of Schumann," Op. 9, 138

Brandenburg, Sieghard, 126

brilliant style, 27, 30, 32, 76, 87, 114, 115

Brodbeck, David, and John Platoff, 126

Bruckner, Anton, 137

Burkhart, Charles, 94n

Burmeister, Joachim, 7

Burney, Charles, 28

cadenza, 30, 75, 87, 89, 114, 115

Castil-Blaze, François Henri Joseph, 28–29

character, 26–30, 72, 125

Charlton, David, 30n

Chatman, Seymour, 33n

Chopin, Frédéric, 62, 126, 136, 137

chorale, 141

circle of fifths, 95–96, 119–21

Clarke, Eric, 20n

Classic: contrasted with Romantic, 135–43; as period label, 4n, 6; as style, 6, 9, 127–28

closure, 67–72, 85, 106, 125, 139. *See also* endings

Coker, Wilson, 12

comic style, 31

commedia dell'arte, 75, 130

concerto style, 31

Cone, Edward T., 58n, 111, 116

contrast, 112–13. *See also* character

contredanse, 32